MUDDY JUNGLE RIVERS

Mobile Riverine Force, Vietnam

When I began taking writing classes at Bemidji State University I was astonished at the interest young students expressed about the Vietnam War. But a universal criticism I encountered was my use of military jargon, technical terms, and acronyms. In the desire to reach a young audience and hold their attention, I decided to use an informal, more personal approach to my story.

I ask forbearance from the army troops and navy men who served on the boats.

Below are three excellent resources to study army and navy unit composition, technical data, and weapons systems. The reader can further explore the Mobile Riverine Force and the areas of operations that are discussed in *Muddy Jungle Rivers*:

IV Corps in the Mekong Delta—Mobile Riverine Force Association: http://www.mrfa.org/

I Corps, Marine Base Camp Kistler, the Cua Viet River, and Cua Viet Naval Base at the river mouth: http://www.pcf45.com/cuaviet/cuaviet.html

The Navy Department Library—explore different history links: linkshttp:// www.history.navy.mil/library/guides/riverine_bib.htm

MUDDY JUNGLE RIVERS

A RIVER ASSAULT BOAT COX'N'S
MEMORY JOURNEY OF HIS WAR IN VIETNAM AND RETURN HOME

WENDELL AFFIELD

SJS

Hawthorn Petal Press, LLC
Bemidji, Minnesota

Published in the United States by Hawthorn Petal Press, LLC.

Library of Congress Control Number 2011944316

Affield, Wendell

Muddy Jungle Rivers: a river assault boat cox'n's memory journey of his war
in Vietnam and return home / Wendell Affield.

Although the author and publisher have made every effort to ensure the
accuracy of information contained in this book, we assume no responsibility
for errors, inaccuracies, omissions, or inconsistency thereof. Any slights of
people, places, or organizations are unintentional. Dialogue is reconstructed
and dramatized.

Paperback ISBN 978-0-9847023-0-5
eBook ISBN 978-0-9847023-1-2
EPub ISBN 978-0-9847023-2-9

Printed in the United States of America on acid-free paper

www.hawthornpetalpress.com

Maps by Mapping Specialists Limited. Madison, WI.
Photographs are property of the author
Book design by TJ Studio, Bemidji, MN

10 9 8 7 6 5 4 3 2 1 First Edition

For

Boat Captain "Buddha" Edward W. Thomas III

He relived it every night.

And the rest of the crew—wherever you may be.

Autumn's rain echoes overhead
as I rock my granddaughter tonight

Another tune, staccato,
lulled you to sleep
on a muddy jungle river

Wendell Affield, "Lullaby for the Lost"

Contents

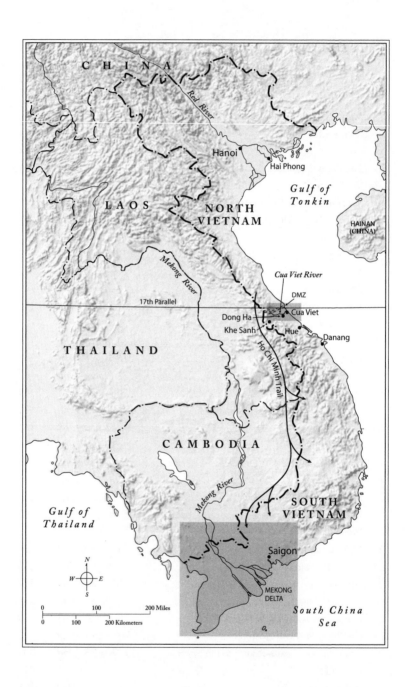

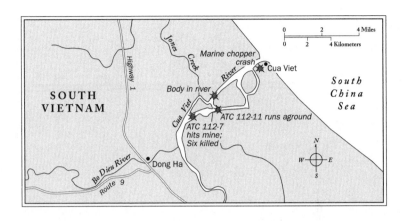

Marine chopper crash

Cua Viet

SOUTH CHINA Sea

SOUTH VIETNAM

Body in river

Jones Creek

Cua Viet River

ATC 112-11 runs aground

Cua Viet

ATC 112-7 hits mine; Six killed

Highway 1

Bo Dieu River

Dong Ha

Route 9

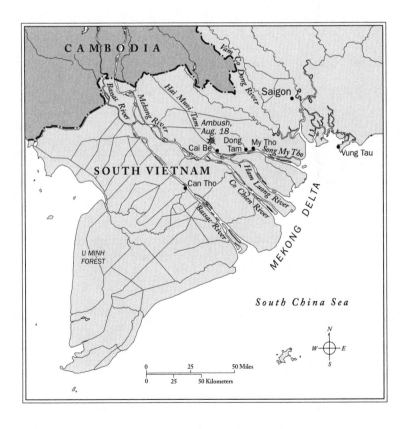

CAMBODIA

Vam Co Dong River

Saigon

Basac River

Mekong River

Hai Muoi Tam

Ambush, Aug. 18

Cai Be

Dong Tam

My Tho

Song My Tho

Vung Tau

SOUTH VIETNAM

Can Tho

Ham Luong River

Co Chien River

Basac River

MEKONG DELTA

U MINH FOREST

South China Sea

Foreword

I met Wendell Affield at a writing workshop in Northern Minnesota. Workshops can be strange settings, for the simple reason that a group of strangers must come together to discuss highly personal work. Wendell's piece was especially charged.

It was an excerpt from a memoir that dealt with his return from Vietnam, where he had served on a gunboat in the Mekong Delta. The piece was striking for its unflinching honesty. He was able to capture the sense of desolation experienced by the veterans of that war with restrained dignity.

But there was one passage that stood out. Wendell recounted an incident in which a number of anti-war protesters stormed a bus transporting him and other wounded veterans, eager to inflict further injury. He described the soldiers within as terrified.

I asked Wendell whether his perception of the events of that day might not be skewed by his intense emotions. Would anti-war protesters really behave in such a vicious manner? Why would they attack wounded soldiers in broad daylight?

Wendell was quietly adamant. He'd been there, and this is what had happened. As we talked, his face reddened with frustration. He told me, quite correctly, that I was too young to remember how it had been back then for returning soldiers like him, and probably too ideologically blinded.

In the end, I issued a few unconvincing bromides about the risks of writing about events that remain so raw, and we moved on to another piece. But I felt terrible. As a teacher, the last thing I want to do is undermine a student, particular one like Wendell, who struck me as an exceptionally gentle soul, and was clearly engaged in a painful personal excavation.

A few months later, rather out of the blue, I received a note from Wendell, along with an article he'd written about the confrontation with the anti-war protesters. Wendell had returned to the scene of the episode, talked with some of the locals, and done considerable archival research in an effort to reconstruct what had happened. What he discovered was astonishing.

As it turned out, the anti-war protesters apparently had confused the bus Wendell was on with one that was transporting members of the National Guard to Chicago, where the bloody riots of the 1968 Democratic National Convention were in full swing. This explained the belligerence of the protesters: they'd thought they were confronting soldiers who were about to descend on their comrades.

I mention all this by way of suggesting the deep respect I have for Wendell, and especially his determination to tell his story accurately. After all, it would have been easy enough for him to dismiss my questions as naïve and presumptuous. Instead, he did what every serious writer must: he investigated further, in pursuit of the truth. This, it seems to me, is the highest duty of any memoirist in this age of fraudulence and solipsism.

I could speak at length here about the merits of *Muddy Jungle Rivers*: its eloquence, its emotional generosity, its urgent and haunting prose. But the book's enduring virtue is that it records, with utmost fidelity, the unspeakable horrors of the author himself, as a young man adrift in the moral chaos of war.

No story is more important to this historical moment, in this country, which has been at war for over a decade now. Whatever rhetoric politicians might use to glorify these military adventures, they boil down to the same story, which plays out all over our country: young men, most of them without many other economic options, are sent far from home, to countries they've never heard of, to fight an enemy they barely know. They move through utterly foreign landscapes as human targets. They endure both tedium and occasional bursts of violent chaos. When they can no longer resist the impulse, they struggle to understand the greater purpose of the risks and burdens they shoulder. And at the end of all this, the fortunate must return home and seek to make peace with what they've seen and done and suffered.

This is the story Wendell has set out to tell. It might be said that it is the essential story of our country. At the very least, it is our saddest.

As you venture into the world Wendell draws so vividly, let me offer one final observation – that the purest measure of our decency as a nation resides not just in our willingness to provide these men medical and psychological care, but to listen when, like Wendell, they muster the uncommon courage to tell us what happened to them.

-- Steve Almond

Prologue

In the snowy predawn of another Veteran's Day, my fingers feather the shards of iron cocooned beneath the numb skin of my sunken scars. My mind wanders back to August 18, 1968, the muddy jungle rivers of South Vietnam, and the ambush on our armor troop carrier. Always, I think about my fellow crewmen and wonder where they are, wonder if they too think about that day.

The jungle was a long way from my childhood home in Minnesota, the farm where I was raised with my eight brothers and sisters. I was in my second tour of duty, only twenty years old, a seasoned cox'n—boat driver, and second in command of our riverine assault boat, a converted LCM-6 landing craft.

When the rockets hit that afternoon, Buddha, our boat captain, was topside, sheltered between the gun turrets and was only peppered with small bits of shrapnel. He was from Maryland and often told stories of growing up on the shores of Chesapeake Bay. He was a career man, the navy in his blood from childhood, and had a mind-set from the old days, where discipline was unquestioned and drinking an inherent trait of the sailor. He was only five years older than me but because of his seniority and bearing, presented the persona of an old salt. I remember how he crawled aboard our boat one night in Dong Tam, drunk, angry that I had received a promotion to the same rank as him. How he sucker-punched me when I mocked his Good Conduct Medal.

Stonewall was the black 20 millimeter cannon gunner. I think he was from Georgia or Alabama. At night, he would lean close to his tape recorder, listening to Aretha Franklin and the tapes of his family's words from home. In the beginning of our tour he was the only man in our crew to attend Sunday services. In April 1968, after Martin Luther King was assassinated, he stopped attending church services and drifted into the Black Power camp. He wasn't outwardly militant, but I remember his sullen looks towards the crew, as if he had something to say but stopped himself. His gun turret was elevated, above and behind the cox'n flat, so he was only lightly wounded by shrapnel in the lower legs on August 18th.

Snipe, the engineman, was from Pennsylvania coal country. I remember the photos of his new wife and the baby daughter he had never met. He took the brunt of Buddha's bully behavior. He was docile, always grease-covered, an easy target. During that last ambush, he was below deck, trying to keep the worn out engines of our World War II vintage boat going. Over the years, I have often wondered why he didn't release the safety latch on the bow ramp when I beached. I think about the lives we could have saved that afternoon had I been able to lower it and debark the platoon of troops we carried. There were at least twenty casualties, killed and wounded, when three rockets detonated among them. At night I still hear the screams, smell the burned flesh and cordite. Remember the blood squishing between my bare toes.

Crow, the starboard .50 caliber machine gunner, was from Alabama or Mississippi. Crow had oily, thinning red hair and always wore rolled up cutoffs and half-laced jungle boots, tongue flapping with each step. He disliked the navy and blacks. On August 18th he abandoned his gun turret. I remember my flash of surprise when he scurried through my cox'n flat and down the ladder to the well-deck. I could hear Buddha, trapped between the turrets above us, voice lost in the cacophony of battle, screaming at him to get back on his gun or he'd kill him, calling him a coward. A black army sergeant came up, manned the machine gun, and was terribly wounded when a B-40 rocket penetrated the one inch armor. He was blown out of the turret and into my cox'n flat. He squirmed on the deck clawing at my bare legs, mewling like a cat with a broken back.

Dennis, our port .50 caliber machine gunner, was from a Wisconsin dairy farm. He was the youngest of our crew. His naïveté was refreshing and the brunt of many jokes. The day we got ambushed, he was wounded but got up and continued shooting. I remember glancing back at him. The battle dressing I had put on his upper leg while Professor manned the helm, slipped to his ankle and blood trickled down his leg onto the deck.

Professor, our radioman, was a college graduate from Ohio and shared the cox'n flat with me. The first time our crew gathered in Coronado, California, for training, Professor informed Buddha that he would not kill anyone, that he was opposed to the war. When we were ambushed that afternoon, Professor and I were wounded by the same rockets. He bandaged me. Later, when Buddha told me to go along the riverbank to the medevac chopper, it was Professor who handed me the 12 gauge shotgun saying, "Just in case."

I looked up into Professor's face, surprised. He hadn't touched a gun since training. At first I refused the shotgun.

My hand was bandaged and my arm in a sling. But Professor insisted I take it, pushing it into my hands. As I dragged the gun through the undergrowth along the riverbank, its weight pulling against my wounded shoulder, I cursed Professor. But now, I wonder what would have happened that afternoon if I had refused the shotgun. If I had decided to leave it there in the well-deck among the blood, bandages, and shell casings. The result of that decision still haunts me.

The memories of those muggy days are never far away, flooding my mind when I hear a gunshot, pass over a river, smell diesel fuel or exhaust, decomposing flesh, or a thousand other triggers. The voices of my crewmen and the soldiers we lost echo through my head.

This is a story of those days in Vietnam. Over decades of sleepless nights, I have gone back to those muddy jungle rivers.

This is how I remember.

1

The Farm

Autumn 1964

Pelt prices dropped the autumn of 1964. Prime skunk hides, winter coat glistening—scraped clean, no skinning nicks, stretched and dried—brought $4.75. Muskrat, weasel, and raccoon pelts sold for considerably less. My older brothers had left the farm; I felt used, having to pick up their share of the barn chores. After scrubbing down and changing clothes, after a liberal dose of Old Spice deodorant, skunk musk and cow smell shadowed me to school. Town kids laughed and girls remained at arms' length.

Post World War II social upheaval was the catalyst that had brought us to the farm. In 1949 my mother, Barbara, was a divorced concert pianist, Julliard educated with four children, living in a tiny New York City apartment. Herman was an army veteran—eighth grade education—living on a one-hundred-sixty acre farm in northern Minnesota. They met through *Cupid's Columns*, a lonely hearts club catalogue. We moved to the farm in October and they were married four months later in February 1950. He was forty-three years old and she was twenty-eight. Both had an impossible dream. She wanted a safe haven for her children and he was lonely and wanted a family. I was two years old that autumn. From the beginning, I formed a strong bond with Herman. I recall riding the steaming silage sled from silo to barn, watching my new father's back arched forward as he leaned into the sled rope, plowing through snow drifts, steam huffing from his mouth as he turned to grin at me. Each morning and evening I went to the barn and "helped" milk cows and feed them.

Chris, five years older than me, was Barb's favorite. Now, I think it was a combination of first son and his love of music. Barb spent many hours teaching him at the piano. That was one of the early triggers of Herman's and Barb's acrimony. Herman expected Chris to help with chores. In her *Cupid's Columns* advertisement, Barb had said, "My children would be a great help to a farmer or rancher." After getting married, she argued that milking cows and cleaning the barn was beneath her son's dignity.

Tim, three years my senior, was often mistaken for Chris's twin. He loved mechanical toys. When he was nine years old his hand was severely injured in the buzz saw while cutting firewood. One of Tim's early memories of that first winter on the farm is of Barb sitting in the front room weeping quietly as piano music echoed from the wind-up Victrola and arctic clippers, sweeping down from the western Canadian plains, rattled loose windows in the old house.

Laurel, a year younger than me, was an infant when we moved to Minnesota. Barb treated her as though she were sacred. Beware the brother who made her cry. Herman was forbidden to touch her.

In those first years I was malleable and tried to please everybody. I was a tag-along to my older brothers but after many thrashings I learned not to accompany them unless invited. As the years passed, my parents' rages became unpredictable and I discovered it best to avoid them. I learned early the solitude of forest refuge.

Barb and Herman would have five children together but their cultural differences were too wide. Verbal sparring grew into physical violence. As a young lady, Barb had traveled Europe, studied music in Paris and at Julliard, and, she claimed, played in Carnegie Hall. Herman had come of age on the farm during the Great Depression. Values of frugality and self-reliance were an inherent part of his character. Money—lack of it—was a constant source of contention.

Isolated on the farm, Barb felt imprisoned. As the years passed, she lashed out at Herman. She accused him of being ignorant; of being dirty; of being a child molester—all untrue. He would listen in silence, his ruddy complexion darkening. At some point Barb would cross a threshold and he'd shout, "Enough is enough." Then, as we children watched, or ran upstairs and hid in terror, he'd unbuckle his belt and the dance would begin. Barb racing around the dining table, taunting, keeping the table between them, until, in a frenzy, he'd switch ends on the belt and begin swinging the buckle end. He would eventually overpower her, beat her, then stalk out of the house cursing; she would be left sitting on the floor rubbing bloody wounds. Twice she tried to escape his brutality, each time forced to return, destitute.

The first escape attempt was in the spring of 1952 to an elegant old home with no plumbing or electricity perched high in the Washington Cascades near the head of Lake Chelan. I was five that spring. We returned to the farm late that autumn.

I think it was the winter I was eight years old. Herman and I were at the Park Rapids Livestock Sales Barn. We'd taken the back seat out of the Chevy and crowded in seven one-week-old bull calves. Since the beginning of calving season Herman had been knocking the new-born male calves in the head with a sledge hammer. But the market had changed and the little veal calves were in demand. On the trip to the sales barn, their little rumps squished against the side windows, calf shit oozed down the glass and got trapped inside the doors. That old car would forever smell like the barn. The calves sold for six dollars apiece.

At the sales barn, farmers always gave away unwanted kittens and puppies. That day I discovered a runt puppy, the last give-away, the one nobody wanted. Her ears drooped like the box flap she was hiding under and I fell in love the moment she peed in my arms. I felt certain she was as excited as me. The little brown mutt's head and her white socked front feet peeked out of my open coat as we stood in line waiting to get the calf check.

"Can I have her? Can I have her? I'll buy food with my trapping money. I'll teach her how to hunt and round up cows."

Herman was in an expansive mood. "I suppose, now that Shep's gone."

"That'll be my dog's name, too. Shep."

Herman had always named his dogs Shep.

Through that late winter, spring, into early summer I played with Shep. One morning, just after school let out for the summer, I was in the garden weeding a carrot row when I heard Shep yipping and Herman shouting. Shep had killed a chicken. Herman, in a fit of rage, tied her to a post and beat her to death with the sledge hammer.

I untied the rope, picked up my puppy and—cradling her in my arms like the day I'd gotten her at the livestock sales barn—carried her out into the forest where we'd played together, her warm limp body tiny beneath blood-sodden fur. I don't remember carrying a shovel with me, but I must have. I remember digging the hole, slashing viciously at roots in the humusy earth until I reached clay. I didn't want scavengers to further ravage her. I tried to straighten her little head—laid her on the side that still had an eye—smoothed her matted fur. I nestled her in my shirt, back feet tucked forward, white-socked front feet folded up against her tummy, nose tucked down by her feet, tail over her face the way she liked to sleep. I slipped the stick we'd played fetch with down between her paws and buttoned the shirt. Sitting under the rustling willow tree, I cradled her against my bare stomach for a time then gently laid the little bundle in the hole on the hillside and shoveled dirt back.

A part of me died that day. Herman tried to regain what had been lost. When one of the sows had piglets he gave me the runt of the litter, a tiny female, and told me if I kept it alive she would be my sow and I would get the money from her piglets. Eventually she did reproduce. I received the money, which Barb insisted on saving for me. I never did see any of it.

December 1959 Barb attempted to escape again, this time to Hillsboro, Texas. Two months later Herman sent us bus tickets to return to the farm. Four months after we got home Barb was committed to a mental hospital, her nine children placed in foster homes. Eventually we were reunited but the weak fibers of family unity had been permanently destroyed.

I now believe Herman suffered from severe post traumatic stress disorder (PTSD) due to combat in North Africa. And Barb—my brothers have always called her schizophrenic—but I've come to the conclusion she was probably a victim of borderline personality disorder complicated by PTSD. On the eve of WWII she was visiting Poland with her fiancée and school friend. She escaped the German invasion. They didn't. It really doesn't matter. Herman and Barb are gone now, too.

As children of post WWII euphoria, we were immersed in stories of North Africa, Europe, and the Pacific island-hopping campaigns. It was the Good War—one to be proud of—and our games reflected that. My two older brothers were Americans. I was relegated to Kraut or Jap (Commie during the Korean Conflict) and was always killed. My younger brother, Randy, was fascinated by Air Force jets that flew over our house on practice bombing runs during the Korean War. Years later he would enlist in the Navy and in 1978, crash, lost at sea, when his P-3 Orion went down near the Azores.

Red Lake Indian Reservation is about fifteen miles north of the farm so cowboys and Indians was naturally one of our war games. Being Indian was my favorite role. I'd race ahead, circle in from the forest behind, and snake through the football-field-size sumac maze, often escaping unscathed. Once, I was hit in the back with a rock grenade, leaving a welt that took weeks to heal. Tim said he saw the bushes wiggling as I squirmed through the sumacs. A decade later that incident would resonate as I crawled toward a medevac chopper beneath foliage along a river bank in Vietnam, enemy voices behind me, gaining. But as a child, the mystique of war and military service fascinated me.

Reading was an escape during the long winter months—no television on the farm. *All Quiet on the Western Front*, by Erich Maria Remarque was a favorite of mine. It's a story of a German soldier in World War One. The protagonist is young, he struggles with adversity; I could relate to his spartan existence. But I didn't understand then the angst, the lost soul of a defeated soldier, tattooed into one's psyche.

When I completed eighth grade in our two-room country school our class traveled into Bemidji for high school orientation. A counselor reviewed my selections for ninth grade electives and said, "You're a farm kid, you take shop classes." He arbitrarily crossed out my wishes for speech, debate, and drama classes. I've never been mechanically inclined and hated shop subjects. Now, I wonder if I'd been allowed to grow in that other direction, what path life may have taken.

The spring of 1964, I was sixteen, left the farm, and rode the rails out to Seattle, Washington. I spent a few weeks with my grandmother then hopped a freight train toward home. That was the first time I met a Vietnam veteran. As I recall, he had just been discharged and was seeing the country—no destination in mind. I remember the confrontation he had with a yard bull at the Seattle rail yard as we waited for an open east-bound boxcar. The ex-Marine's rage frightened me when he wrestled the guard's club away and beat him with it. We jumped off the train in Montana, earned some cash bucking bales for an old rancher, hopped back on a freight car, returned to Minnesota and spent the rest of the summer working a carnival. But that's another story.

That autumn I returned to high school and stared out the windows. I'd lost all interest. Chinese dynasties, algebra equations, disassembled big blocks, and dissected frogs had no chance against the open spaces and freedom I'd discovered the past summer.

November of 1964, trapping season was in full swing and I was disgusted with my predicament at home. At school, on the first anniversary of President Kennedy's death, there was a moment of silence followed by our history teacher reading Kennedy's inaugural address. The challenge of his words resonated in my mind. "Ask not what your country can do for you—ask what you can do for your country."

The Gulf of Tonkin Resolution had been passed that August, authorizing President Johnson to send troops to Vietnam. The teacher spoke of communists overrunning South-east Asia and moving down the archipelago to Australia just as the Japanese had tried twenty-five years earlier. As I listened, I realized what I could do for my country. I could join the military and help stop the spread of communism. I turned seventeen that autumn, anxious to escape the farm, anxious to go to war before it was over. Like the WWII movie heroes I'd seen, I would return a hero, medals on my chest, perhaps a few strategically placed scars to authenticate the awards.

New Year's Eve 1965, after the evening chores and supper, Barb and Herman were having an argument. Unnoticed, I slipped into my school clothes, pulled on my good coat, and walked out of the house. I hitchhiked to Phoenix, Arizona and lived with my brother, Tim. Two months later, many unpaid traffic tickets later, we'd worn out our welcome in Arizona and returned to the farm. The Monday we returned, Herman ordered me onto the school bus. I rode into town and walked nine blocks to the recruiter's office where I knocked on the Marine Corps recruiter's door. Naturally I would be a Marine. They built men and were the most heroic. I knocked a second time—no answer.

I stepped down the hall and knocked on the Navy recruiter's door.

"Enter," barked a voice. I walked in and a first class radioman in dress blues greeted me.

"Do you know where the Marine recruiter is?"

"No. Why, are you thinking of enlisting?"

"Yes sir."

"Just between you and me, the Marine Corps sucks."

And he had me. Because I was only seventeen, Barb signed permission for me to enlist. A week later I was sworn in and on my way to naval boot camp in San Diego, California.

Herman was proud I'd enlisted. He spoke nostalgically of his time in the army. Barb—I think she was just happy to see me committed to something. In early 1965 Vietnam had not reached our isolated corner of the world. They had no idea what my future might entail. And I was thrilled to be in the military.

Fate often plays, unrecognized at the time, a pivotal role in life. Late winter 1968 during the Khe Sanh siege, our riverboat division was transferred from the Mekong Delta north to the Cua Viet River near the Demilitarized Zone between North Vietnam and South Vietnam. One night during a North Vietnamese artillery bombardment, I sought refuge in a shell hole with a Marine and listened—between explosions—to the man curse the Marine Corps and the horrors he'd seen. The Marines suffered very high casualty rates during the Vietnam War. I realize now, had I enlisted in the Marine Corps at the dawn of our build-up in 1965, I'd have served multiple tours of duty.

2

In the Navy
4 March 1965

Boot camp was a clash of ethnic and regional values. As company commanders went, I believe ours was quite mild. We had about twenty Filipino recruits in our company who always clustered together at the far end of the barracks. I remember the company commander walking up behind them while they were chattering in their native Tagalag language. He slapped one across the back of the head, skidding the terrified boy across the floor. "You're in America now," he shouted. "Speak English."

But there were others that I didn't understand, too. A few college boys who'd dropped out of school and enlisted, they were friendly. Southern boys who acted tough yet formed a clique. Black boys, most were very quiet, a few seemed outspoken—I wasn't familiar with the term militant then. I kept a low profile. This was a different world than I'd imagined when we had played war back on the farm.

Three weeks into boot camp I got in a fight.

"You boy, shine my shoes. I want to see your teeth glow on the toes when you're done," commanded a southerner to a black kid sitting next to me.

The kid had set his Blue Jacket Manual—the book of traditions and basics of naval life—down and picked up the shoes.

"Shine your own fucking shoes. He's busy studying for the test we have tomorrow," I had blurted out.

"What the fuck are you, one of them northern do-gooders? We take care of your kind where I'm from."

I scrambled up from the centerboard bench I'd been sitting at and dodged the book he flung at me. "I don't want trouble—we'll both end up in the brig if we get caught."

"Too late, asshole. I'm going to teach you a lesson."

I stood then, waiting as he advanced. I flipped my book—underhand, between his raised fists and hit him in the face. It distracted him for an instant and I kicked him high and hard in the stomach, knocking the wind out of him.

"You scrounges got that much energy?" asked the company commander who had silently witnessed the confrontation. "I have a little project for you."

And so went the next three days. Carrying buckets of sand, double-timing across a hundred yards, dumping them, filling the buckets, then sprinting back. At 1400 hours we had to start refilling the holes we'd spent the morning digging. We finished for the day when the ground was raked smooth and inspected by the Marine guarding us.

Naval boot camp does not strive to break the recruit and instill that killer urge. Rather, it teaches tradition and discipline and focuses on selecting men for the hundreds of specialized duties necessary throughout the Fleet. I remember the batteries of tests and the boredom I felt as I glazed through them. Failing dismally, I was assigned to the deck division and went directly to a destroyer, USS *Rogers* (DD 876), after boot camp.

I enjoyed the wide variety of tasks and was soon singled out for training. A quote from an early performance evaluation, "Affield is highly effective and reliable. Needs only limited supervision." I was sent to Water Survival and Pilot Rescue school. As I recall, out of about thirty students from several ships, five of us passed the rigorous class where we spent 12-14 hours a day in the water.

Shortly after that, I was assigned to the ship's landing force party. We were trained by Marines in the hills of Camp Pendleton, north of San Diego. It was a grand game with real guns and blank ammo. I remember how I basked in an old gunnery sergeant's praise when I charged an ambush. A few nights later, dug in atop a marl knob, the Marines charged our position in a rainstorm. My M-1 rifle jammed and the old sergeant stood over my foxhole firing into the air. "You're dead, asshole." Then he walked away laughing. My gun unjammed, I glimpsed him in a flash of lightening and fired in his direction. The next day, sitting in a classroom as we listened to a critique of our defensive perimeter, the sergeant limped in. "I catch the bastard who shot me with a plug last night, I'll have his ass." We all laughed.

A few months later the USS *Rogers* left on a WestPac cruise—acronym for West Pacific, synonymous with Vietnam. We left San Diego in late January 1966 and returned in August.

I saw my first dead American while we patrolled the Gulf of Tonkin.

We were at General Quarters—we'd come close to shore searching for a downed pilot. I was dressed in a wetsuit, ready to drop over the side to help him. He had limped his shot-up F-4 Phantom out over the water before he'd ditched. The plane must have disintegrated on impact. As our ship eased through the debris field, the top of an open parachute was spotted about thirty yards off the port side. The phone talker relayed the captain's order, "Swimmer over the side." I was on the seaward side of the guardrail, one leg hooked inboard. At that instant a geyser shot skyward twenty meters off the ship's stern. Another artillery volley bracketed us. An explosion of spray off the port side drenched me. The ship lurched forward and white foam churned from her screws. We jumped into the gun mount and returned fire at the enemy guns firing on us from behind sand dunes. We set a record that afternoon—twenty-seven rounds per minute fired over the next seven minutes—until we steamed out of range.

I recall how my hands shook as we picked up the still-warm, three-foot-long shell casings that cluttered the deck outside the gun mount. The gun crew laughed and talked faster and louder than usual—a tight, high-pitched laugh. Somebody pointed out that I was still wearing my wetsuit and a fresh burst of laughter washed over them.

Late that night, while standing bridge watch, I toured the ship to check watch stations. I looked in on the skeleton gun mount crew. One man began laughing. My eyes shifted to the instigator. He was staring at me through the red nightlight illuminating the closed mount; soon others burst into laughter. My mind locked on what I'd seen bumping against the side of the ship moments before incoming artillery had splashed around us—the upside-down helmet, still sheltering the hollowed out pilot's skull, white tendrils of flesh swaying in the pink-tinted water cupped inside. A chill passed through me, knowing that in a few seconds I would have been down in that green-hued tepid water as the ship lurched away, sucking both of us into the vortex of the seething wake created by the ship's huge propellers.

As weeks passed, the memory dimmed and became irrelevant. I was young. Nothing like that could ever happen to me.

Several months later, before returning to the United States, we stopped at Yokosuka, Japan to off-load our remaining ammunition. My appendix ruptured while on a working party carrying high explosive 5"/38 projectiles to the supply ship we were moored next to. I was left behind in a hospital. Several weeks later I returned to the United States and the USS *Rogers*.

June 1967 I was transferred to the USS *Samuel Gompers* (AD 37) pre-commissioning detail. The *Gompers* was new construction in Bremerton, Washington. It was easy duty but a much larger ship with many more officers, therefore more discipline and structure. One day while waiting on the pier for my turn to use the pay phone, I watched a black boatswain's mate third class—the same rank as me—come down the gangplank of the USS *Pueblo* (AGER 2) and over to the phone booth. I commented on what a nice looking ship the *Pueblo* was and how I had transferred from a destroyer to the *Gompers* and decided I liked a smaller ship and would rather be at sea or overseas than stationed stateside.

"We're getting ready to leave Bremerton. How would you like to switch duty stations?" he asked excitedly. It wasn't unusual for enlisted men to switch duty stations if their qualifications were equal. He was newly married and didn't want to leave his bride in Seattle.

"Sounds great to me," I said. "You submit the paperwork." I gave him my name, service number, and the division I was in on the *Gompers*. Three days later my division officer called me to his office and told me the request was denied because I didn't have a top secret clearance and there wasn't time to apply for one before the *Pueblo* was scheduled to leave port.

At the time I thought it odd for a boatswain's mate third class on a research vessel—that's what the *Pueblo* was—to need a top secret clearance. That was the day I saw a notice posted on a bulletin board looking for volunteers to man riverine assault boats in the Mobile Riverine Force (MRF).

3

Riverine Assault Boat Crew Training

Autumn 1967

Late autumn sun flashed off low swells rolling across San Diego Harbor. Salt mist feathered the open decked ferry as it ploughed through a tourist launch's wake. The tour director's voice echoed across the water. "Off our starboard side, secured to a mooring buoy, is a warship similar to the USS *Maddox*, the ship that started the Vietnam War." Leaning against the ferry's guardrail, a waft of sea teased my nose as I gazed beyond the breakwater.

I ignored his words and looked across the water at the haze-gray destroyer as she came to in the ebb tide, glistening in her fresh coat of paint. Polished brass turnbuckles and gun barrel plugs flashed while in-harbor pennants waved from signal halyards. On this Sunday afternoon, only a skeleton crew stood watch. A sailor monitored hawser tension at the forecastle as the ship swung from the buoy. Two figures stood beneath the awning of the quarterdeck amidships visiting, while another seaman—an apprentice probably—stood watch at the stern. Swirling water sparkled as the outgoing current flowed past. She was beautiful, that sleek silhouette, and I imagined her knifing through calm seas toward a clear horizon, dolphins racing along side. She reminded me of the destroyer I had transferred from and I was startled to realize I felt homesick.

"Those are 5"/38 twin gun mounts fore and aft," declared a voice. I looked around and discovered that he was speaking to me.

He was a likeable, easy-going kid and I think his nervousness made him talkative. His name was Dennis and he had grown up on a dairy farm in Wisconsin—he'd enlisted in the navy soon after high school graduation so he wouldn't get drafted into the army. His white hat was cocked back and he reminded me of my younger brother. He was about five-feet eight-inches—a couple of inches shorter than me—slimmer, with light brown crew-cut hair and milk-fed cheeks; barely old enough to warrant a razor. His dress-white uniform still had the mark of boot camp wash tables, hand-scrubbed and air-dried. He was attempting to impress me as an old salt, but his Seaman Apprentice shoulder patch and the dark, crisp green of the still-creased seabag gave him away. He looked down at my seabag with its three years of wear and asked timidly if I was being transferred to Coronado Naval Station.

"Yes," I said nodding my head, "For training with the Mobile Riverine Force, for river patrol boat duty in Vietnam."

"That's where I'm going. Our drill instructor had a Purple Heart—he was on a river patrol boat. He had three fingers missing and walked with a limp. He laughed when he saw my orders. Said I'd have a Purple Heart by the end of my tour, too. I don't want one."

His eyes searched mine as he bit his lower lip. I remembered how I'd felt just out of boot camp going to my first ship. Not knowing anybody, the butt of practical jokes by young sailors who had recently been subjected to them themselves. Fear of the unknown. I smiled and told him to stick with me—we'd figure things out together.

Dennis' recruiter had assured him that he would be trained as an electrician and never see Vietnam. Two kids from his high school—a year ahead of him—had been killed in Vietnam the past year. His eyes shifted to the green steel ferry deck as he shuffled his feet and struggled to light a *Kool* in the harbor breeze. He seemed embarrassed that he had revealed so much to a stranger. I showed him how to hold the match between his trigger finger and index finger then push the match head down on the strike pad with his thumb while simultaneously forming a cup with the other hand. I explained that this blocked the wind and shielded the glow at night. He coughed when he inhaled.

I stared at the aft port side of the destroyer, remembering the day in Tonkin Gulf, and told Dennis the odds of getting hurt were slim. Half an hour later we arrived at Coronado Naval Station.

A hoarse voice echoed through the low-ceilinged barracks as we entered. "That's bullshit. I was a seaman on the USS *Constellation* CVA 64 in 1962. If those friggin Russians hadn't loaded up their missiles and left Cuba, we would've blown them out of the water single-handed. The *Connie* had the best air wing in the fleet. We followed them red commie bastards half way back across the Atlantic."

"I don't think—," a voice began.

"Yeah. That's right. You don't think," the louder voice overrode. "You snipes should stay in the engine room with grease up to your asses. You don't know what goes on topside. You get a breath of fresh air and you're giddy as a seaman recruit in a Tijuana whorehouse."

I maneuvered down the aisle between two rows of bunks toward several sailors. When I reached them, the loudmouth focused on me.

"Where are you coming from?"

"Pre-commissioning detail, USS *Samuel Gompers*, new construction up in Bremerton," I replied.

"Have you ever been to sea? Who's that kid? He looks like a puppy trailing you." He said it with a sneer as he glanced around, his eyes demanding approval from his audience. He glowed in their chuckles and grins, but I sensed an undercurrent of intimidation. They probably wondered when it would be their turn to be singled out.

"Yeah, I did a WestPac tour on a destroyer," I said, as I locked eyes with him. Who the hell does he think he is, I wondered, King Neptune?

He stood there with his hat pushed back holding an empty beer glass. He leaned forward, lifted it to his thick lips, and a rivulet of chaw juice oozed out, down the inside and outside of the glass and over his knuckles. In the other hand he clutched an unlit cigar between gnarled fingers. His paunch bulged under a sweaty T-shirt and tattooed arms were supported by elbows resting on the tops of the two bunks he stood between.

Face tilted down, lips on the dirty glass, eyes locked on me, he mumbled, "Which one? What's your rate? Shit, you don't look old enough to leave home yet."

Back on the farm there was a tattered book about mythological creatures—this guy reminded me of the hunchbacked drooling ogre.

"I was on the USS *Rogers*, DD 876." Dropping my seabag to the floor, I turned so he could see my insignia and ribbons. "I'm a boatswain's mate third class. On the *Rogers* I stood bridge watches, was a ship's swimmer, and rifleman on the ship's landing force party. During general quarters I was the pointer in the aft 5"/38 gun mount."

Caught off guard he paused, searching for a comeback. "Why did you leave the *Gompers*? That should have been cushy duty."

"Oh, it was. Seattle is a great liberty town, but there were so many recruits on the *Gompers* I felt like a baby sitter. And there were a couple of loudmouth lifers I wanted to get away from, so I volunteered for this."

"You're nuts. Welcome to sunny Coronado. My name's Thomas—I'm going to be a boat captain. Take your puppy and grab a bunk."

I picked an empty bed as far from Thomas as possible and surveyed my surroundings. We were all strangers, coming from duty stations across the world; from seaman apprentices like Dennis, straight out of boot camp, to a grizzled World War II veteran, nearing retirement, not happy about this turn of events. Kicking off my shoes, I lay back on my rack and listened as two old timers passed down the aisle.

"I already been to Vietnam. 1944, I was on a cruiser—shelled a Jap base in Cam Ranh Bay. Let them gooks keep it, I say."

"I spent three years in Korea shuttling troops and freight up and down the coast, freezing my ass off, getting shot at. I don't need this bullshit. Listen to those friggin kids over there playing grab ass. They don't have a clue what they're in for," complained a bald-headed gunner's mate.

Gusts of rain blew across Coronado as we gathered for orientation. At the front of the auditorium, a huge map of Vietnam was projected onto a screen. The speaker was a Boatswain's Mate First Class—short, stocky, with a chest full of ribbons and three hash marks. A career man. He'd spent eighteen months in Vietnam as an advisor to the South Vietnamese Navy Riverine Force.

He explained the concept of the U.S. Mobile Riverine Force, the combined Army/Navy unit we were training for. Our mission would be to patrol the rivers and transport army troops to operational areas. When on joint operations, after disembarking the troops, each boat would patrol a sector of the river and act as a blocking force so the enemy couldn't escape or infiltrate from behind.

He briefed us on the history, geography, and culture of Vietnam. From the Chinese invasion 1,500 years ago, to the French defeat at Dien Bien Phu in 1954, to the current American efforts in 1967. His droning voice soon had heads nodding as he explained how stemming the flow of weapons and men from the communist North Vietnam Army (NVA) was beyond the capability of South Vietnam's army and navy.

He said the NVA moved through neutral Laos and Cambodia transporting weapons. They crossed the border into South Vietnam and developed large arms caches and reinforced Viet Cong units. War materiel was also smuggled down the coast of the South China Sea and dropped at staging points in the south.

Projecting a large map of Asia, he showed us where the Mekong River originated in the Plains of Tibet, flowed south to Vietnam and spilled into the South China Sea. A new slide, a blow-up of the Mekong Delta, revealed a maze of waterways. With a pointer, he directed our attention to major rivers we'd be operating on—the Bassac and Mekong. He pointed out the network of tributaries and canals, many of which were navigable only during the monsoon season. When we broke for lunch there was a collective sigh of relief.

"A man could get fat at this billet. Do they always feed this good? Those slides of Vietnamese farmers in the Delta you showed us—those gooks sure are skinny." Without looking behind me I recognized Thomas's voice.

"They tell us we need to have empathy for the gooks. When I first heard that word I thought it was something you caught. Something a shot of penicillin would cure," the instructor said. "From what I saw over there, a bullet is the best cure for empathy."

"The Enlisted Men's (EM) club doesn't open until 1600 hours," complained Thomas. "I don't think I'll make it that long."

"I keep a bottle of Jack Daniels in my desk," the instructor said in a low voice. "We'll tap that before this afternoon's session."

"Why the hell do they waste our time on all this crap?" Thomas said, toothpick dangling from his mouth. "Who gives a shit about where the Mekong comes from or who those gooks worked for a thousand years ago. I want to get my boat crew and begin training."

"We'll hit the club at 1600 hours and drown this bullshit, then I'll tell you what it's really like over there."

A freckled seaman stood at our table and asked, "Did you guys stay awake this morning?"

He set his tray down and pulled out a chair. "This pisses me off. I just spent two years on an oiler and requested Subic Bay—to work in the motor pool—I'll be fucked if I'm letting anybody shoot at me."

"What refueling ship were you on?" I asked. "The destroyer I was on probably resupplied from your ship."

"I was a snipe—always down in the engine room when a ship came alongside to refuel."

"Where's Subic Bay?" Dennis said.

"It's in the Philippine Islands—best liberty I ever had. Get a girl all night for twelve dollars."

"What for?"

"What for—where the hell do you come from? What do you think for?"

I'd been to Subic Bay several times. I thought it was the dirtiest port in the Orient and had the scroungest girls. "Why did you leave the oiler?"

"I liked Subic Bay so much I stayed until I ran out of money then went back to the base and turned myself in. The navy flew me home—my ship didn't want me back—so I was busted to seaman and sent here. "The name's Crowell," he said, through a mouthful of food. "I hear the EM club opens at four o'clock."

"You mean 1600 hours," Dennis said.

"Kid, you are a real boot—1600 hours, four o'clock— who gives a fuck how you say it, just so the club opens."

Crowell's curly-red hair was matted to his sweaty forehead. I was surprised to see the skin on top of his head when he leaned forward to eat. His uniform looked slept in and his white hat, sitting upside down on the table, had a gray dirt band inside the rim. Black horn-rimmed glasses camouflaged blond whisker shadow. He spoke with a southern drawl and reminded me of the kid I'd gotten into trouble with in boot camp.

"I wonder if they'll miss me this afternoon if I sneak back to the barracks and take a nap. I could use a few winks before the club opens," Crowell said.

That afternoon we learned that approximately half of South Vietnam's population lived in the Mekong Delta region and it was a rich breeding ground for communist insurrection. Since the French left in 1954, communist influence had grown in the rural areas—which was over ninety percent of the Delta. By late afternoon, minds numb with facts nobody cared about, the instructor closed his presentation and directed us to the EM club. "They don't check age. If you're old enough to go to Vietnam—you're old enough to drink."

That evening I sat with Crowell and Dennis and listened to Thomas, the instructor, and two other career men brag about past exploits—one trying to out-do the next. Thomas did well, but the instructor topped his story. He told a story of a Vietnamese navy lieutenant he'd been stationed with on a river boat who had been captured and tortured. How he—the instructor—discovered a pack of dogs pulling at the man's carved, burn-tormented body.

Thomas couldn't top that story. I don't think he wanted to try. He took a sip, raised his glass and said, "You know the difference between a fairy tale and a war story? One begins, 'once upon a time,' the other begins, 'this ain't no shit.'" It raised a feeble chuckle but conversations trailed off.

The next morning, boat crews were assembled and I learned that Thomas would be the captain of the Armored Troop Carrier (ATC) I would be stationed on in Vietnam. Great friggin birthday gift. October 30 was my birthday, twenty years old—one more year, I could drink legally and vote. Why was I so lucky—getting that character for a boat captain?

Our ATC had a seven-man crew.

Eyes settling on me, Thomas said, "Affield, you did a WestPac cruise, you're Boatswain's Mate Third Class. You're the cox'n and in charge of the crew. You make sure all work is done." He was obsessed with hanging names on people. He called me Afe—like 'safe' without the 's.'

Thomas glanced down at his notes then eyed a black Gunners Mate Seaman and asked his name. "Stonewall. That's an unusual name—he was a Confederate. You're tall. You look like you could handle the 20mm cannon."

Stonewall nodded wordlessly.

Shifting to Dennis he frowned. "You're a little shit, where are you from? What's your name?"

"Wisconsin. My name is Dennis."

"Dennis—I like that—Dennis the Menace. Those gooks better look out for you. Think you can handle a .50 caliber machine gun?"

"I think so."

Next, Thomas looked at Crowell; from grungy white hat

to scuffed shoes. His red, two day whisker growth sparkled in the early morning sun. With a high-pitched nasal twang, Thomas, mimicking the cartoon character Roadrunner, said, "Well, well, well, ain't we a fucking beauty—red-on-the-head-like-the-dick-on-a-dog."

Crowell, no—Crow. You're a mess. Take a shower, shave, get into a clean uniform."

"I don't have any clean uniforms left."

"You red-headed turd, you better get your shit together. Do your laundry, then get your ass back. You're assigned to the other .50 caliber machine gun."

Thomas then focused on a sailor who reminded me of a trapped raccoon. He was short with a receding hairline. His close-set eyes were locked on Thomas. He was clean-shaven and his uniform shined but I sensed hostility before a word was spoken.

"So you went to radioman school. Where'd you graduate in your class?" Thomas asked.

"I graduated first in my class. I want you to know I didn't volunteer for this duty. I will not kill anyone. I'm here to man the radio. That's it." He hunched forward in self-defense and I imagined, like the trapped animal, bristles rising beneath his shirt.

"You fat fuck. You better start looking for a new billet," Thomas spit the words as he bent forward, face six inches from the radioman. "When we get in the shit, if you don't shoot, I'll drop you myself."

"I'm not going to fight with you. I'll do a good job on the radio. That's why I'm here," replied the radioman, holding his place.

"What the fuck are you, a college boy? A protester? You're older than these other kids. How old are you?"

"I'm twenty-three. I graduated from Ohio State. I have a B.A. in history and planned to go on for my Masters when

I got a draft notice so I joined the navy. I don't think we belong in Vietnam, that's why I won't shoot."

"Well, well. A professor—a B.A.—sounds more like BS. You're on my radar you fat little fuck. If I catch you slacking, you'll be in the hurt bag. That'll be your name—Professor." Shaking his head in disgust, Thomas moved to the last man.

Instinctively, I felt sorry for the man. He reminded me of a scared dog. He had cowered beneath the barrage against Professor. Now he cringed as Thomas turned to him. Patchworked acne scars masked his dark complexion. Greasy brown hair straggled out from under a worn hat. His shoes were scuffed and looked as if they'd never seen a spit shine. His eyes dropped to the asphalt when Thomas questioned him.

"So you're a Snipe. Have you ever worked with 6-71 Marine diesels before?"

"No, but I studied them in school."

"You better learn those friggin engines inside and out. I don't have time for mechanical problems. You're responsible for all mechanical and electrical maintenance on the boat. If you don't know it, you better find someone to teach you. Fast. And clean up—you smell like an oil slick."

"I'll do the best I can," Snipe said.

Thomas glared at us. "I'm going to drive you hard. You're going to learn teamwork. You're going to learn to do each others' jobs. When somebody gets wounded or killed in a firefight you'll be able to take over their position. We're going to be the best trained crew and the most squared away boat in the squadron. By the end of our tour we'll have the highest gook body-count in Vietnam. If anybody has a problem with that, they'll deal with me."

Great birthday present, I thought again—having Thomas for a leader for the next year.

Early next morning, our class boarded several large landing craft equipped with an assortment of weapons our river assault boats would be armed with. We left Coronado Naval Station and crossed a short stretch of ocean to San Clemente Island. I welcomed the warm autumn sun and open sea after days in the classroom. The Gunners Mate instructors, another boat crew, Thomas, Crow, Stonewall, and I hugged the weather side of the boat—the side blocking the wind—as ocean spray shot up from the blunt nose and across the open well-deck. Seagulls followed along, snapping up bits of discarded food as we picked through the bag lunches prepared for the voyage.

Dennis, Snipe, and Professor lined the lee side of the well-deck, drenched with spray as they leaned over the gunnel vomiting. When the boat dipped on the down-side of each swell between gusts of ocean spray, Crow jumped behind them, pulled a deep drag from the cigar he was puffing, and blew a cloud toward them. He leaned near Professor and blew directly into his pallid face, triggering another bout of heaving.

"Knock that shit off Crow, I want those boys healthy when we get there," Thomas yelled across the well-deck.

"I'm just having a little fun," Crow yelled back as he blew a cloud into Snipe's face.

"You want fun? Throw that fucking dog turd over the side before I feed it to you, then we'll all see some fun."

Crow pitched his cigar over the side, muttered something unintelligible about fucking wimps, then sat down by me.

The southern portion of San Clemente was the naval firing range. Cross-training was emphasized. Several of the instructors had recently returned from tours in Vietnam and stressed the fact that we must be proficient at every duty in the event of casualties, reinforcing what Thomas had said.

A Gunner's Mate First Class stood at the front of the boat. "Fire short bursts, three to five rounds to find the target, then longer bursts. Don't hold the trigger down. The weapon will overheat and wander off target. Continue firing until those little fuckers are wasted."

He stepped to the side of the well-deck where a .50 caliber machine gun was mounted, grasped the handles, sighted down the barrel for an instant, then fired. Even though we expected it, everyone jumped. With the first burst, sand spit up in front of the target on the beach two hundred meters away. The second, third, and fourth bursts sent the target reeling and smoke drifting across the well-deck.

I watched and listened. On the *Rogers* everything had been long-distance. Even the day we were shelled we never saw our enemy and once we were inside the armored gun mount firing back, it seemed like just another exercise. I couldn't fathom being shot or shooting at somebody.

There were things about the instructors I didn't understand. I began watching one near me. His eyes darted constantly—I soon realized why. If a gun started firing and he wasn't expecting it, he recoiled and ducked. He seemed detached. As the afternoon progressed, I noticed him staring out to sea, as if watching something only he could see. I tried to start a conversation with him.

"Where were you stationed when you were over there?" I asked.

He glanced over, never made eye contact. "I was up north."

"I was in Danang about two years ago on a destroyer," I told him. "I spent the afternoon circling the ship in our motor launch, watching for enemy swimmers who might try to attach a mine to the ship."

"Did you catch any?"

"No, all I remember was getting bored and cold and wet."

He looked out from under the drooping brim of his faded blue hat. "Get used to it. Another twenty-two days and I'm done with this shit and home free."

He turned his back to me then, signaling an end to the conversation. The next morning our boat crew began firing the weapons.

I was familiar with the .30 caliber machine gun. When my turn came to fire the .50 caliber and 20mm cannon, I was surprised at my reaction. During the short bursts of power my body echoed each thud. The roar consumed me. I felt invincible. I watched the tracers arc shoreward as targets and sand surrounding the impact area came alive. No one could survive that onslaught, I reasoned to myself. As I watched other crew members firing, I tried to understand the sensation that swept over me during those moments. I realized it was power. A sense of complete power.

When I was young, on early autumn mornings before school, I would sneak down to the lake behind our farm and shoot migrating ducks. Using a single-shot 12 gauge shotgun, I'd creep through willows to the lake's boggy edge where feeding mallards swam in groups near the shore. I would wait patiently until three or four ducks were in a row, then fire. Rarely, did I kill less than three. In the instant before I fired, I would hesitate as I watched them beyond the bead on my rust-stained, pitted barrel—and the feeling of omnipotence as my finger tip caressed the trigger. I recalled the flash of remorse as the birds flapped their death throes, brilliant green feathers glittering with air-borne beads of water in early morning sun. The following day I'd return for more.

The Honeywell grenade launcher delivered death in innocent-sounding bloops that a sharp eye could follow from barrel to target. HE, high explosive rounds, had a kill radius of fifteen meters. The little olive-green launcher reminded me of the hand-crank meat grinder we had back on the farm, only this grinder turned out 40mm grenades. My left hand aimed the launcher from a handle mounted on the back while the right hand turned the side-mounted crank. One turn of the handle launched four belt-fed grenades. We were taught to launch two, watch where they landed, adjust up, down, or sideways; then fire a few more. When on target, fire for effect. I loved that weapon.

"Afe, you're good on that thing," Thomas grinned.

"It's almost like tossing a football long distance," I told him. "My eye follows it from the barrel. I can feel where it's going to land."

One of the instructors who was listening stepped in. "That's good shooting. But on the rivers you don't usually worry about a trajectory. The action is so close that you aim straight or just above. Let the grenades detonate in trees above the bunkers and spray down."

We spent several days at San Clemente Island. Warm, cloudless days with calm seas. Each day we went out and fired the weapons. Late afternoon we moored at the island naval base, disassembled the weapons and cleaned them. We learned their nomenclature and how to maintain them. Time flowed leisurely. We got to know one another and learned to operate as a team. In the evenings we gathered at the EM Club.

Thomas seemed jealous that I had done one tour in Vietnam already and was only one rank behind him, though he had seven years in the navy compared to my two and a half. He didn't stop to consider that he had served during peacetime when advancement was slow. By 1967, with the Vietnam War escalating, more petty officers were needed, therefore advancements were accelerated. The navy promoted a man through a process of recommendations and written tests in the individual's specialty. For Boatswain's Mate rate there were a wide range of specialized knowledge—from duties on tugboats to aircraft carriers, from weaponry to navigation, from cargo handling to cable splicing.

"Hey Afe—on a cargo ship, what's the boom called over a hatch?" he asked.

"I don't know. Like I told you, I served on a destroyer. Ask me anything about that," I replied.

"You dumb shit, it's called a hatch boom. How the fuck did you pass the test? I know that question was on it," he mocked, as other sailors grinned in silence.

"I read a lot. What's the maximum range of a 5"/38 HE round?" I retorted.

He looked at me and silently mouthed, "Fuck off."

Crow was such a suck-up. Each day he smuggled liquor aboard and shared it with Thomas. He was an artist at slipping away from work details.

Everybody agreed that Stonewall was the acknowledged expert on the 20mm cannon. The first positive words I heard Thomas say. "Your mama named you right—Stonewall Jackson was a marksman too." Stonewall nodded without a word.

Thomas grudgingly admitted that Dennis was very good on his .50 caliber. "You little shit. When the gun fires, you lift right off the deck. I'm going to strap an ammo crate to each foot. You will be a menace to those gooks."

Besides taking his turn at firing the weapons, Professor practiced radio etiquette and learned to monitor different bands and call-signs from radiomen on other boats. No more was said about his philosophical position, but Thomas watched him. He good-naturedly accepted his nickname and smirked a little grin when addressed. I thought he was proud of it.

Thomas zeroed in on Snipe when he fired the guns. "You useless fuck, you couldn't hit the side of a barn with a shovel full of shit if you were locked inside. Try turning those coke-bottle glasses upside down. That might help."

He told Snipe not to waste any more taxpayer money shooting the big guns. "Stick to the .30 caliber. That's what you'll have in the well-deck to shoot. We'll all be dead before you'll be needed above deck—by then it won't matter."

I think Snipe was trying to learn about the engines. I noticed that he spent time at the back of the LCU visiting with the engineman. More than once I saw him come out of the engine compartment. If Thomas noticed, he made no mention of it. One evening at the EM Club, Snipe told me that he had gotten married while home on leave but now regretted it.

"She hasn't written me a letter since I got to Coronado and when I try to call her, she's never home," he lamented.

"It's only been about eight days," I told him.

I thought Snipe's constant worry about his new bride was distracting him—affecting his performance. He was homely and I wondered what kind of girl would marry him. It was a fact that some women married men scheduled for Vietnam in hopes of collecting their $10,000 life insurance. A nice paycheck for a few months of marriage.

One morning we cruised around the end of the island and discovered a new target—a WWII liberty ship hulk anchored between the shoreline and us. An F-4 Phantom jet screamed down out of the early morning sun, cannons blazing, and strafed the ship. The roar of engines and echo of firing hit us with a light concussion. The plane swooped down over the wreckage, then up—gone in an instant—the old ship left smoldering. We stared, transfixed, as other jets followed. After releasing bomb loads they pulled skyward as their bombs pulverized the burning hulk. Smoke drifted low across the morning swells.

San Clemente Island was shrouded in fog our last day. Target shooting was cancelled and we were ordered back to

Coronado. Mid-day found us transiting the open sea through thick haze, everybody damp in the open well-deck. Visibility was zero as the boat eased over glazed swells.

Suddenly there was a shout. "Watch out! There's a boat coming toward us!"

Through drizzling fog I watched the apparition take shape. It was a gray whale with crusted barnacle patches. The whale rubbed against us, apparently disoriented in the fog. The dark gray, slope-humped mass loomed a few feet higher than our gunnel and I reached out and ran my hand along the slick, rippling flank. My fingers brushed over a rough spot, a clump of barnacles. Perhaps he thought we were one of his pod. In another instant he was fading into the mist.

We returned to Coronado Naval Station late in the afternoon and found orders directing us north to Whidbey Island, off the coast of Washington State for survival training.

That next morning I went to the post office and Snipe had fourteen letters. We all had something—everybody except Thomas. I think he was jealous of Snipe that day. That afternoon, strapped into web seats along the walls of the aircraft, we couldn't hear a word over the loud engines as we flew to Whidbey Island.

The summer of 1964 when I rode the rails from Minnesota to Seattle to see my grandmother, we had visited Whidbey Island for a day. As a young woman, she had spent summers on the island where her husband's family had a dairy farm called Greenbank. In the 1930s they began growing loganberries. By the summer of '64 when we took the ferry across the harbor and explored the island, the estate was called Greenbank Berry Farm.

Now, as we flew over the island, I tried to locate the road we had traveled and the old homestead on the sandy coast. I searched for the big red barn, but didn't spot it.

Survival, Evasion, Resistance, Escape (SERE): Capture and escape seemed top priority. If captured during a firefight, that was also the best time to escape. At that point you were closest to friendly forces—it was also the most likely time you'd be executed if you attempted escape. As you were moved away from the battle scene, the odds of escape diminished. If you did escape at some point, follow the river flow. It would lead you to the coast.

The training, originally designed for naval pilots, was directed by Marine Corps personnel who role-played Viet Cong soldiers. Psychological effect of captivity was stressed. After several days with no food and very little sleep, we would be captured, imprisoned, and interrogated.

Four days later, I was evading our "Viet Cong" enemy. Low, dark clouds scudded overhead as I crept through the forest. I felt at home stalking across the pungent damp earth, my senses heightened as my eyes scoured the area ahead of me. I spotted an "enemy soldier" and dropped to the ground where I lay still as a new-born fawn. Ferns rustled behind me. Several minutes passed. I knew he must be very close. The odor of fresh-broken ferns mingled with the fir needles scratching my cheek.

The forest floor reminded me of my deer lick back home. I had saturated a rotting stump with saltwater far back in the forest at the base of a ridge near Horseshoe Lake. I could sneak up, lie on the ground, and look down to the lick—the deer never aware of my presence. No one else knew about the lick.

Pine needles stuck to my cheek when I turned my head. Through the ferns I spotted a double-knotted shiny black boot close to my face. It kicked me in the side.

"Stupid Amelikan pig. You told not to move. You mine now."

He ordered me to my feet and told me to go out to the trail. When I reached it, I found most of our class standing around, joking. Most of us had gotten caught, but a few made it through undetected. We began hiking south.

Without warning, "Viet Cong" soldiers jumped from camouflaged positions along the sides of the trail, fired bursts into the air, and declared us prisoners of war (POW). They pulled black hoods over our heads then ordered us to place a hand on the shoulder of the man in front of us and march. I was cold and hungry, but not scared. I knew this was a game and would soon be over. I was thirsty. I hadn't had a drink since I finished my salted beef jerky. It was late afternoon by the time we were ordered to halt and strip off our uniforms.

Naked, bag over my head, I was hit with a blast of icy water from a high-pressure hose. The cold water was numbing in the November wind. I cupped my hands below my chin as I tried to deflect some water up under my hood. I was tripped. Hands wrapped around my neck and grabbed me by the arms, pinning me.

"Ahh, Amelikin thirsty? Dlink. Dlink." And they held my hood while the hose nozzle was pushed up. High pressure water, trapped inside my hood, penetrated my ears, nose, and throat. I couldn't breathe—inhaled water—coughed—inhaled more—panicked and kicked at my assailants. I was cuffed alongside my hooded head, making my ear ring. Then they released me and walked away laughing. I lay shivering, gasping for breath as I listened to them torment others.

"You a big boy." A kick thudded to my left. "You the asshole that thought parachutes a joke?"

"Blacky." A kick thudded beyond my hooded head. "Why you want to kill Vietnamese while white men burn your neighborhoods?"

"You a big one." Kicks thudded to my right. "Why you shaking—you scared? We just little gook fuckers—keep that hood down, asshole."

Footsteps approached, kicked me in the side—not hard—just enough to intimidate. "Stupid Amelikan pig. Get dressed." He yanked my hood off. Shivering into wet fatigues, I surveyed my surroundings.

We were clustered in a grassy area in front of a POW camp. The compound was about two hundred feet square enclosed by twelve-foot barbed wire walls with a guard tower at each corner. There were three sandbag-reinforced log bunkers inside the prison yard. Outside the compound were several low buildings. A lieutenant was senior man of our training class and took charge once we were locked in.

We stood in formation and counted off. All boat crews were present.

From a guard tower, the prison commandant addressed us with a microphone. "Amelikan pigs, you will stand at attention." He paused and sipped from a steaming mug of coffee then bit into a sandwich. "You will not enter the bunkers. In the morning, I will visit with each of you."

As November darkness settled, my stomach cramped and I began shivering. Floodlights illuminated the prison yard. We remained in formation while loudspeakers blared in scratchy voices. The tapes, the accent foreign—perhaps French—reminded me of Tokyo Rose propaganda I had heard in World War II movies. But these had a new message, for today's world. "The United States criminal aggression is white man's war. Wealthy upper class Americans become richer and more powerful at the expense of the poor working classes who have been drafted to do their dirty work. How many millionaire's children or college students are in your unit? You black boys—why do you fight when you cannot even sit in the same café as the whites?" The scratchy recording blared on. "Come, join us. Many of your countrymen and women come to Hanoi. They see the damage done by your bombs."

We laughed and saluted the recording with our middle finger as we booed and cursed the traitors to America. We stood in formation through the black November night. We did calisthenics to stay warm and marched inside the perimeter to stay awake.

A drizzling dawn crept upon us. Fistfuls of carrots and celery flew over the fence. Guards stood in shadows beyond the fence, laughing as we scrambled for them. Our lieutenant ordered us to turn all food over to him. He divided it into equal portions for the boat crews then distributed it to the boat captains who in turn divided it to their crews. Thomas gave me a three-inch stalk of dirty celery and a half carrot. I chewed slowly, stretching the meal into a one-hour feast.

A hard sun burned the cloud cover off but it was a damp, hungry day. Guards began pulling small groups out of the compound for interrogation. They marched us to a small building and separated us.

My guard shoved me into a small, unpainted room; bare except for a desk with a high-backed chair, the back facing me. Another plain wooden chair stood in front of the desk. A naked bulb dangled from the ceiling on an electrical cord— just like the torture scene in a movie. With the muzzle of his AK-47, I was prodded toward the chair.

"Sit, Amelikan pig." He left the room, closing the door behind him. I sat wondering what would happen next, when the high-back chair swiveled. An effeminate "interrogator" slammed his pistol, muzzle toward me, on the desk.

He doesn't look very tough, I thought.

"How many men in your unit, pig?" He opened a drawer, casually raised a knife. "What your boat captain's name?" He spoke softly, squinting through slitted eyes as he thumbed the gleaming blade.

I stared at him. We had been instructed in the Military

Code of Conduct. We were obligated to give only name, rank, and serial number. "Afe, BM3, 9140521," I said.

Gently, almost in a whisper, he probed. "Amelikan pig, how many in your unit. You can disappear. No one will ever know. Your countrymen have abandoned you, they don't care. I spit on Geneva Convention. You are criminals. What your boat captain's name?" He grabbed my wrist, pulled my hand toward him. With a light stroke, he shaved the hair from the tattoo on my arm.

"Afe, BM 3, 9140521," I repeated, telling myself this was just a game. He had no power over me. He couldn't really hurt me.

Licking thin lips, he pushed his chair back and stood with a smile. He holstered the pistol and stepped behind me. Grabbing my hair, he snapped my head back. I felt the cold edge of the blade as it slipped down my cheek to the side of my throat. In a low, gentle tone, he said, "I ask you one last time Amelikan pig, how many in your unit?"

This is a game. He's forbidden to hurt me. "Afe, BM3, 9140521." But he was right. If this were the real thing, he could slit my throat and no one would ever know.

He removed the blade, yanked me to the floor by the hair, and pushed me forward with his foot, shouting, "Comrade, throw this criminal in the box. Soften him up."

I was shoved out the door into the hallway. The guard prodded me in the back, down the narrow passageway toward the back of the building where I stumbled into sunlight.

Five wooden boxes rested on the ground—they reminded me of children's coffins—dull black in the hard light. They were approximately two feet wide, two feet deep, five feet long, with a hinged top that locked with an iron clasp. Three guards sat on the shaded porch drinking coffee while two walked between the boxes with clubs. Randomly, one would strike a box. "Stay awake Amelikan pig. Don't get too comfortable."

The senior guard pointed to the box at the left end. "Pull that pig out, throw this one in."

The steel clasp was unlatched. Dennis climbed out and glanced at me. He rolled his eyes in an expression I interpreted to mean, *this wasn't bad*. But he was smaller than me.

The guard saw us smirk and screamed, "You think it funny, pig." He clubbed me on the back, knocking me down. I looked across the box and saw Dennis was on his hands and knees gasping for breath. His guard had knocked the wind out of him. I was kicked in the side and told to get up. I glanced over to several boxes I hadn't noticed before. They stood upright—approximately three feet wide, three feet deep, four and half feet high.

I was pushed forward. "Into the box, pig—now."

I stepped into the box wondering how the hell he expected me to fit.

"Kneel, pig." He pushed me forward, down, my shoulders wedged between the walls, my face scrunched to the floor. He slammed the lid and jumped on it while I heard another guard latch it. My knees were jammed into my stomach, my leg muscles stretched tight. I couldn't breathe. It was pitch black. I realized I was holding my breath. Slowly releasing it, I took bearings. It was actually warm in the box and I sensed a bit of light creeping in from tiny ventilation holes above my head.

A sharp blow on the side of the box made me throw my head up, cracking the back of it against the lid. "Stay awake, Amelikan pig."

I listened for footsteps so they wouldn't startle me again.

A muffled shout broke the silence. "Hey, let me out. I'll tell you whatever the fuck you want to know."

The guards laughed. "Open box comrade. That Amelikan criminal wising up."

One of the boxes was opened. "Man, that friggin box is too small for me."

I recognized the voice. It belonged to Mays, the captain of another boat. "You got a cigarette?"

I listened intently.

"Man it feels good to stretch my arms, this cigarette do taste great."

I heard a new voice approaching—sounded like my interrogator. "Ahh, dis da Amelikan who forsakes his comrades? How many men in your unit, Blacky?"

Silence. Then Mays' voice. "This cigarette sure do taste great."

The interrogator, his voice rising, asked again. "How many men in your unit Blacky?"

"You talking to me, you fucking gook?" I heard Mays laugh gleefully.

The interrogator, pissed, made no attempt at mimicking an accent. "Lock that asshole up, back in the box. You think this is just a game?"

We shouted encouragement as we listened to him being forced back down into the box. The guards descended on us with clubs, pounding our boxes in frustration.

My box was opened.

"Out of the box, pig." The guard grabbed me, lifted me up, then released me and I toppled to the ground. Both legs had fallen asleep. He looked down laughing. "Amelikan forget how to walk? How many men in your unit?"

I look up at him and repeated my name, rank, serial number.

"Into the cage with you, pig." He reached down, pulled me up and half dragged me to the larger boxes. Opening the door, he shoved me in. These were more miserable than the last ones. I couldn't stand or sit. I had to lean against one side with my knees flexed. My leg muscles were soon screaming. I bent over and lowered myself to the floor, knees against the far side of the box with my legs bent double. I felt them going numb. I didn't want that to happen again so I stood up and bent my head and shoulders forward with the top of my head resting against the far side of the box. I was thankful this was only a game. I didn't think I would survive the real thing. I promised myself that if I ever were in a position to be captured, I wouldn't be taken alive. Then I thought of our heavily armored boats. There was no way the Viet Cong could get near me.

The door opened. "What your boat captain's name, pig?"

Again I repeated my name, rank, and serial number. The senior guard yelled over, "Throw him back in the compound."

In the compound, I was interviewed by the lieutenant. "Did you tell the 'enemy' anything?"

"No sir. Only name, rank, and serial number."

We stood in small groups rehashing our experiences, laughing about Mays. By late afternoon all the interrogations were completed—one man had broken and told his interrogator his boat captain's name. He would be sent back to the fleet.

Our POW training was over. Euphoria flowed through the bus as we rode to the naval station mess hall. We'd survived SERE training. We convinced ourselves that we could survive real captivity. Listening, I was reminded of the too-loud laughter that night two years earlier on the *Rogers* in Gulf of Tonkin.

That afternoon we left for Vallejo, California where we would begin our hands-on boat training at Mare Island Naval Station.

The barracks at Mare Island were built during World War II—two-story wooden structures wrapped in faded yellow stucco with large bare windows and hardwood floors. Inside, it smelled like my little country school, old wax and resinous red shavings used to pick up dust.

Our days at Mare Island began at 0500 hours with Reveille. We were dressed and on the parade ground by 0530. A half hour of calisthenics warmed us for the five-mile run around the base.

Late one night at the EM club, Thomas sat hunched over his whiskey at a table with several other boat captains. As usual, they were boisterous with Thomas leading the way. He leaned forward, head scrunched into his shoulders. Liquored eyes squinted against rising cigar smoke. Jimmy, a pear-shaped boat captain next to him laughed and said, "Thomas, you remind me of a Buddha I saw once up in Kyoto."

Everybody burst out laughing—he did look like a Buddha statue—his head set on stocky shoulders, the scowl, the tight eyes, the round belly when he leaned forward. He skewed his face, spit into his cup, and smiled a crooked grin, miming what a Jim Beam loving Buddha must look like.

I think the incongruity was lost on most of us. Professor may have chuckled to himself, juxtaposing Thomas to Buddha. Thomas liked the name, perhaps felt linked to a divinity. Maybe felt that in the scheme of things—being captain of a riverboat—he warranted such an exalted title. He began signing his name "Budda" Ed Thomas. Professor must have gotten a charge out of the fact that he didn't know how to spell it. From then on, Thomas was known as Buddha.

Autumn slipped into winter. Our uninsulated barracks reminded me of home where pee cans froze solid in the hallway outside our upstairs bedrooms. I didn't think California got so cold—some mornings I could see my breath. Burrowed into my covers for five more minutes of warmth, I'd listen to the world stir around me. Early one Sunday morning I eavesdropped on an exchange.

Buddha coughed, hawked phlegm, and asked, "Where the hell you going so early in the morning?"

"There's a sunrise church service in town," Stonewall said. "Then a Thanksgiving breakfast."

"Well, say a little prayer for the Buddha," he rasped. "I'll put a good word in for you."

We learned small unit tactics—how to operate in concert with other boats. Corpsman taught us first aid; how to seal sucking-chest wounds, place a tourniquet, bandage wounds, inject a morphine syrette, cut white phosphorus or napalm out of flesh.

We were told what to look for on the river. Point-detonating floating mines camouflaged by vegetation that exploded when you ran into them. Beware of scuff marks on the riverbank that covered wires snaking up out of the water leading to submerged command-detonating mines—triggered as you passed over. We were taught how to spot camouflaged enemy bunkers along the riverbanks by watching for wilted foliage, leaves hanging unnaturally, fresh dirt, unusual openings in vegetation along the dense, low-hung riverbanks. Early December we moved to operating the boats.

An ironclad gunboat out of the Civil War, trapped inside a steel cage—that was my first impression of the Armored Troop Carrier I would be driving in Vietnam. It was a converted LCM 6, Landing Craft Mechanized—like the landing craft in WWII movies hitting the beaches of Normandy and Iwo Jima. She was painted the same dull green as an army tank. No graceful, jutting bowline for slicing through waves. The only recognizable features were the well-deck—the open compartment where troops stood—and the high, ribbed bow ramp, the flat front that dropped when they stormed ashore. Even the well-deck was altered by a dark green canvas awning designed to protect troops from the elements. The steel cage was composed of iron re-bar to detonate rockets before they reached the one inch armor plating.

"Keep that awning laced tight," the instructor said. "When grenades are tossed at you from riverbanks they'll bounce off and into the water before they detonate."

The Sacramento River Delta is similar to the Mekong Delta. Each morning we cruised for about two hours to our training area—south in Mare Island Strait, turning east into Carquinez Strait, then across Suisun Bay and into the slough.

Suisun Slough must be a wintering ground for northern birds I thought, as we swung into a canal. A red tail hawk cruised back and forth above a mud flat, just like the ones above our hay fields back on the farm. Sparrows and kestrels flitted about in the scrubby brush along the shoreline. I glimpsed red-winged blackbirds in stunted cattails. As we moved up into the canal, mudflats changed to sandy banks and trees began to replace brush along the banks.

"Keep your head down," Buddha shouted as a flare trailed over our boat and shots rang out.

"Corpen niner, corpen niner," blared the boat's radio, three feet behind me. That was my cue to swing port ninety degrees, hit the riverbank, drop the ramp into the face of the ambush, and land troops.

The instant the boat nosed into the bank I pulled the lever to release the ramp but it didn't drop. From behind me, Buddha shouted, "Drop the ramp. Afe, drop the friggin ramp."

"I did," I yelled back.

"Snipe, did you release the safety latch on the ramp?" Buddha said.

"It's stuck. I can't get it loose."

"You dumb fuck. When Afe swings toward the bank, you know you're supposed to release it before he tries to drop it." Without pausing for breath, Buddha continued, "Afe, you're broaching, straighten out. Crow, Dennis, Stonewall, why aren't your turrets turned so your guns are facing the bank?"

I looked to the side and discovered the boat had swung to starboard. The tide was going out and the current had carried the boat's stern over. The boat straightened when I kicked the port engine forward, swung the helm to starboard and surged against the sandy bank.

Boat crews gathered ashore and the instructors critiqued our performance. Nobody had spotted the telltale signs they'd left for us along the bank—footsteps, freshly cut trees, a few branches lying on the bank. The games continued for several weeks. Information trickled back from Vietnam, where riverine operations continually evolved. We worked on new tactics to offset enemy advances. Mines became a growing concern.

The blank ammunition fired at us caused no damage but the flares were dangerous. They disintegrated when striking the boats and splattered bits of smoldering magnesium which often hit somebody. The instructors must have been aiming at us when they fired. One young sailor had a flare explode near his face and was shipped to the hospital. We heard later that he was blind—poor kid, I thought.

Christmas weekend Dennis, Professor, and I, dressed in civvies, went down to San Francisco and visited Haight Ashbury. We stepped out of a taxi and onto a sidewalk swarming with long-haired young people dressed in baggy, brightly colored clothing. Everybody was talking, singing, swaying. A melody seemed to float—about "flowers in your hair." It was a popular song that winter and I found myself humming along—sweet smoke seemed to waft with the music.

"Hey man, got a quarter?" a bead-decked bearded man asked. Dennis handed him one. "You guys in the navy?" A small crowd was gathering round to see the short-haired black-shoed outsiders. I was surprised. They knew we were in the military but rather than bad-mouth us, they sympathized with us.

"Yeah man, my brother's in the army—got drafted. Says it really sucks, I told him to go to Canada but he won't do it."

We walked up one side of the main street and down the other, into a park. I watched a girl sitting beneath a eucalyptus tree reading aloud from a book of poetry. Legs curled inside a long dress, her toes peeked out and her granny glasses rested on the tip of her nose. She glanced up, gazed beyond the music, the sweet smoke, the laughter, and the jokes and for a fleeting instant our eyes met and she smiled. I realized then, she was writing—her eyes floated down, retracing, doodling, taking ownership of her discoveries. From a Berkley '67 bag she pulled a dictionary. From a hidden pocket, a handful of popcorn for the squirrels chattering nearby. As the critters nibbled treats, the girl devoured words, flipped pages, wrote, crossed out. I watched her a moment longer, then turned away.

On our return trip to Mare Island we rode in silence. Dennis was the first to speak. "When I get back from Vietnam I'm coming back here."

"They don't seem like the antiwar protesters back in Ohio," Professor said. "They seem like a bunch of aimless kids."

I was confused. I wondered what they did for a living— they couldn't live just bumming money—but I thought Dennis might be right. I felt comfortable in that park, watching that girl under the big tree.

It was a curious encounter. Everything was so compressed. In San Diego and Seattle I'd seen hippies, but nothing like this. Growing up in the sheltered farm environment and enlisting soon after turning seventeen, I'd traded that isolation for the Navy. This flower child culture I had stepped into left me feeling empty and these long-haired people my age left me wanting something.

Graduation day. The base commander praised our commitment to country. He emphasized the critical role of Vietnam in the battle against communism—if Vietnam fell, then Laos, then Cambodia, then Thailand. Where might it end? Our sacrifice would insure the future democracy of South Vietnam and the world. He proclaimed the Vietnamese our brothers. We were a wall against communism. Our instructors, all veterans of Vietnam, stood behind him smirking.

We had six days before our flight to Vietnam. I flew up to Seattle to visit my grandmother and Marian, a girl I'd been dating the previous summer. Granny was a die-hard Republican and anti-communist. Her parting words were, "Kill a commie for me, dear." Marian drove me to SeaTac airport. Long afterward I would remember her tear-filled eyes as I entered the loading ramp for my red-eye flight to San Francisco.

That was the last time I saw either of them.

When I returned to Mare Island, I learned that North Korea had captured the USS *Pueblo*. They claimed it was inside their territorial waters, gathering intelligence. Rumors were flying.

We were going to invade North Korea.

The North Koreans had executed sailors from the *Pueblo*.

General Douglas MacArthur was being recalled to active duty and the U.S. was going to nuke North Korea.

I recalled my encounter on the pier in Bremerton. If the USS *Pueblo* was an intelligence-gathering ship, I now understood why the third class boatswains mate I'd wanted to swap duty stations with had needed a top secret clearance.

"That cowardly son of a bitch. That's the first U.S. ship

captured in over a hundred years," Buddha ranted, referring to the *Pueblo's* captain.

Late morning our class was transported to Travis Air Force Base, near San Francisco, for our flight to Vietnam. We were scheduled to depart early afternoon with a refueling stop in Anchorage, Alaska but our flight was delayed several hours then rerouted to Fairbanks.

Mini-skirted stewardesses greeted us as we boarded. Our uniforms were tropical whites because our destination was Kadena, Okinawa, a tropical island south of Japan where we would catch a hop into Tan Son Nhut, near Saigon, Vietnam. Taxiing down the runway I remembered what our instructors had said, "Some of you will be killed, some wounded."

Buddha and his buddies had a poker game going at the rear of the plane. The low hum of conversation was interspersed by sudden shouts of a winning hand. One man seemed to be a constant winner. I could tell by Buddha's tone he was getting irritated.

I was awakened by a cockpit announcement, "Ladies and gentlemen please fasten your seatbelts. We're descending into heavy cloud cover and expect turbulence."

Snowflakes whipped by as the plane thudded onto the runway. A blizzard was screaming in from the north and there would be no flights out of Fairbanks until the front passed. Braniff Airlines issued each of us an orange blanket because our tropical white uniforms would be no protection from Arctic winds. There were no open barracks on base so we were bussed to hotels downtown.

Windswept Fairbanks reminded me of Bemidji in the dead of winter except here, late-night bars blaring country music seemed to line ice-glazed streets—conversation buzzed from loggers, miners, truckers, oil field workers. We stood out in our tropical white uniforms, cocooned in orange capes. After hearing our destination was Vietnam, our money was no good—free drinks—free meals. By the third day, the storm had blown itself out and we returned to the base. The aircraft buzzed with animated chatter as sailors relived the past few days. One young sailor was the envy of others. He had struck up a friendship with two sisters who wanted a blond haired baby. After three days he sounded relieved to escape.

The Tet Offensive, triggered on January 31, 1968, had been raging across South Vietnam for about sixteen hours when we landed in Okinawa. Rain beat at the aircraft as we taxied toward the terminal. Tan Son Nhut, Vietnam was under rocket attack so our final flight was delayed. Soldiers milled about the terminal. Incoming flights from Vietnam arrived continuously, off-loading troops directly from the field—mud-covered, many still carrying weapons. Buddha returned from a meeting and called us together.

"Listen up. Viet Cong are attacking all over Vietnam— it's supposed to be a holiday truce but the little gook fuckers lied and now they're getting their asses kicked."

Two days slipped by, waiting for our final flight. The terminal was trashed—cigarette butts, Styrofoam cups, papers, assorted bits of clothing cast aside. Everything was coated with monsoon mud—nobody seemed to care.

Home bound troops chanted, "You'll be sorry," as they passed us in search of a place to lie down. They clustered in small groups and I once again heard that strange, high-pitched tone, the fast talk, forced loud laughter. They were still on an adrenaline rush, incredulous that they'd escaped, only a few hours removed from a world we could not then comprehend. When they settled down, I was amazed at how comfortable they appeared, sleeping soundly on cold muddy concrete. Finally, our flight was announced—no mini-skirted stews on this leg.

4

Tan Son Nhut, Vietnam

3 February 1968

In the beginning, Tan Son Nhut was a village near Saigon. The French constructed a dirt airstrip in the late 1920s. During WWII the Japanese Imperial Army occupied it. After the war, the French returned to Vietnam and the airport expanded to accommodate civilian and military flights. In the mid 1950s the South Vietnamese Air Force (SVAF) was formed and headquartered out of Tan Son Nhut. After the French defeat at Dien Bien Phu in 1954, after they left Vietnam, the United States Air Force mentored SVAF into the 1960s with an increasing American presence visible. By February 1968, Tan Son Nhut was a huge military base; headquarters for MACV, US Army 3rd Field Hospital, and one of the busiest airports in the world.

We approached the Vietnamese coast in the night. Engine pitch deepened as we began to descend—the plane banked sharply and dropped at a steep angle to avoid enemy anti-aircraft guns that might be positioned beyond the runways in the jungle. We hit the tarmac with a tire-flaming thud. In shadowed flashes I glimpsed wing flaps shuddering as smoke puffs swirled from squealing tires.

"I thought I was going to lose my cookies," Buddha said.

Flares swayed in the distance like dancing northern lights, casting a distorted glow through the plane's concave portholes. When the doors opened, smoke, fuel fumes, and decay seeped into the aircraft. Raw sewage odor reminded me of Victoria Harbor in Hong Kong.

In the distance, boom followed flash from out-going artillery as we left the airfield. The bus convoy was led by an armed jeep, with another bringing up the rear, two armed guards on each bus. Heavy metal mesh covered the open bus windows to prevent grenades from entering.

"I feel like I'm swimming in a septic tank, it's so humid. What's that smell?" Stonewall asked.

"That's Vietnam—it gets so thick you can chew it—get used to it," said the bus driver.

"How does he know where he's going without his headlights on?" Crow asked, as our bus trailed the darkened jeep.

"We've made this trip so many times we can drive it in our sleep," said one of the guards. A flicker of light illuminated his strained face. Gunfire cracked in the distance. "Probably a sniper. They get a lucky hit once in a while—but not often at night," he added, as if reading our thoughts.

The other guard chuckled. "You Navy boys give Charlie a nice target in those white uniforms. You stand out like Maggie's drawers on a rifle range." Charlie was a slang term for VC derived from the military phonetic alphabet, Victor Charles.

At our barracks we exchanged tropical white uniforms for green fatigue trousers, blouse, and jungle boots. I tucked my sea bag at the end of an empty bunk and lay on the bare mattress, wincing at the flash on the cracked stucco wall as the barracks shuddered with each out-going artillery salvo. The night was filled with distant explosions. Flares hovered in the distance and red and green tracers streaked across the sky—gooks used green, we were told.

Armed guards were posted at our barracks because we'd have no weapons until we reached our boats. Rumor had it that Viet Cong had infiltrated Tan Son Nhut so all Vietnamese civilian help had been barred from the base. Even South Vietnamese Army troops were looked upon with suspicion. Buddha said we'd be transported south to the Mekong Delta via helicopter but at the moment we were low priority. They were engaged in the Tet offensive and the defense of Saigon.

Morning sun burned hot in the cloudless sky. The constant thump-thump-thump of helicopters and the distant roar of aircraft seemed to make the air shimmer.

"Afe, get the crew together," Buddha said. "They're not letting any gooks on base to help in the mess hall so we're only going to eat twice a day. Everybody stay in a group this morning when we leave the barracks."

By afternoon it was well over one hundred degrees. The barracks reminded me of the steel hayloft back home. After loading hay onto wagons and hoisting it into the loft, we would level it in late afternoon and evening. The steel roof absorbed the day's heat, trapping it, and we couldn't escape until the job was done. This heat was the same only more humid.

"There's a new John Wayne movie we can go watch called *The Green Berets* if we can scrounge up some money," I said to our boat crew as we returned from afternoon chow the second day.

"Lucky's loaning money," Buddha said. "Five for seven, ten for fourteen, payable payday." Lucky—Buddha had sardonically nicknamed him—was the card player who had cleaned him out.

"Just getting into air-conditioning will make it worth it," Crow said. Between last-minute partying in California, the days in Alaska, and the layover in Okinawa, everybody was broke.

Lucky's business was booming. "Give your name and your boat captain's name to my bookkeeper and don't make me come looking for you on payday because the price will go up," he announced to the line forming at his bunk.

I borrowed forty dollars—sixteen dollars was high interest for two weeks but I thought, what else was there to spend it on?

Buddha borrowed one hundred and wasn't happy about it. "It's a shitty deal to borrow my own money. His friggin luck's going to change. Come payday, I'll win it back."

That afternoon, in a cool theater, we watched John Wayne kill Vietnamese communists while the theater floor vibrated from out-going artillery on the other side of the base. I recalled his heroics in *Sands of Iwo Jima* and again felt that surge of patriotism. I empathized with the little boy when his dog was killed. Around us, many laughed at the battle scenes and dialogue.

"Look at the starched uniforms those assholes are wearing in the bush."

"Where the fuck are the mosquitoes?"

"I ain't never seen no bitches like that one over here."

"John Wayne better stick with westerns—he don't know shit about this hole."

"I've never seen a gook that I'd share a fighting hole with—can't trust the little fuckers. I say let them keep this sewer."

"I'm waiting for a shot of gooks dropping their guns and running—let's get real here."

"Yeah, and how about a shot of them stealing. Little fuckers take anything that ain't tied down."

"Makes you wonder why we're here, don't it?"

"Fuck, I'll take the extra sixty-five a month to sit and watch John Wayne jerk off."

We walked back to the barracks, heat rising from the sun-softened asphalt. Everybody seemed down on the Vietnamese. I asked Buddha what he thought. Why everybody around us hated the people we were helping.

"Don't dwell on that bullshit. We're here to kill gooks—that's all you have to worry about."

Professor looked over, rolled his eyes skyward and shook his head.

I didn't know what to think. Stopping communism was not going to be as easy as we'd been led to believe. Back in school the history teacher hadn't spoken of the Vietnamese not wanting our help.

On the third day, restrictions lifted and we went into Saigon. Mid-morning we entered a local joint and ordered drinks. Troops were three deep at the bar, shouting, drinking—most with weapons, many directly out of the field.

Three prostitutes approached us. One girl placed her hand on my back and laughed. "Ahh, VC get close." Chattering in Vietnamese to her friends, they investigated my back, giggling as they fingered it. I was wearing a fatigue blouse I'd worn during training. A flare had been fired at our boat from a mock ambush, striking the sidewall of the cox'n flat and splattering bits of magnesium onto my back. It had burned small holes in the shirt before I'd realized it was smoldering. One of the girls, louder than the others, cackled.

Suddenly she was pushed away, her assailant punching her face as he rushed her, knocking her to the floor. The army trooper, well over six feet tall, blurred past me—muddy, unshaven, sleeves ripped from his shirt, his arms and face pocked with scabs. He was drunk, and as he stomped her face and body he kept screaming, "Fucking VC bitch. You're dead—dead."

The man's friends pulled him away and I stared in horror at the girl lying on the floor, a low moan bubbling from her lips. He had stomped her face and it looked crooked. Her hands clutched ribs. Pink froth bubbled from her mouth. As the drunk was dragged past me he glared and shook his head in disgust, "Stupid fucking new guys."

One of his buddies explained. "He lost three friends yesterday. Bitch VC threw the grenade."

The prostitute sobbed as the Vietnamese bar owner prodded her with the toe of his cowboy boot. Other girls helped her up and pushed her out the door into the hot noonday sun.

The next morning our boat crew was choppered to Dong Tam, the base we would be operating from. As we flew south, the countryside appeared tranquil. Sitting on a web seat, I peered over the door gunner's shoulder and watched ant-sized figures work in rice paddies. Popsicle-stick-size sampans dotted the rivers.

"Why is it all dead along the riverbanks down there?" I shouted to the gunner as we passed over a brown area.

"You see the thick vegetation along the riverbanks we just passed over? They spray herbicide to kill that shit so the gooks can't hide in it."

5

Dong Tam

8 February 1968

Dong Tam, a U.S. Army/Navy base, was built on sand dredged from the Song My Tho, the north branch of the Mekong River. As our chopper settled down, fine sand blasted up. We jumped to the ground, crouching low to avoid the blades as we struggled away carrying our seabags. Wading through the ankle-deep slippery sand reminded me of the first warm, slick snows of winter. Away from chopper turbulence, biting flies attacked us. They seemed to favor the sun-reddened flesh on the back of my neck.

Three men, stripped to the waist, on what we learned was shit-burning detail, derisively welcomed us to our new home. They directed us to the Navy command building where we turned in our orders and were assigned to a sandbagged plywood hooch. The diesel/human excrement slurry smoke hung low in the muggy morning air.

We spent the next five days waiting for our boats to come in. They were out on operations fighting the Tet 1968 battles. The troops at Dong Tam loved us—fresh meat to fill sandbags. We reinforced bunkers and thickened existing barriers around plywood hooches—protection against incoming rocket and mortar rounds. Boat crews paired off, one man holding the bag while the other filled.

Our third morning at Dong Tam we were escorted to a locked, steel-sided hut. Seabags, boxes, duffle bags, and personal effects cascaded from benches to the floor, cluttering the hooch. We were given forms and told to catalogue all items in the room.

"Take care of these belongings like they're yours because one day yours might end up here," the Yeoman in charge of the detail told us as he explained how to fill out the forms.

The hooch was the collection point for personal belongings left by army troops and sailors who had been killed or wounded. Our job was to pack them for return to next-of-kin for those killed or forwarded to hospitals where the wounded were convalescing. We spent two days sorting, glimpsing the private life of strangers—letters, pictures, tapes, souvenirs, uniforms, and civilian clothes worn on R&R. A damaged picture troubled me. It was a crewcut man, his arm draped over the shoulders of a young boy in a baseball uniform, looking down smiling proudly. Brown stains had turned the man's smile into a frown. I showed it to the Yeoman.

"Pitch it," he said. "I told you. Don't return anything with bloodstains."

That night we hugged bunker walls as incoming mortar rounds exploded and sand trickled down. I hunched in a corner thinking that if we got a direct hit and the roof caved in, there might be a small space left open where the two sides joined. It was impossible for me to distinguish between friendly and hostile artillery, machine gun and small arms fire around the perimeter.

"How do we know which is the VC shooting?" I had stupidly asked.

"They're the ones that hurt," replied a voice in the dark to an audience of giggles. There was that laugh again, I thought, flinching at a near-miss, as sand trickled into my hair.

When the all-clear sounded, I emerged from the bunker and stood watching one of the plywood huts smolder, destroyed by a direct hit. The base was shrouded in smoky haze accented by tongues of flame in the damp night air. I tossed in my bunk, wondering what had happened to the crewcut man. What the future held for the young boy?

Late the next morning, I stood with our crew at water's edge squinting out over the river and swatting sand flies. Two army green ships were anchored far out in the river—the USS *Benewah* and the USS *Colleton*. The *Benewah* was to be our mother ship.

"Afe, where the hell is Stonewall?" Buddha said.

"I think he went to church service this morning." I watched the column of boats swing from the river into the small man-made harbor at Dong Tam.

The third boat swung shoreward and I saw ATC 112-11 painted on the front corner of her bow. Tango boats they were called—abbreviated from the military phonetic alphabet Alpha Tango Charlie used for radio communication. Ours was Tango 11—our radio call-sign would be Tango one-one. (River Assault Division 112's full call sign was "Plain Genius," so ours technically was Plain Genius Tango one-one.)

She rode low in the water, a tattered flag limp on her mast. I recalled my first impression of the armored troop carrier back in Mare Island when we were training. How it looked like an Ironclad—a gunboat out of the Civil War. Light breeze kicked up. The flag ruffled and a cloud of diesel fumes washed over us. The rusted bow pushed sand forward as she beached. The newly submerged engine exhaust outlets near her stern gurgled in protest. Cables squealed as the bow ramp lowered to the sand and we stood peering into the well-deck of our new home.

Army troops rose sleepily from the deck, picking up gear they'd used as pillows. They emerged from the shadows; weapons cradled, slung, or clutched. Packs, flak jackets, bandoliers, canteens slung across a shoulder or hung from an arm—too tired to sling them. Mud-caked men squinted in the harsh morning light and shuffled off the boat.

"Fuckin weather. It either cooks you or drowns you," complained a tired voice.

"You men clean your weapons, get cleaned up, then get some chow. Don't forget, there'll be a memorial service at 1800 hours tonight," a sergeant said as the men filed off the boat.

They shuffled past me and dragged their feet up the beach through loose sand—I was surprised how young they were, about nineteen or twenty—my age. I stood in the hot sun and caught snips of conversation as they slogged by.

"Poor bastard would've been better of dead."

"Easy for you to say, you didn't—"

"My feet are as rotten as that gook's guts. I've got to get them cleaned up."

"Five friggin men. We keep this shit up we'll all be gone in three weeks."

"Screw it, just screw it. I've got sixteen days left in this shithole. I'm not going back out."

"You better get that puncture looked at. It's turning red."

"Fuck it. Let it get infected."

I was surprised at their attitude—reminding me of the comments I'd heard during the *Green Beret* movie. So many Americans sounded disgusted.

With the troops off-loaded, Buddha stepped onto the ramp and I followed down into the shade of the canopied well-deck. They had left it a trash dump of mud, empty C-ration boxes and cans, and cigarette packs. The boat crewmen's bunks—steel framed racks with a canvas bottom laced in—weren't triced up against the bulkheads as they should have been when transporting troops. The air mattresses that belonged on the racks were lying on the mud-covered deck—two of the seven were deflated. The racks and air mattresses were filthy with stagnant crusted muck. I glanced at the *Playboy* magazine on the little table across from the ladder leading up to the cox'n flat. It was an old one—November—back at Mare Island we had joked about the Thanksgiving "feast" centerfold.

"Hey, welcome aboard. We were wondering when you guys would get here with this friggin Tet Offensive screwing things up. We've been out for eight days and running on no sleep for two. The VC stirred up some shit but they're paying dearly for it," the boat captain said. "Why don't you spend today cleaning up the boat, refuel her, and take her out on a run. Tomorrow my crew will come aboard and spend the day with you. We'll go out, fire weapons, and go over radio codes. My engineman can show yours around, get oriented. Right now we've got to eat and sleep."

"Sounds like a plan," Buddha said, standing at the foot of the ladder leading from the well-deck up to the cox'n flat. "I'll look for you at the club later this afternoon. We can discuss things while my crew cleans up. Afe, take notes for repair work while we tour the boat." The boat captain looked at Buddha as he and his crew gathered a change of clothes.

"Snipe, come into the engine compartment with us," Buddha said, as he moved toward the back of the boat, bending down beneath the five foot overhead, passing crew lockers on both sides of the short passageway. He undogged the hatch to the engine compartment and swung it open, Snipe and I close behind. "What the fuck. What's all the water in here?"

"The packing around the shafts is bad. We backed into a submerged tree two days ago and I think one of the screws got bent—the constant vibration is raising hell with the packing," shouted the engineman as he dug in his locker behind us.

"What's all this shit caked on the engines?" Buddha yelled back as he opened his knife and scraped a crusted mass that looked like pistachio green vomit.

"Probably ham and limas. We were warming cans of C-rats on the engine blocks when we got ambushed yesterday. Everybody forgot about them until they started exploding," said the engineman. "That bilge pump has been going non-stop for two days. I'd keep a close eye on it. We need to get this old boat put on skids, check the shafts to make sure they aren't bent, put new screws on and re-pack the shafts."

"Snipe, you go up with him and meet whoever you have to deal with. I want it taken care of ricky-tick—then get back here and clean this compartment up—get that crusty shit off the engines and the bulkheads. I expect it to shine when I come back in the morning."

"You might want to change oil and check the gauges first," said the engineman as he stood in the open hatch, listening. "I haven't had a chance to change it for two weeks and the port temperature gauge is running hot—oil pressure seems screwed up on the starboard engine but I think it's just a faulty gauge. Right now, I wouldn't worry what it looks like back here. Just keep the engines running. You might find yourselves called out on an operation with ten minutes notice. I'd recommend topping off the fuel and getting that packing fixed for starters."

"Afe get fuel topped off—Snipe get those engines squared away," Buddha said, stepping out of the engine compartment, returning to the foot of the ladder leading to the cox'n flat.

From the open hatch above, a humid down-draft of "I Dig Rock And Roll Music" washed over me along with a plague of biting flies as I climbed the ladder. It ended at the cox'n flat, the small compartment I was committed to spend the next twelve months in.

I was inside a steel shell about five feet wide by five feet long. Narrow slits in one inch armor plating allowed me a restricted view of the surrounding area. Directly in front of me, at waist height was the helm and console. On the face of the console were tachometers, temperature gauges, and oil pressure gauges for the two 6-71 Marine diesels that powered the boat. On the left and right sides of the console were the shift and throttle levers; port and starboard. A combined mechanism, the throttle linkage came up through the shift levers and was connected to molded brass handles that looked like upside-down stirrups. Engine rpm's could be adjusted at the twist of my wrist while pivoting the levers down for reverse or up for forward.

"Turn that friggin hippie racket off," Buddha said from the ladder as his head came above deck near my feet. Climbing into my compartment, he motioned toward the boat's radio, set into the bulkhead. "I want to hear what those boat captains heading out on patrol are talking about."

All I heard was garbled static.

The cox'n flat was tight with two of us. Professor stood on the ladder, his head level with the deck we stood on. Buddha grunted, bent down, and stepped aft into the area between the two .50 caliber machine gun turrets. Professor climbed into the cox'n flat, checked the radio, then kneeled down by the small-arms locker. Buddha told him to inventory the weapons and the ammunition because he would have to sign for them when he took command the next day.

"This place is a pigpen Afe—I want it cleaned up," Buddha said, sending an empty C-ration can across the compartment with his foot. "Stonewall, Crow, Dennis—get up here, check your weapons." Crow and Dennis climbed the ladder, brushed past me, stepped around Buddha and stood in their turrets, racking firing mechanism back and forth, checking the action, and swiveling the turrets.

"Where's Stonewall?"

"I told you—he went to church services this morning," I said, as Buddha stepped forward into the cox'n flat again.

"Church," he echoed at a loss for words. He nodded toward the hinged steel plates in front and on the sides of my cox'n flat as he wiped his forehead with his olive drab shirt tail. "Open those armor flaps and get some ventilation in here. It's like a friggin oven—and clean this console. I can hardly see the gauges they're so full of coffee stains and ashes."

The departing captain, listening from below, stepped onto the ladder and poked his head above deck. "Like I told you, we've been going for eight days, the last two without sleep. Fuck you—I don't need to apologize to you. See how it looks twelve months from now when you rotate back to the World—if you last that long."

"Well excuse friggin me," Buddha mocked sympathetically.

"Hand me my radio," the boat captain said reaching toward me. "I was going to leave it, but not for that asshole. The port .50 caliber needs a new barrel, it got overheated yesterday. The starboard grenade launcher is jamming—but you might want to clean up before you get your weapons squared away," he added, as he descended the ladder, radio in hand.

"Well, well, well, ain't we touchy?" Buddha whispered as he stepped onto the ladder and climbed down.

The instant I lowered the armor plates, gusts of fine sand joined the flies. I looked out the front of my cox'n flat through the bar-armor—a grillwork of 5/8 inch re-bar welded to a framework, three inches apart. The framework was mounted about two feet out from the one-inch steel armor. Bar-armor was positioned to detonate incoming rockets before they could penetrate our inch-thick steel plating. The VC used Russian and Chinese-made armor piercing anti-tank rockets—B-40's, B-50's, and Recoilless Rifles. The B-40's were the most-used. The rocket's 82mm warhead burned through the armor and sprayed molten iron through the compartment it entered.

"Afe, come down here," Buddha called from the well-deck.

I heard him grumbling as I descended the ladder from the cox'n flat. The rear fifteen feet of the well-deck, sheltered from above by the cox'n flat, served double duty. Between operations it was living space for the boat crew. When transporting troops the racks were supposed to be lashed against the bulkheads. If casualties were taken during firefights, they could be lowered and the wounded placed in them. Aft of the racks was a small table bolted to the deck on the port side with empty ammo crates for chairs. We walked to the front of the well-deck, across the still lowered ramp, and onto the beach to inspect exterior of the boat.

"Tighten the lacing on the canopy. Remember what the instructor at Mare Island said? About keeping it stretched tight so grenades would bounce off if the gooks threw them at us from shore? It's too friggin hot out here. Let's get in the shade." Back at the table in the well-deck, he pulled out a clipboard and began writing as he talked. "Put Snipe, Dennis, Crow, and Stonewall on the starboard side racks and lockers—you, me, and Professor will be on the port side. Dennis and Crow are responsible for the port half of the boat topside. Stonewall and Professor, the starboard side. You're in charge—if the work isn't done to my satisfaction, you'll be doing it." He ripped his scribbled notes off the board and handed them to me just as Stonewall stepped into the well-deck.

"Where the hell have you been?"

"Church services."

"Church services—why waste your time?"

"Faith is not a waste."

"Faith—don't preach at me, you'd do better putting your faith in that 20mm cannon," Buddha laughed. "Afe, that's the name for this boat, *Satan's Wait'n*. Sand that other character's name off and get my name and boat name on it."

By late afternoon, against a fresh rectangle of flat yellow paint, just below the 20mm cannon turret was our new logo, in blue letters—THOMAS BM2—below that, SATAN'S WAIT'N.

Buddha and the other boat captain apparently reached an understanding. Early next morning they came down to the boat together complaining about rot-gut whiskey. With the old crew and ours onboard, I raised the ramp and backed off the beach. I steered out the narrow harbor mouth—boat basin they called it—toward the south side of the river. The cox'n from the old crew explained some of the idiosyncrasies of our boat as we cruised.

The boats had flat bottoms with steel guards surrounding the propellers to protect them from underwater objects. Toward the front third of the boat, the bottom tapered up for sliding onto the beach. With this old tub, sometimes he'd just hold the bow against the high riverbank while troops crawled out of the well-deck on the sides of the ramp. This boat rode bow-down because the hull leaked and the engineman had to siphon the compartment beneath the well-deck once a week with the portable pump. He laughed when he saw I had cleaned the console.

"Me and the radioman spelled each other two days straight on that last operation. C-rat coffee and cigarettes kept us awake. The second night I fell asleep driving and hit the riverbank—scared the shit out of everybody—dumped my coffee all over."

One hundred yards before I reached the far bank I swung to starboard.

"Commence firing," Buddha ordered.

Dennis opened fire with short bursts from his .50 caliber machine gun. Stonewall fired his 20mm cannon. In the well-deck, Snipe fired a .30 caliber machine gun into the jungle. Gunfire echoed through my cox'n flat as cordite fumes clouded the boat.

"Cease fire, cease fire," Buddha yelled from where he sat between the two .50 caliber gun mounts. In the lull of firing he reached over the top of the gun turret and I heard his knuckles rap on Dennis' helmet to get his attention. "Dennis, try your Honeywell." Mounted above each .50 caliber machine gun was the Honeywell grenade launcher that fired belt-fed 40mm grenades. They were hand-crank-powered by the gunner.

I heard the dull thumps of three rounds leaving the barrel in rapid succession as I steered the boat parallel to the bank. The first round splashed in the water near the riverbank. The others exploded in foliage just above the waterline.

The captain of the old boat crew was standing topside near Buddha and from my cox'n flat I heard him say, "That's the one that's been jamming on us. Something's worn inside and the belt holding the rounds slips when they feed in. We'll make a list of repairs that need to be done. Hopefully they'll get her up on blocks before you go on an operation. Have your cox'n swing around, fire the other side."

"Swing her around, Afe," Buddha yelled down to me. "See how fast you can swing her."

I reached up and in one sweeping motion down-throttled both engines, pivoted the shift levers from their up position, back and down and turned the throttle control handles at the ends of the shift levers full throttle in reverse for ten seconds to slow the forward motion of the boat. I spun the helm full a' port with my left hand as I threw the starboard engine forward again with full throttle as I continued full throttle on the port engine. The boat swung sluggishly to port. I could hear the boat captain explain to Buddha about the flooded compartments and how the seams needed to be rewelded.

"Commence fire," Buddha said, as I straightened out on the return run. Stonewall's 20mm cannon belched in short bursts. Crow's .50 caliber fired three short bursts then jammed—I could hear him cussing as he ejected unfired cartridges from his gun, spewing them across the small compartment.

"Knock that shit off. One of those could detonate when they hit the deck," the boat captain yelled at Crow. "Start firing the Honeywell. When you're in an ambush you don't have time to play with your weapon—just put rounds out."

I watched Crow's 40mm grenades arc shoreward and impact in several short series of explosions. He was on target and Buddha and the boat captain complimented him on good shooting. Snipe and the engineman were still firing the .30 caliber machine guns from the well-deck.

With this firepower, plus the platoon of army troops we would carry on riverine operations against the communists, I again felt the sense of omnipotence I'd experienced while firing the 20mm cannon during our training. But those discarded personal belongings strewn around that Quonset hut nagged at me.

"Cease fire," Buddha shouted. Everybody stopped firing topside but apparently they hadn't heard him in the well-deck. "Professor, stick your head below and tell those knot-heads to cease fire," Buddha shouted, his face near the opening behind us.

The radioman knelt down, leaned forward, and stuck his head through the hatch. "Cease fire, cease fire." Laughter echoed up through the hole as the two enginemen yelled at each other, hollering to compensate for the ringing in their ears and the adrenaline of firing the guns.

"That's the first time I've seen Snipe happy," Professor commented, shaking his head in disgust.

That afternoon we returned to Dong Tam. I topped off the fuel tanks while Buddha submitted a list of repairs he and the old boat captain had put together. The departing cox'n showed me where to go for restocking fresh water storage tanks and replenishing C-rations. He gave me a list of suggested ammunition quantities we should keep onboard. The old crew cleaned out their lockers and the boat was officially ours.

We beached near an ATC equipped with a small helicopter landing pad—mounted above the well-deck—for medical evacuations. Buddha returned later that evening and told us repairs would be put on hold because we were going out the next day on an operation. We were standing on the catwalk, a two-foot-wide walkway inboard of the re-bar gunnel that ran along each side of the well-deck from bow to stern.

"Are we restocked and ready to go?" Buddha asked, as we walked aft.

"Yes," I told him. "But Snipe says our bilge pump is barely keeping up with water leaking in right now—he's worried about what will happen when we start traveling at full speed for hours."

The boat captain on the medevac boat beached next to us overheard our conversation. "I have a portable gas-powered water pump you can borrow," he said. "Your boat has been leaking bad, but we just haven't had a chance to slow down." He was a big man—as big as Buddha—ruddy round faced with a German accent. He stepped across to our boat and over to the rack holding our mine-sweeping gear. "You need to get a new cable for your sweep gear. They snagged a mine and triggered it four days ago. See how it shredded the strands. I'm surprised it didn't rip the drag off." He spoke softly as he fingered the sharp steel strands of the damaged cable that had a grapnel-like contraption clamped at the end.

Buddha thanked him and we wrestled the portable pump from the stern of his boat to ours. "Keep these jerry cans of gasoline below deck—stashed below the waterline so if a rocket comes through it won't pierce them," he told us as we transferred four five-gallon cans across and passed them down through the hatch to the storage compartment at the stern of the boat.

Next day we moved out to USS *Benewah* (APB 35), mother ship for the 2nd Battalion, 9th Infantry Army troops we'd be operating with. Our boats tied four and five abreast to pontoons attached to the ship's side. The *Benewah* was designed to house our boat crews too, but early 1968 the *Benewah* must have been over capacity because on Tango 11, as for many other riverboat crews, our boat was our home.

Our boat division seemed to run non-stop. In the dark of night, columns of boats eased out into the river, cruised for several hours, then turned into nameless canals and tributaries. At times I'd nose the bow of our boat onto the river bank, drop the ramp and watch our platoon of army troops disembark and disappear into the jungle. Then we'd patrol a section of river while the troops were inland slogging through rice paddies and canals searching for Viet Cong. We stayed out three to four days then returned to the *Benewah*. Our boat didn't fire a shot nor did we receive enemy fire, though others in our class became casualties.

We saw our first dead communists—killed by air strikes, artillery, and earlier riverine operations. Spread armed, face-up, leg bent back, shrapnel wounds pitting face and chest—

another, face down, mud up to his ears, fingers grasping the earth. Bodies, hanging into the river from destroyed bunkers dug into banks, bobbed gently in our passing wake.

"Those little fuckers don't look so dangerous now, do they," Buddha said, from his shelter between the gun mounts.

A black army sergeant stood on the ladder and shouted up to us, "This was a bad spot—killed five army guys and screwed up about thirty sailors."

I watched flies swarm up as the wake from the boat in front of me washed over the bodies. A breeze rustled the few leaves still hanging on the shredded brush along the bank— wafting dead smell towards us through the armor slits.

I recalled the elaborate death-throes my brothers and I had performed when playing war—clutching our chest, spinning on one foot with head thrown back, flopping to the ground in a convulsive finale. Now I saw, there was no drama in death. And the smell—we'd never discussed what the dead might smell like.

6

Life on Tango 11

20 February 1968

Another warm morning on patrol. Sun flashed through nipa palms as our wake lapped at dense jungle foliage hanging into the river. The ever-present aroma of decaying plant life reminded me a bit of fresh plowed fields back on the farm. I had to smile—right now it was probably below zero in Minnesota—and those plowed fields were beneath several feet of snow.

I was in the well-deck warming a C-ration breakfast when Buddha shouted down that a sampan was approaching. It was my turn to go aboard. I loaded the shotgun and climbed out onto the catwalk. It was a typical sampan. The wooden boat was about eighteen feet long; larger than others we'd searched.

"*Li dai, li dai,*" I shouted, gesturing with a wave for the sampan to approach. What a strange culture, I thought. At home, waving my hand indicated farewell. Here, it was a signal to come. I would be searching for weapons, medicine, booby traps—anything that might be used in the VC war effort. Any male eighteen to forty raised suspicion. They should be crippled or ARVN—Army of Vietnam. The only other option was VCS—Viet Cong Suspect.

Professor was at the helm and the gunners stood on the catwalk with M16's covering the sampan— when a sampan was against our boat, machine guns barrels didn't depress low enough to cover them.

Buddha stood above, on the ledge that bordered the gun turrets, cradling a shotgun, overseeing the operation. "Swing to starboard—put that gook between us and the riverbank."

Professor maneuvered to keep the sampan between us and the nearby bank. It would be caught in crossfire and shield us if we were fired on from shore. That wasn't much comfort for me—I would be on the sampan. I stood poised on the gunnel of our boat, shotgun in hand, ready to jump. As it approached, a middle-aged woman tossed a frayed rope to Stonewall, screeching at him in a high-pitched rebuke.

"Yeah, yeah, whatever, Mamason," he replied, shrugging his shoulders.

Crow caught the stern line and tied it to our bar armor. I dropped two fenders—tires secured to ropes—over the side. They buffered between the fragile wooden hull of the sampan and abrasive re-bar that shielded our boat to the waterline. The old man at the sampan's tiller shouted at the woman. She whirled and shouted back at him, betel nut juice dribbling out the side of her mouth. The old man went silent.

"Get'er done Afe," Buddha said, waving his shotgun barrel over the sampan like a wand.

I stepped over our bar armor rail onto the rocking deck of the sampan. There were four people on board; a man and woman, a boy fourteen or fifteen years old, and a girl about eight. I recalled our training and motioned for them to move to the stern—they made a better target if grouped, the instructor had told us.

"Check for I.D. and hidden weapons, Afe."

I could see that the girl and boy didn't have anything

concealed—their clothes were plastered against their bodies by the wind. I motioned them to the stern.

"Frisk the other two—that gook bitch doesn't look very happy—I don't trust her."

The old man was shaking. Scared, I thought. With the shotgun in one hand I ran my other hand up his legs to his crotch. They were known to conceal a grenade between their legs—I brushed across his front, back, and beneath his arms. "He's clean but he smells like a dead fish," I said, glancing up at Buddha.

"Check that bitch close—from her look, she'd slit your throat in an instant."

I looked at her. She glared back—reminded me of Professor the first time he met Buddha. I tried to tell her with my eyes that I didn't enjoy what I was doing—it was my job. I bent forward and ran my hand up between her legs—she smelled more like wood smoke—not the dead-fish smell of the old man. She didn't make it easy for me—pinched her thighs together so I had to poke my fingers in front and back to make sure nothing was hidden.

"Are you having fun?" Crow joked, from a few feet away on our boat.

I looked over at him. "Fuck you Crow. I know this is your speed. Want to trade places?"

"Get on with it Afe—Crow, shut the fuck up—this isn't a game," said Buddha.

I think the woman knew I was uncomfortable. When I slipped my hand across her baggy top—across her rib cage, she leaned down and forward and I suddenly had a small breast in my hand.

"Yeah, get it on Afe," Crow shouted.

"I told you to shut the fuck up," Buddha said from above, lashing out with his foot, barely missing Crow's head.

"She's clean," I said, glancing up again at Buddha as I

motioned her toward the stern where the others stood. "But she doesn't smell much better than Papason."

"Okay. Go through the boat so they can get on their way."

The bow jutted upward four feet above the waterline and had a compartment reaching from the V front, back three feet. I removed the lid and found miscellaneous gear for the boat; ropes, a propeller, a few rusted engine parts, caulking, old fishnets. I worked my way toward the stern, lifting loose floorboards—nothing but stink from old fish and wet hull. Moving back under the canopy I found compartments on both sides with a walkway through the middle. I lifted the cover from the starboard side compartment and found twelve one-gallon jugs of dark liquid with rice straw mats protecting them—like shields in a liquor case. These were the first gallon bottles we'd found on a sampan.

"I think I found some *nuoc mam*," I shouted through the sampan canopy to Buddha. "There's lot's of it—a dozen jugs."

Nuoc mam was Vietnamese fish sauce. While cruising the river we often passed barrels mounted on stilts along the banks. When we approached from down wind, we smelled them before we saw them. They were filled with fish, layered in salt. Sun percolated the concoction and juices dribbled into a container from holes in the bottom of the barrels. The juice created from the decomposing fish was filtered, spices blended, aged, filtered again, and bottled. The fish sauce was very strong smelling and very spicy. Vietnamese ketchup, our instructors had called it, because everybody used it.

"Maybe they're hauling it to market," he shouted back. "Keep going."

I opened a jug out of curiosity and lowered my nose to it. I jerked back as the pungent sauce scorched my nostrils. The woman cackled at my reaction. I replaced the lid and put the jug back in place. Be calm, I said to myself—we're supposed to treat these people with respect.

Moving to the port side, I removed the cover and found several woven baskets filled with dark brown rice. I wormed my hand down through the rice to feel for hidden items— we had been warned that sometimes the VC put snakes at the bottom of rice baskets.

"Stonewall, keep your gun on that bitch—take the safety off—she's twitching," Buddha said. "She's nervous about something."

I was still under the canopy but looked aft when Buddha spoke and I could see her glancing around. I moved onto the next basket. I pushed my hand into the third basket and felt something soft about three inches below the rice. I glanced aft and saw the woman's eyes locked on me.

"There's something under the rice," I shouted up to Buddha.

What is it? Pull it out—dump the basket."

"Suppose it's booby-trapped—remember how they warned us?"

"Call the bitch back by you. Take your gun off safety and level it at her. Make her dump the basket—that way she's screwed if she's playing games."

I backed up and waved my hand, shotgun leveled at her. "*Li dai, li dai*," I said, motioning her to come under the canopy. When she stepped forward I backed up—don't ever get close enough for them to grab your weapon before you can shoot, had been an oft repeated warning. I motioned with the muzzle for her to up-end the basket. She grabbed it and flipped it over, scattering rice and a bundle of black clothing into the narrow passageway.

"I wonder if they're VC uniforms—this might be a supply boat with all the rice and *nuoc mam* on it," I shouted up to Buddha.

"Get that bitch back to the stern where I can see her. Professor, call in for an ARVN interpreter—tell them what we have. Afe, collect their I.D cards."

I motioned the woman back to the stern. I followed through the passageway beneath the canopy and stood with the shotgun leveled at her stomach, demanding, "I.D, I.D." They understood that English and produced identification papers. The man and girl had tattered cards, water-stained and difficult to read. The woman and the boy had crisp, fresh cards. I heard a radio transmission and Professor's reply to it.

"Afe, we're going to tow them back to Dong Tam," Buddha shouted down to me. "Hop back aboard. Let's get them hooked to our stern and head in."

As we maneuvered the sampan to our stern, the girl began crying and the old man clutched his tiller, eyes wide beneath his straw hat. The woman screeched something at the girl and she looked up at me and cringed—sniffling to stifle her outburst. She wiped a dirty sleeve across her face, smearing tears and snot. The boy moved closer to the woman and glared at me. The woman spit betel nut juice on the side of our boat.

"Those ARVN interrogators will rip that bitch a new asshole," Buddha commented as I climbed up and stood by him.

I looked aft and watched the sampan bob in our wake, wondering if she really was a VC. I hadn't given any thought to women being communists.

About a week later, during a beer party on the USS *Benewah* pontoon, while drinking my two allotted beers, I listened to an interesting conversation between an army sergeant and a navy boat captain.

"I hate those friggin boats. I feel like a sitting duck going up the river," complained the sergeant. He gulped a swallow, grimaced, and continued. "Look at this rusty friggin Budweiser—looks like one from the Korean War."

"I've got better stuff stashed in my locker if you'd care to join me," the boat captain said. "But I think you're wrong. I'd rather be on my boat than dug into a muddy hole waiting for a round to drop on me."

"If that happens, it's just a bad break. But the odds are better dug in."

"I don't think so—shit starts falling. I'm behind armor— I can shoot back while I speed up and dodge incoming."

"Yeah, like that Tango boat a few weeks ago? Fucked up fourteen of my boys and four sailors. You call that good? Top speed of that slug going into the current is about four miles an hour—shit, my grandmother could out-swim it. And that B-40 burned through his armor like a Zippo on a sheet of shit paper."

Late that night, deep-throated hacks and cursing alerted me to Buddha's approach as he struggled to climb onto the boat from the front corner. "Afe, where the fuck are you? You think you're good as me?"

"I'm right here," I yelled back. "What the hell are you talking about?"

"Don't play games with me."

"I don't have a clue what the fuck you're talking about," I said, as the crew listened from their racks.

"You didn't know you were promoted to Boatswain's Mate Second Class?"

"I took that test way back in June on the *Gompers*. I'd forgotten all about it."

"I don't know what this fucking navy is coming to. Snot-nosed kids taking over the world."

I smelled his whiskey breath. I crawled out of my bunk and told him to transfer me—he was Second Class too—and now that I was the same rank as him I didn't think we should be on the same boat. It would create conflict and besides, this snot-nosed kid had more medals than he did if he didn't count his lifer Good Conduct Medal which obviously was a joke. He stared at me with that look I had seen the first time I'd met him, head lowered, eyes glaring from the top of the sockets. Suddenly his hand whipped up and slapped me. I flew back against my bunk, rage souring my mouth at being sucker-punched as blood trickled from my nose.

"I'm boat captain and you'll do what I say. You're going nowhere." He lay back on his bunk as if nothing had happened. Five minutes later he was snoring.

Nothing came of the incident. I didn't report it. What was there to say? Buddha pushed more responsibility on me. Professor took notes at the boat captain meetings and kept the crew informed, and Buddha had more freedom to drink more and sleep in as we patrolled the rivers. I expected to be transferred when the system realized there were two second class boatswain's mates on the same boat, but it never happened.

A routine did evolve as the weeks slipped by. If we were going into a narrow river, or transporting troops, Buddha performed his duties admirably. We all wore our protective gear—flak jackets and helmets. In tight canals I'd even put my armor shields up, sealing the cox'n flat in one-inch steel, Professor and I slow-baking in our little green oven while Buddha sat above and behind us, between the .50 caliber turrets, barking commands.

"Afe, watch that submerged tree off to starboard."

"Professor, don't miss any radio calls."

"Snipe, have you cleaned the bilge pump screens lately?"

"Stonewall, cover that mound on the north bank. It looks suspicious." And the gunners in their turrets swiveled slowly fore and aft, guns barrels traversing the riverbanks, grinning at the charade.

When troops weren't on board, and when we didn't feel threatened—which became more frequent as days passed—

another facet of the routine developed. Buddha liked to volunteer us for supply runs which gave us a chance to pilfer a case or two of food; frozen steaks were popular, or soft drinks for mix. Dr. Pepper was a favorite—it tasted okay warm. Ice was a rare treat.

Base Interdiction Defense (BID), called bid patrol, was another choice assignment. We circled the mother ships at a distance, pitching concussion grenades into the river to deter enemy swimmers, watch for floating mines, searching sampans—not allowing them near the big ships. It was a very low risk time. It was a livable system for the crew—Buddha allowed us to drink onboard, too.

In the day's heat, our uniform consisted of cut-off fatigue trousers. No underwear, no shirt, usually barefoot or flip-flops. On bid patrol, two men were on duty—one driving, the other stationed above deck as lookout. We loved it. When Buddha wasn't around I was in command of the boat and stayed topside, escaping the roasting cox'n flat. I had a relaxed arrangement with the crew; one hour shifts on the helm monitoring the radio while steering. Snipe didn't have helm duty because nobody wanted to get involved with working in his engine room. One cloudless hot day drifted to the next.

"What time is it?" Buddha's phlegm-clogged voice demanded. "Who the hell's cooking spaghetti this early in the day?"

"It's 1030," I heard Snipe's voice respond. "I'm grabbing some lunch before I shut down the starboard engine."

"What are you doing to it?"

"Changing oil. The water pump is leaking. I have a new gasket for it and I want to re-do the packing—it still leaks. I think the shaft is bent. They replaced the propeller but it still vibrates and the packing works loose every three to four days."

"I don't like having an engine down while on patrol."

"I did the port engine yesterday. It'll only be down about an hour if all goes well."

"Who the hell told you you could shut it down?"

"Afe."

"Afe, why didn't I know about this?" Buddha hollered up to me.

I climbed from topside down into the shaded well-deck. "I mentioned it the other night when we were playing cards. Remember? I told you some of the other boats were doing engine maintenance while on bid patrol. There's never time to get it done otherwise, and you didn't object," I lied.

Scratching his head while hacking up and blowing to-baccoey wads of phlegm over the side he mumbled, "Yeah, but I don't like it done while I'm sleeping."

I watched him make coffee over an empty C-ration pound cake can that was perforated with air holes top and bottom. It was about the size of a tuna fish can with the lid cut off and tabs bent in to rest a second can on. Buddha filled a cleaned out spaghetti & meatball can with water from our fresh water supply tank. Then he broke off a small chunk of C-4, an explosive that burned very hot. I was surprised to see his big hands tremble slightly as he worked. He dropped the fuel into the can-stove, lit it with his Zippo, then set his water on. When it started steaming, he stirred in a packet of instant coffee and sugar.

"We're getting low on booze—keep an eye out, try and get some today," he said, opening a can of pecan cake. "Fruit cocktail—Afe, see if you can find a can in that mess."

We had a box of loose cans, leftovers from previous meals we saved for trading or snacking on. Rummaging out a can of peaches I tossed it to him.

"I better get topside. There's a sampan heading our way," I said, motioning up river at a small boat in the distance.

I climbed the ladder into the cox'n flat, opened the small arms locker and grabbed a shotgun. After climbing topside through Crow's .50 caliber mount, I cradled the shotgun in my arms as the sampan approached.

"*Li dai, li dai*," I shouted, waving my hand toward it. I recognized the old papason as he drew near. A ten year old boy was his spokesman. I was amazed how these kids picked up our language. Laced with profanity, their vocabulary was limited to phrases used to barter.

"Hey, hey, sailor, numba one," sing-songed the skinny boy as he pushed black hair from his eyes. His right arm ended eight inches below the elbow and the leaking stump left streaks on his face where he brushed his bangs. "Whiskey, rum, smokes, girls—I got—you want."

We were always well-stocked with cartons of American cigarettes. We paid about twenty-seven cents a pack in Dong Tam or on the *Benewah*. They were in high demand by the Vietnamese—hot bartering merchandise.

The old man forced two girls out from beneath the canopy. They wore once-white thigh-length capes that were tied at the neck, now stained and torn. They stood clutching the front together trying to cover themselves. I recalled how shocked I'd been two years earlier in Hong Kong, the first time I'd seen young women displayed like merchandise. Now, they were just two more whores.

The old papasan pushed them forward. One was in her mid-twenties—old and worn—an eye missing. Milky fluid oozed down her cheek from a chancrous socket and a scar ran across her face and nose. I wondered what had happened. She reminded me of the girl in Saigon. The other girl was young and nervous and I wondered at the circumstances that condemned her to the life of a river-borne prostitute.

"No girls," Buddha told papasan. The old man argued through his interpreter as he pantomimed how great they would be with exaggerated, lecherous gestures, pushing them forward, pulling the younger girl's cape open. She pinched her knees together and turned her hips, but the old man slapped her ass and said something. Turning towards us, she looked skyward and spread her legs as the old man slid his hand from her knees slowly up over her front, across her brown belly, between her bare breasts to her chin where he gently wiped his finger across her lips. Buddha repeated, "No girls—booze."

The old man grinned a toothless smile as he slipped several bottles of liquor from beneath a canvas cover. Buddha, the master negotiator, began haggling with papasan, through the interpreter.

"One carton Salems—one bottle," the kid said.

Buddha shook his head in disgust. "Numba ten—three packs," he said, mimicking the kid's broken English, ripping a carton open, holding three toward papasan, reaching for the bottle. The old man shook his head "no" as he spoke rapidly to the boy.

"Eight packs," the boy said.

They haggled back and forth. I stood above, shotgun cradled in my arm, barrel aimed over the sampan and Buddha. The girls sat near the stern of the little boat and laughed at Buddha when he mimicked the kid.

"What the fuck's so funny," he barked, looking over at them. They went silent, grins frozen as they looked up at me. Buddha was back into his argument with papasan, the girls forgotten. I winked at them, smiled, and shook my head, no. They stared back—straight-faced—silent.

Morning sun drew sweat beads on Buddha's forehead as he negotiated for the liquor. It was a game—price wasn't the issue. A compromise was finally reached. Four bottles of whiskey at six packs of cigarettes each, two bottles of rum at four packs each. The old man reached under his seat. I swung the gun barrel down. He grinned his toothless grin up at me as he pulled out a bag—a large bulky package of marijuana; rolled joints—enough to keep us stoned for a week. Six cartons of cigarettes, he motioned to Buddha.

"No dope, *didi mau, didi mau*, get the fuck away from the boat," Buddha yelled, flicking his hand in a down and up motion, as if he was shaking mud from it. He reached his leg over the bar armor and kicked at the little boat. I stood above watching, thinking how different the Vietnamese were from us.

"Why didn't you get that dope? I could've sold it on the *Benewah* and made some big money," Crow said.

"Yeah, and get your ass and mine thrown into LBJ." LBJ was the army prison in Vietnam. The acronym stood for Long Binh Jail and a pun on Lyndon Baines Johnson. The prison was notorious for racial viciousness that went on behind the razor-wire walls.

"They don't send sailors there," Crow said.

"I ain't about to find out. You want to fuck with dope, you find yourself a new billet. I catch any on this boat you'll go over the side with it."

We resumed patrol, our stash of booze tucked below. Hard liquor was forbidden on the boats, but almost everybody stocked it. Rumor had it that the Viet Cong laced poison or crushed glass in liquor acquired on the black market, but like their presence, it was an invisible threat, easy to overlook.

Buddha finished his breakfast then went back to the stern and dropped his shorts. He sat on the bar armor—bare ass over the water—and relieved himself as he hooted at passing sampans. "Numba one," he'd shout toward passing boats, laughing as he pointed down at his turds splashing in the river. I was still self-conscious and preferred going early morning before river traffic got heavy. After relieving himself he washed up in a pail of river water, shaved, then inspected the boat.

Daily, he'd grumble about the piss-poor job I did supervising the crew and how they weren't keeping the boat ship-shape as he pointed at trails of rust running across the green paint. I no longer argued with him. He could see that the rust was caused by water constantly splashing up from waves, wakes, rain—he knew painting couldn't be done on a wet surface. He rambled and bitched his way around the boat, back into the well-deck where he entered the engine compartment and complained to Snipe about some imagined problem. Then he climbed the ladder to the cox'n flat, studied the gauges, and with a non-committal grunt, asked Professor what boat was going to relieve us and when. He moved back and checked the gun turrets. Each day there would be some make-work project he would initiate.

"How many boxes of M79 rounds do you have belted up, Dennis?"

"Five cases."

"How about you, Crow?"

"Yeah, I have five, too."

"When's the last time you pulled those .50's apart—gave them a good cleaning, put new barrels on them?"

"We did both of them two days ago when you told us to," Dennis replied.

"When we're done with this BID patrol, I want to go over to the island and fire all weapons—including the hand guns—that'll give you boys something to do." He crawled up into the 20mm cannon turret, stepped on the cocking stirrup twice then crawled out and told Stonewall it needed oiling.

"I just cleaned and lubed it this morning," Stonewall said.

"Well, put more oil in the receiver. It looks dry." He bent

down, moved back to the cox'n flat and stepped onto the ladder leading to the well-deck. "Afe, when we go back in I want to double our supplies, I've got a feeling something big is coming."

I followed him down and watched as he opened a can of Dr. Pepper, took two swallows, then trickled Jim Beam into the small triangle hole. He swirled it around, sat on his bunk, back against the still-cool bulkhead, and yawned. "This is the life, Afe. Get the cards out. Crow. Professor." he shouted, as he shuffled the stained titty cards. "Take a break. Get down here and play cards."

Like a dysfunctional family, we found a livable comfort level. Buddha ruled and I was the buffer for tantrums. The crew and I pacified him by going along with his tangents.

Morning was the best time of day. We'd silently crawl out of our racks in the well-deck, cook our coffee and breakfast on the stern, whispering our way through the morning until that first grunting hack of phlegm alerted us.

And so the days went. Card games among the crew never lasted long. Buddha loved to read. Louis L'Amour was his favorite author. We'd nap between watches. Afternoons drifted into evenings. We sipped drinks and listened to country western music—Buddha's preference. Nobody got shit-faced drunk, aware that we had watches to stand. An added advantage to these patrols; the breeze on the wide river kept the biting flies and mosquitoes away. It was a peaceful time—an interlude—but we couldn't know that, then. Dennis began reading Buddha's books when he was done with them.

Professor received a packet of books from home and offered to let me read them. *The Quiet American* caught my attention because it took place in Vietnam. I couldn't understand why the U.S. would send such a naïve man as Pyle—a CIA operative—to work with the Vietnamese. His obsession with Phuong didn't make sense either. There were plenty of beautiful women in Saigon. I commented to Professor about how the author must not like Americans—how he portrayed them as simple, how they didn't understand Vietnamese culture.

"Phuong and Pyle are metaphors," Professor said. "Phuong represents Vietnam. The story is really about Colonial exploitation of third world countries. Remember how Phuong is with Fowler—the old man? He represents the old Colonialism of France, but they leave. Then she switches to Pyle. He represents American power and how inept we are, then she goes back to Fowler after Pyle is killed. She—South Vietnam—will bend whichever direction is most profitable."

"It kind of reminds me of *The Ugly American*," I said. "We read that in school. I remember how manipulative the communists were, lying about who the rice was from."

"Yes, it's similar. But remember how most Americans took advantage of the Sarkhanese? That book is a metaphor too. Even the title is a twist of irony."

I shrugged and didn't answer. Metaphors and irony didn't interest me but I decided that Pyle got what he deserved—being dumb enough to go out on a dark bridge in an obviously VC controlled area—he had just been dumb-assed lucky the night he and Fowler had spent stranded in the Delta when the VC blew up the watchtower they were hiding in.

"Remember those people on that sampan?" Professor argued. "The two prostitutes and the crippled kid? What good have we done for them? I'd be willing to bet they'd be better off if they'd never seen an American. We're not doing a damn thing for the common people."

I couldn't argue with that. But I thought of the poverty I'd seen in other countries; Japan, China, the Philippines. Surely we weren't responsible for that. Besides, the communists had been in Vietnam since 1945. Why hadn't they done more for the people? We usually had these conversations in the evening, on the back of the boat—where Buddha couldn't listen.

"Walter Cronkite said that Vietnam is a lost cause. We'll end up like Korea," Professor said one evening.

"Who's Walter Cronkite?"

He looked at me like I was dim-witted, "You've got to be kidding—he's the biggest television news broadcaster in the world."

"We didn't have television back on the farm."

We returned to the *Benewah* from an operation and found suspense high, rumors rampant. A boat division was being transferred to a river bordering North Vietnam. Buddha and Professor returned from a boat captain's meeting with the facts.

"We're going north. The Marines are kicking ass at a place called Khe Sanh. The river we're going to is the most heavily mined in the country. Artillery from the North comes in most nights in the area we're going to. Afe, get those supplies doubled—pack extra cases of ammo and grenades above the well-deck behind the bar armor on that ledge in front of the cox'n flat—wherever there's room. I want C-rats tucked between the bar armor and the steel plating below the gun turrets and on the sides of the cox'n flat. Professor, double our first aid supplies, salt tablets, malaria pills. I'll get another case of morphine syrettes. Snipe, I want you to beg, borrow, or steal two spare screws—propellers—don't come back aboard until you have them."

7

Northbound to the Demilitarized Zone

29 February 1968

Leap Year—everybody was bummed. We'd spend the extra day in Vietnam. That afternoon, beneath dark clouds, we left Dong Tam for Vung Tau, where we would load aboard a northbound transport. We followed the Song My Tho River east to the coast, into the South China Sea, then turned north into rolling whitecaps. For the next twenty-five miles our heavy boat didn't ride over waves, but pushed through them. She dipped in the hollows, then smashed into the next oncoming wave, forcing a solid sheet of water to shoot up over the flat bow. It was a constant struggle to keep the sluggish boat from broaching. The helm squealed as I spun from port to starboard, trying to maintain control. I closed the armor plates, blocking the deluge sloshing in on us. Buddha wanted a clean boat. Now he's got one, I thought.

He sat above and behind us, yelling orders. "Keep that bow into the wind Afe. If she broaches we're screwed. We'll go down like the *Connie's* anchor."

I glanced back and up through the opening and laughed. He was scrunched down between the turrets in an attempt to dodge the water spraying over the bow, but some of it was coming down on the awning covering my cox'n flat, rolling back, and washing over him. With his helmet down and his sunken eyes and big nose plastered against the opening behind me he looked like a Bill Mauldin WWII cartoon character. For an instant, the screws were out of the water when we crested a swell. They screamed in protest, rattling the whole boat.

Snipe, oil-smelling and drenched, crawled up the ladder from the well-deck and yelled up to Buddha, "Water's pouring in so fast the bilge pumps can't keep up."

"Well take your shoes off and roll up your pants. Pretend you're at home," he yelled back like a maniac against the wind and spray.

"What should I do?" Snipe asked, looking at me.

"Everybody's below. Have them start bailing with empty ammo boxes."

The column of boats in front of me ploughed into waves and disappeared into troughs—only soggy ensigns and identification light masts visible above the crests—then they'd rise slowly on the next swell, framed by spray exploding from their bows.

"Everybody's nuts up here," Snipe said, with a shake of his dripping head.

We swung into the harbor at Vung Tau after dark, tied to a pier and went to the mess hall. The food reminded me of being back aboard ship. Fresh milk—not powdered—chocolate or plain; ice cream, all we could eat; fresh roast meat. We gorged ourselves, then went to a transit barracks where we showered and rolled up in dry blankets. The next morning we cleaned the boat and laid our clothes out to dry.

Late afternoon we circled on rolling swells, waiting our turn to enter an LSD (Landing ship (Dock)). From my cox'n flat I watched seagulls floating along side our boat scavenging scraps of food Snipe threw to them. One swooped in, snatched a morsel, settled in the water to eat it, then dropped it. I had to laugh—not gooks or seagulls would eat C-ration fruitcake.

"Afe, watch how those boats go in. Look at that one. I think it's Tango 7. Dumb ass. He hit the stern door of the ship. There must be a crosswind curling around the back pushing the boats sideways. Watch, there goes another one. He did the same thing—they're not paying attention."

Sitting in his sheltered cove above and behind me, Buddha explained again where we were going. Top brass had come to the conclusion that there wasn't much action in the Delta anymore because Westmoreland had lured them up north to Khe Sanh.

"Three weeks ago we were told that they were beat up so bad during Tet that they skipped back across to Cambodia," I said.

"Yeah, that too," Buddha replied. "But now they've come to the conclusion that North Vietnamese Army (NVA) replacements are only going as far as Khe Sanh. Once that blows over they'll get back on the Trail down to the Delta."

I remembered the Ho Chi Minh Trail from our training lectures. It was almost mythical—a path that originated in North Vietnam and meandered through Laos and Cambodia, just across the border in those neutral countries where the United States couldn't officially touch them. The Trail snaked south—ending in the Mekong Delta, branching off along the way—with a never-ending resupply of men and materiel. It had started during the war against the French in the 1950's as a path, with hand and bicycle-transported supplies. By 1968 it had grown to a thoroughfare with heavy trucks and rest areas. Rumor had it the North Vietnamese even used elephants.

Buddha continued on, repeating a mixture of facts and rumors he'd gleaned. Our boat division had been selected to move north to the Cua Viet River—a river about six miles south of the DMZ. The Marine Corps didn't have the resources to keep it open and it was a vital artery for transferring supplies from the coast, inland to Dong Ha, in support of the on-going Khe Sanh offensive, which was near the Laotian border. The Marine base at the mouth of the river was subjected to incoming artillery, big stuff, 122mm. On the river, mines were the biggest threat. And we could expect ambushes from shore with heavier weapons than used in the Delta. Our mission was to keep the river open. Minesweeping, keeping the banks secure from ambushes, checking sampans—we would be busy. Our division would be part of Task Force Clearwater.

"Tango one-one, you're next in," blared the radio.

"Take her in. Afe, remember. Stay to the port side. Keep the bow angled into the wind. Let it push you to the center—once you're inside the ship you can jockey for your berth. Crow. Dennis. Drop fenders over."

The LSD's stern doors were open wide and the dark hole of the flooded cargo deck reminded me of a cave mouth. I eased forward, revved the starboard engine gently to keep my bow to port and, as Buddha had predicted, the wind and current carried me forward into the flooded hold. I eased into position, third boat along the starboard side—next to Tango 7.

"What the fuck were you trying to do, rearrange the ship's stern?" Buddha yelled across. The Tango 7 boat captain outranked Buddha and the division commander assigned them tasks that Buddha coveted. From my cox'n flat where I was busy holding our boat in position, I glanced across and saw the Tango 7 captain flip Buddha off.

With the LSD's cargo hold full with riverboats, the stern doors closed and sealed and the deck pumped dry as our boats settled. I could feel the ship get underway. It was a strange sensation in that dark hold, almost vertigo as down-drafting diesel fumes filled the compartment. I was used to seeing the horizon as the ship rolled. High overhead interior lights came on. My eyes adjusted from the bright outside sunlight and I could see figures moving about on other boats.

"Afe, secure the small arms locker."

While in Vung Tau, waiting for the LSD to arrive, the boat captains had attended a meeting. The LSD captain was worried about all the weapons on our boats and the racial unrest on his ship. Buddha had told me that he trusted Stone-wall, but you could never tell when a couple of dozen black sailors got jiving after dark on the fantail. He'd seen it on the *Connie*; individually they were fine, thrown into a cluster they just—were different. I knew. I'd seen it on the *Rogers*. Stonewall knew. There had been black boat captains at the meeting.

"Don't worry Buddha, I won't frag anybody," he said in disgust.

"I'm not worried about you but some asshole might sneak on here once we leave."

"You think that piddly-assed lock'll stop somebody? They'll pop it like a ripe zit." I sensed an undercurrent in Stonewall's tone and wondered about it. I had noticed how at night he would change the radio station to, as Buddha called it, jive shit, when he was on watch. From his bunk in the well-deck Buddha would look up toward the hole leading to the cox'n flat where we kept the radio.

"Who's got the next watch?" he'd say, when one of us acknowledged that we did, he'd whisper. "Change that sta-tion. Get rid of that friggin jive."

I didn't think he was a racist. He just didn't like the mu-sic. He refused to leave Peter, Paul and Mary or the Beatles on—fucking hippie protesters he called them. He would tol-erate Tom Jones and Neil Diamond. I didn't care for the jive songs either—couldn't understand most of the lyrics.

With boats secured, we moved topside. Stepping out onto the main deck we discovered a black Marine guard at the hatch. I found a sheltered nook, sat down and leaned back against the bulkhead. With a gentle breeze and warm sun on my face I watched the Delta coastline shrink until it disappeared in our wake.

Shipboard sailors were in awe of our boats and us. I recalled how amazed I had been when I was on the *Rogers*, patrolling in the Gulf of Tonkin, when Swift Boats came alongside. From our ship's deck we'd look down at their little boats, the machine guns, the relaxed command structure, and envy them. Usually, all they wanted was a bucket of strawberry ice cream. They traded soccer size glass balls, broken free or stolen from Vietnamese fishing nets set out in the Gulf.

These deep-water sailors had never seen anything like our army-green armored assault boats—or sailors like us, longer hair, cut-off fatigues, jungle boots, tennis shoes, or barefoot. It was hard not to strut. I had a hand-made machete I'd traded an old papason two packs of cigarettes for. He'd used it for chopping coconut husks. The sailors were hungry for war stories so we accommodated them.

I created a profitable war story. "I'm going to tell you a story, and it ain't no shit." The sailors listened raptly as I wove the tale. "A few weeks ago I was searching a sampan. When I bent down to pull open a compartment door in his fish-stinking little boat, the friggin gook pulled a machete from under a rag and was on the down-stroke over my head when Crow took him out with the 12 gauge. That old fuck flew overboard and churned in the water like a sturgeon that'd been gaffed."

"What did you do when you pulled him out?" said a wide-eyed sailor.

"Pull him out?" Crow said—he'd been standing nearby, listening. "Afe grabbed the machete, leaned over the side and wacked the old fuck."

"He didn't get in trouble?"

"Why would he get in trouble? That's what we're here for—to kill gooks."

"What happened?"

"Not much. We took the other two prisoners, sank the sampan, hauled them back to the ARVNs for interrogation," I said.

"What's ARVNs?"

"South Vietnamese Army—I kept the machete though, figured I'd bring it home with me."

"No shit. Can I see it?"

I played hard to get. Dennis, Crow, and Stonewall stood, nodding heads, reinforcing my tale. I finally conceded and went below. The story spread and when I returned there were several more sailors who wanted to see the machete. The big knife had a three-foot-long rusty blade and a bamboo handle wrapped tightly in black fishing twine. I apologized for the dark stains—I'd rinsed it off afterwards but the blood had already dried, I explained.

"How much for it?" a sailor asked.

"It's not for sale," I said, lightly feathering my thumb across the nicked blade.

Crow stepped into the action again. "I didn't realize that you'd chipped the blade when you chopped the old fucker's skull." He reached out and touched the dented edge.

"That happened on the second swing when he grabbed the gunnel—skinny-assed arm—blade went all the way through and wacked the side of the boat."

"I'll give you a hundred dollars for it," declared a voice.

"Hey, I talked to him first. I'll give you a hundred and twenty five."

"I guess—just don't tell anybody."

We watched shipboard sailors chip paint, sand hot pitted metal, primer it, then repaint Navy gray. The endless routine made us appreciate our position, but the hot food, fresh milk, fruit, ice cream, hot showers, air conditioned living compartments, and the safety of the ocean was their reward and we envied them that.

Buddha and the other boat captains listened to Marine Corps radio transmissions and to the Marine detachment stationed on board the LSD. Incoming artillery was the biggest threat up north where we were going. The North Vietnamese dropped shells unexpectedly; random strikes. You don't hear the one that gets you, they said. Only those falling short or whistling over. The boats had no defense against a direct hit but the odds of a round landing directly on a boat was just fucked luck—nothing to be done about that, they said. The radio reported a mining on the Cua Viet River—boat destroyed, crew killed. That was just bad luck, too. If you drove over a mine, not much you could do—just pucker up.

I couldn't sleep that night so I wandered the ship and reflected on my first tour in these waters. I thought about the hundreds of bridge watches I'd stood. How I'd started as aft lookout, fresh from boot camp—a position impossible to screw up—watching the ship's wake. Twelve months after enlisting, learning, being in charge of an enlisted watch section, the pride I felt in accomplishment. Memories flooded back as I stood in the shadows on the port wing of the bridge and listened. The low hum of the darkened bridge. The faint green glow of the shielded radar screen. The helmsman's face caught in the reflection of light from the compass in front of him.

"Mind your helm," barked a voice from the starboard wing of the bridge. The helmsman had been daydreaming and allowed the ship to drift a few degrees off course. The officer of the deck had checked him. I glanced aft and in the moonlight, saw the long gentle curve in the phosphorescent wake as the helmsman corrected his heading.

"Aye, aye, sir," replied the helmsman. I slipped away with a smile. Some things never changed, I thought.

I found my way down to the mess deck and had a midnight snack; strong acidic coffee, a cold spongy apple, sticky caramel rolls. I sat, feet up, thumbing through old magazines, knowing I'd be tired the next afternoon. About 0300 hours I wandered to the stern and watched the wake glisten into the distance. I discovered Snipe, Dennis, and Professor on the fantail and asked why they weren't in their bunks.

"We've never been to sea before except crossing to San Clemente. It's so calm up here we decided to watch the ocean," Professor said.

"Night on the open sea," I sighed.

Professor started talking then—about where he'd gone to college and the things his old friends were telling him in letters. Snipe, Dennis and I listened as he spoke of college protests. He told us about a big draft protest at Oakland in October of the past year called Stop the Draft Week and how some of his friends had participated in the big Washington, D.C. march.

"Why are they protesting? If they're students, they get deferments—they've got nothing to worry about," I said.

"Look where it got me. I enlisted in the navy three weeks after graduation because I knew I'd get my draft notice and didn't want to end up in the army. It's not just that—look around. These people just want peace. Ho Chi Minh begged the United States to help him at the end of World War II. But instead, we supported the French when they re-invaded Vietnam because we were worried about French support against expanding Russian communist influence in Europe."

"What did France in Europe have to do with France in

Vietnam?"

"The French are treacherous. America and Britain learned after two World Wars that they couldn't be trusted. At the end of World War II they were completely defeated. Communism and a rebuilt Germany were on the rise. France was in terrible condition economically. The United States was afraid that if we didn't support them in Vietnam that they'd turn toward communism in France. Russia predicted communism would rule the world, blackmailed us with threats of nuclear annihilation."

"Well it worked," I said. "In the early '50s when I was a little kid we had bomb drills and marched to the basement of the little school I went to."

"That was government propaganda—what in heaven's name would the Russians bomb northern Minnesota for?"

I shook my head and laughed. "You've got a point there, I guess."

"Like I said," Professor continued. "Ho Chi Minh asked the United States for assistance at the end of World War II. When we turned him away, he went to the only other places he could—Russia and China. Think about it. China wasn't communist at the end of the war. Mao didn't take over the country until 1949 when Chiang Kai-shek was cornered in Formosa. The point is—Ho only wanted independence for Vietnam—he's their George Washington."

"I think that's stretching it," I said. "George Washington wasn't a communist."

"No, but he was a slave owner and people like McCarthy claim that communism is no different than slavery."

I knew I wouldn't get the last word in with Professor. He always had a come-back. The scary thing was, they often made sense. I went silent and watched dawn arrive.

It crept in with a faint sting of salt spray moistening my tongue and left a taste of vast open reaches—the water and sky became one with the horizon. For a time I couldn't tell where the sea ended and the sky began. Pale pink shadows developed into golden red hues as the granite sea rolled west, waves dancing atop. Below the high cirrus clouds, screeching gulls soared on thermals. I discovered three flying fish on deck. On the *Rogers*, the Filipino mess stewards had searched topside decks at dawn, retrieving the small fish, a delicacy for the captain's breakfast.

Reveille piped through the ship. Off the port side I could see the coastline silhouette. As the ship approached the coast, sea traffic picked up. A large, ocean-going junk slid past, sail billowing, bow jutting skyward. A small sampan, three tubs in tow, prepared for a day of fishing. The sampan was heavily loaded—papasan and three children. I watched them shrink into the distance. He disconnected the tubs and placed a child in each one with a fishing line and bait. I'd seen it many times when I was on the *Rogers* in these waters; the papasan would circle from tub to tub, transferring fish the children caught into the sampan. At dusk he'd gather them.

8

Cua Viet

2 March 1968

Seawater took on a light brown tint from sediment washed down from distant plains and mountains—a sure sign that we were approaching the mouth of a large river. The ship's company was piped to morning chow. Boat crews went first because we would be off-loading in two hours. This would be our last breakfast of steak and eggs, fresh fruit, and pancakes. Comments were ruefully cast that this was our "last supper." After eating I hurried topside, anxious for a glimpse of our destination. Now the coastline was distinct—I could see breaking waves against a background of pale sand dunes and green brush.

Forward motion of the ship decreased and the loudspeaker piped a call to attention. "Now hear this, all boat crews to the cargo hold. Ships' company, prepare to off-load," blared the boatswain's voice from the ship's bridge.

"Once we're out of the hold I want everybody ready, helmet and flak jacket on," Buddha said. "Afe, raise your armor—gunners, check everything. Snipe, when I tell Afe to start the engines, I want you in the engine compartment to make sure everything's running properly."

We were ready. I felt a rush of fresh air when the stern doors opened. Water rushed in, refloating our boats.

From above, Buddha's voice echoed down through the cox'n flat. "Standby to start engines. Start your engines. Hold your position."

I pushed the ignition buttons for port and starboard engine and felt the boat quiver as the diesels came to life.

"Back down. Hold her steady." Swells began rolling into the compartment, tossing boats like corks in a whirlpool.

I threw both engines into reverse and attempted to back out straight but incoming waves and turbulence from other boat's propellers made it impossible. It was a good thing our fenders hung over the sides because I bounced against the boat on my port side, pushing him against the ship's starboard bulkhead before he ricocheted back against me. For an instant the image of the two squat boats banging against each other reminded me of two sumo wrestlers I'd seen in Tokyo. The stern of the ship loomed above as we eased out of the hull into daylight. Away from the ship, we joined the growing circle as the division formed up. I quickly discovered that the swells and waves were much higher than they appeared looking down from the ship.

With the last boat out of the LSD, we formed a column and proceeded west toward the river mouth. Heavy swells pushed our stern, creating a corkscrew affect. The coastline came into focus; the river mouth; men and machines moving—the 3rd Marine Division—the unit we'd be operating with.

As I steered toward shore I reflected on how our boats were converted LCM 6's—landing craft used during World War II. What tales of past beachings could this boat tell? Was this suspense what our fathers felt a generation earlier, approaching foreign shores in this boat; the fear to be faced and overcome? Was this boat used in the Atlantic or Pacific? Had it traveled these same swells twenty-five years earlier toward some island in the South China Sea? I thought of the mechanic at the John Deere dealership back in Bemidji. He'd been a Marine Raider during WWII—had gotten wounded in hand to hand combat on Tarawa. Might he have ridden this boat when they'd assaulted that beach? From my cox'n flat I watched little eddies as the flood tide—incoming tide—confused the brown, silty water pushing against our boat.

Buddha's voice interrupted my thoughts. "Look sharp, Afe. I don't want to end up like those boats."

Off the port side, two hulks nestled in white sand dunes, testimony to the treachery of these winds and currents. One looked like a Swift Boat, the other, an LCM 8, the same kind of boat we'd ridden from Coronado to San Clemente Island the past October during our gun training. As we pushed into calm water, inside the shipping channel, I was surprised at how wide the river was—over half a mile. Looking west, I could see a village and scrub trees. The river must turn south, I thought. I looked to the north bank, the desert-like sand—about six miles from North Vietnam.

A dredging barge was at work between me and the north bank—a never-ending task we learned—clearing constantly shifting sand bars. We entered a turning basin, a large deep-water area where ships could back away after off-loading cargo. I passed the stern of an LST, a large ship that opened at the bow. It was beached against a fifty-yard wide concrete ramp that angled down into the water. Forklift tractors raced in and out of her cargo hold with pallets of supplies, stacking them in a large staging area up from the ramp.

"That's why we're here," Buddha shouted. "So those supplies can get up to Dong Ha. This is a real bottle-neck. Look at those piles. I saw another LST heading this way about half an hour ago. Afe, see that dude on shore, waving? I think he wants us to follow him."

A man on the concrete ramp waved a tattered red rag, motioning us to move west. I passed the LST and saw two LCM 8's nestled near her. The forklift tractors were loading directly off the ship and onto the two smaller vessels. I passed the end of the concrete apron and swung toward the beach.

"Welcome to Cua Viet, the arm-friggin-pit of Vietnam," the flag man said, flag hanging at his side.

"Does this wind ever stop?" Buddha asked, as a powdery gust drifted across the boat.

"Each day, from 1600 to 1605. I'm in the shitter with the door locked."

The man pointed out the refueling pier west of us—now I understood why diesel fumes permeated the air. I glanced back and watched rainbow-colored fuel from the weeping storage tanks swirl seaward atop the brown water. Just up-river from the refueling pier a South Vietnamese flag waved over a military base surrounded by coils of concertina wire. I asked if they operated with the Marines. In the Delta we rarely carried ARVN troops.

"They generally operate independently. We have to bail them out sometimes when they can't run fast enough. Don't trust'm when they come begging. We get shelled damn near every night, sometimes during the day, and those assholes never get a round dropped on them. The NVA probably have a forward observer stationed there to spot for them. That's why this fuel pier is close to their base. Less chance of getting hit. Actually, it's a naval base but I rarely see a boat there," the flag man said.

Buddha left for a boat captain's meeting and I stepped ashore to survey our new home. I stood ankle deep in sand and watched a dust devil swirl across the beach. It filtered between pursed lips and left a gritty film in my mouth. The sand reminded me of the Delta, but here, vegetation was stunted compared to the lush tropical jungle down south. Beyond the pallet-clogged staging area I could see the corrugated metal roofs of several hooches.

Snipe came up to me. "The way this stuff is drifting onto the boat, those bilge pumps will be like liquid sand blasters."

I was thankful not to be in Snipe's spot. I had come to the conclusion that Buddha didn't know anything about engines and to disguise his ignorance he barked at Snipe for petty visible things in the engine compartment or the well-deck, yet he was helpless when it came to mechanical problems. Snipe was worried about the packing—the seals where the propeller shafts went through the bottom of the boat's hull— how the sand would grind in and cause greater seepage.

"Get that portable pump back on board," I told him. "That's about the best insurance."

"He told me he needed it because of an electrical short in his bilge pump system, he's afraid of it cutting out—his pumps kick on every twenty-five minutes because of cracked welds in the hull below the engines," Snipe replied, in reference to the portable water pump we had borrowed earlier.

I watched Buddha approach, his arm looped around a bundle. He was moving faster than usual and called ahead to me. "Afe, get the crew together for the low-down. We're going upriver in three hours."

He told us to fill the sandbags—the bundle—and stack them in the well-deck against the bow door. They would serve a dual purpose; added protection from rockets and increase our weight so we wouldn't flip if we hit a mine.

The same guy who'd flagged us earlier approached the boat. "I'm supposed to guide you guys up the river. Who's in charge here?" I looked up from where I was bent over holding a sandbag Crow was filling and nodded toward the open bow of the boat.

"Buddha. He's up in the cox'n flat."

I could hear voices but couldn't distinguish what was being said. A few minutes later Buddha and the guide came down the ladder and over to where we were stacking the filled sandbags. "We're supposed to eat before we go up-river. This guy will show us around. Leave those bags. You can stack them after we get underway."

We listened to our guide as we walked across the concrete ramp, up past the staging area piled high with supplies, then back into sugar sand. He said the sailors called this base Cua Viet but the Marines called it Camp Kistler. I noticed how the hooches were tucked into a deep sandy swale south of the staging area. "Most of the incoming rounds go over us or drop on the staging area. That's the mess hall," he said, nodding toward a low, sandbagged hooch with a three-foot–wide screen wrapped around it and sandbags stacked four feet up on the walls. Inside, it was raw wood, bare studs and plywood with a steam table and Navy mess cooks doling food onto compartmented steel trays.

After eating, on our return trip to the boat, the guide pointed out hooches we would find useful. They looked like they were punched out with a cookie cutter: studs, plywood, screen, corrugated roof, and heavily sandbagged. Every building had a screen door on a powerful spring that sounded like a rifle shot each time it slammed. "Helps keep the flies out," our guide said. He pointed out the sandbagged, radio-antennaed shelter of our Task Force Commander.

"I left the best for last—the EM Club. Actually, it's just a beer hooch but the beer is always cold and they never run out—two bits a can."

"The wind sure raises hell with these trees," I commented nodding toward some scrub pines with most of the foliage stripped and branches snapped.

"Yeah, those trees were hit by a North wind—we call it 152mm NVA artillery—it raises hell with the landscaping."

He pointed out bunkers to be used if we were caught ashore during incoming artillery barrages. I glanced from the mess hall to the nearest bunker—about thirty meters— that should be an easy sprint, I thought.

When we reached the boat, everybody went to their battle stations and the guide stood in the cox'n flat with me and Professor. I joined the column and we proceeded up-river toward Dong Ha. I commented on how wide the river was and he laughed—said that would change. The boat's radio came to life and ordered all boats to put out sweep gear.

"Did you hear that?" Professor called up to Buddha.

"Yeah, stick your head below and tell Snipe to put it out."

Professor knelt down, stuck his head through the hatch and yelled, "Snipe, hey Snipe, put the sweep gear out."

Snipe didn't answer so Professor went down the ladder to find him. A few minutes later he returned and called up to Buddha, "Snipe's on his way back to the stern—he was in the engine compartment. He's worried about the engines sucking up sand in their coolant systems."

"You're lucky," the guide called up to Buddha. "Sounds like you have a squared away engineman."

"Yeah, I'm real friggin lucky with Snipe."

When the sweep gear hit bottom and dug in it was like pulling two skiers out of the water with an under-powered outboard. I increased RPM's as the drag pulled the stern down.

"It's great having you guys here. Last week we couldn't get a convoy through to Dong Ha. NVA blocked the river at a narrow spot up ahead. I've never seen a boat this heavily armored. Does that bar armor really work?"

"I hope I don't find out," I said, as we swung south past a burned out village.

"See how we favor this side of the river, here," the guide told me as I followed the lead boat to starboard. "The sand bars constantly shift. If you stay on the outer side of curves, the water is deeper—stronger current. The tide is out now. See how that one in front of you is kicking up sand. Problem is, the NVA know that too."

"What's that over to the port side?" Buddha asked. I looked over and saw what looked like the bottom of an LCM 8.

"They hit a mine two days ago. Two killed—haven't found one of them—probably washed out into the gulf by now."

"If we flipped like that, we'd be screwed," Buddha said.

"Mines are a bigger threat than ambushes or snipers along here. You'd be wise to keep the crew topside. At least the first run of the morning—they'd have half a chance, anyway. Like you said, down below, you're screwed."

"I can see beyond the riverbank," I told the guide. "Down in the delta, jungle hung right into the river. We could be twenty feet from a bunker and not see them. What's back in that paddy?" I said, motioning toward a burned out machine.

"That's an APC, an Armored Personnel Carrier. That one caught a rocket—killed four guys. The Marines use them for transporting troops. They're amphibious but sometimes they get stuck in the sandy riverbanks. Once in a while one swamps while crossing the river—then they're screwed. They go down like an anchor."

Our column of boats turned north into a smaller river, passing a cemetery on the point that jutted out. The guide said it was a favored sniper and ambush site.

"Kind of handy," Buddha commented. "The gooks don't have far to go to get buried."

"You're not dealing with VC up here," the guide said, looking up between the turrets. "These boys are North Vietnamese Army regulars—you respect them or you won't be around long."

Ahead, a bridge spanned the river. "Route 1," the guide said. I followed the lead boat in a wide, arcing turn so we wouldn't have to pull up the sweep gear. As I turned, traffic crossing the bridge kicked up dust clouds. The wind carried the reddish tinted powder down into the cox'n flat and coated my console.

"During the monsoons it turns sticky, like clay, about impossible to get through," the guide said.

On our return run to Cua Viet our guide pointed to a small canal flowing into the main river. It reminded me of the canals down south because about fifty meters in from the mouth, thick vegetation lined both banks. He said that it was called Jones Creek and it came down out of the DMZ. The Marines had been—still were—in heavy contact with the NVA north of us along the creek. We proceeded east on our return run. Buddha left his shelter between the gun mounts and went forward into the well-deck. Moments later he stuck his head up through the opening to the cox'n flat and told the guide to come below.

"Just follow the boat in front of you Afe. Kind of hard to screw that up."

Passing the graveyard on our return trip, I looked to the west, wondering where that river led as it disappeared beyond the curve. We hugged the sandy bank on the north side and I watched Marines swimming below watchtowers on the south side. Professor commented on them, saying he felt much safer on the boat than ashore. I agreed. We followed along, swung north through another narrow channel as I watched a farmer follow his yoked buffalo plowing a rice paddy beyond the diked riverbank.

"We had a one bottom plow like that back on the farm," I told Professor as we both watched the farmer. "Three years ago when I left, it was lying in the orchard with other abandoned horse-drawn equipment—probably hasn't been used since about 1930. There was a four-inch-thick crabapple tree growing between the handles."

"He's a good example of why we shouldn't be here," Professor said, watching the man wrestle his wooden plow around at the end of the paddy. "They live in a different world. He's doing what his ancestors did three hundred years ago. They don't know any other life. All he's interested in is enough to eat and safety for his family—democracy is alien to his values. He's been forced to pay taxes and obey a power above him for so many generations it's the natural way of things."

When we arrived back at Cua Viet, the last LST of the day was backing out into the turning basin. Our guide said that the channel coming in, where we'd passed through earlier, was only about two hundred feet wide and ships didn't like navigating it after dark.

That night I strapped on a .38 caliber pistol and went up to the shower hooch. While I waited for a stall, two Marines asked if I wanted to sell the pistol.

"I'll give you two hundred dollars for it."

"I can't sell it. It's part of the gear on our boat, it's not mine," I explained.

"Gear? Bullshit man. Everybody loses shit. Tell'em somebody stole it."

"I can't do that. Besides I need it."

"Man, that's bullshit. I seen them boats. Ain't nothing can get you with all them guns sticking out."

When my turn came I unbuckled the .38, kicked out of my shorts—hung them on a nail just outside the stall—and stepped into the shower. As I reached up to close the tattered curtain I glimpsed an arm shoot toward the peg and grab my pistol belt. I lunged out, grabbed the other end in a tug-o-war.

The man looked at me and laughed. "Shit man, if I'd only waited 'til you got soap in your eyes."

"Yeah," I laughed back. "You fucked up."

Dropping his end, he and his buddy walked out laughing. I pulled the shower curtain closed, gun hanging from the pipe the shower nozzle was attached to. When I returned to the boat I warned the crew about thieving Marines.

That evening Buddha and Professor went to a boat captain's meeting. Buddha stayed at the beer hooch. Professor returned and told us that the next morning we would all make a run west to Dong Ha. On the return trip, boats would peel off to patrol sections of the river, overlapping ends with the boat on each side of them.

Dawn broke cloudless. Seagulls screeched as they flicked through the rising sun. I stood at the stern relieving myself and watched a massive ship beyond the channel we had entered the day before. Was it the battleship *New Jersey*, I wondered? We'd heard she was off the coast somewhere up north doing shore bombardments and supporting ground forces. I returned to the well-deck, opened a can of eggs and ham. Buddha explained that the first run up river was the highest risk; the greatest chance of hitting a mine the NVA may have planted during the night.

To share the risk, a new boat rotated forward each day. Our ten boats patrolled two columns abreast—once every five days wasn't bad odds unless you were in front. Lead boat was a high-risk position because it would pass over a mine before the mine sweep gear, which dragged sixty feet behind the boat, made contact. The boat crew would wear lifejackets and ride topside, except for the cox'n. They'd hunker down on the inboard side of the boat—away from the nearest riverbank. If the boat was mined, odds of survival were better getting blown overboard rather than trapped inside.

"Afe, leave your armor flaps open. That'll give you a chance to get out."

Alone in my cox'n flat, following the boat in front of me, my mind drifted to the sampans headed seaward. What must they think of these huge steel hulks creating wakes that almost swamped them? Passing a steep riverbank—unusually high—I thought, what a great ambush site. At Dong Ha we turned around. As we proceeded east, boats dropped from the column in their designated sector. Our section of the river was adjacent to where we'd watched the farmer the day before.

"Everybody, stow your lifejackets and get in your gun mounts," Buddha said, as we dropped from the column. "Snipe, check those bilge pumps."

For the next three hours he stayed above deck at his battle station and the gunners remained in their mounts. We could see aircraft maneuvering and bomb explosions to the north. Professor studied the map and discovered we were near the mouth of Jones Creek. Yesterday's guide had told us another small tributary nearer Dong Ha was Jones Creek.

By midmorning I heard Buddha snoring. The farmer unhitched the scrawny water buffalo and left her to forage in the dry paddy. He hiked inland toward the brown-slabbed hut beyond the dike. Professor turned the radio on to "Come On Down To My Boat Baby," and Dennis, Crow, and Stonewall sang along from their gun turrets. Buddha woke up. "What the fuck? It sounds like a hippie rock concert up here. Shut that shit off or find something decent. Man it's hot here. Afe, I'm going below."

I was near the end of our sector and began a wide turn. With a sick feeling I felt the boat rise for an instant then lurch as it scraped bottom. Cutting hard to starboard—toward the wide part of the river, I gunned the engine and felt her crawl higher on the sand bar.

"You dumb fuck, why are you out of the channel?" Buddha screamed from above.

"I'm in the channel. I've turned fifteen times in this spot," I yelled. "Snipe, get the drag gear in so I can back down."

Buddha had been listening to the exchange and yelled

down, "Professor, you get on the radio. I can see Tango 7 coming this way. Call him for a tow."

"Tango seven, I see you heading our way. We ran aground. Can you help us?"

"This is Tango seven. The tide is out. I'll back toward you until I start kicking up sand, you'll have to get the tow-line to me."

"Roger, Tango seven. Tango one-one, out."

Professor raced down the ladder and crawled out of the well-deck. I glimpsed the top of his head as he went astern to tell Buddha what was going on. I could hear the dog gears clicking as Buddha cranked the mine sweep gear in. The noise stopped for a moment as Professor was relayed the news.

"That chicken-shit bastard! Tell Afe he got us stuck, he can swim out to that friggin coward. You stay in the cox'n flat and steer once we're hooked up."

Professor returned and told me what Buddha said. I shrugged. He was right. I'd run aground—besides, I was a ship's swimmer.

Buddha had the rope laid out on the stern. "That chicken-shit won't back any closer. You get this line over to him." I looked across at Tango 7. She was about fifty meters away.

"That shouldn't be a big deal." I jumped from the stern of our boat into the river. It was only about three feet deep. I hooked my arm through the spliced eye and waded toward Tango 7.

I heard a dull thud and moments later a mortar round whistled down between me and Tango 7. Flinching, I crouched in the water.

"Incoming mortar rounds," the Tango 7 boat captain screamed at me. "You have twenty seconds to get here or I'm leaving—get your ass up and moving!" His voice jarred me back. I hadn't realized I was crouched in the river, water up to my chin.

Rounds splashed nearer as the NVA walked them toward our boats. I pushed through the water trying to escape.

I heard Buddha scream. "Hurry Afe! You can do it."

A round fell near, drenching my face and hair, pushing me sideways—down into the brown water. A weed-rope clung to my arm when I got up. I screamed and brushed at it thinking it was a snake. They said there were lots of them in this river. Hands grabbed the towline and secured it. Tango 7 surged forward as a sailor pulled me aboard.

The boat captain and I crouched on the stern below the 20mm cannon and watched as Tango 11 backed at full power. Sandy water churned forward on her sides as mortar rounds fell closer. The towline stretched and brown water beads rolled off as the line sang like a taut guitar string. Tango 11 refused to budge.

The Tango 7 boat captain shouted for his cox'n to back down, then swing to port—see if he could get an angle to pull from. I jumped to the stern and gathered in towline as Tango 7 backed up. Buddha must have thought we were leaving because he stood up and yelled—shaking his fist at us. Tango 7 swung to port and surged forward, this time gaining speed before the towrope tightened. Stretched tight, it popped out of the water. The Tango 7 captain and I laughed when Buddha fell as Tango 11 broke loose from the river bottom. Grudgingly, the grounded boat slid back. I watched sandbags we'd filled the day before sail out the sides of the well-deck as the crew lightened our boat. Suddenly she was free and backing toward us. Three mortar rounds, in rapid succession, splashed around the two boats as they came together. Beyond the scrub-pine-shrouded riverbank where the mortars were being fired from, I watched a helicopter shoot rockets then make four strafing runs. No more mortar rounds fell. The two boats came together and I tossed the tow rope to our boat. I jumped back to Tango 11 and listened to Buddha and the Tango 7 captain discuss the situation. When we pulled away Buddha looked at me.

"You okay?"

"Yeah."

"You looked pretty lonesome out there when those rounds were coming down."

I watched the farmer in the dry rice paddy kick up a tiny dust cloud as he followed his plow. We stood together at the stern of the boat and I told Buddha about another time I had been terrified.

It had been the summer of 1964, when I rode the rails out to Washington from Minnesota. I was in a boxcar with three other guys. It was a hot day and I was sitting in the open doorway as the train sped through a scrub area of Montana where narrow steel bridges spanned arroyos. I was half asleep with my feet swinging in cadence to the swaying train and the rhythm of the clacking wheels when we crossed one of those narrow bridges. The train was going about forty miles an hour and my foot hit a steel brace on the sidewall of a little bridge. Luckily, I was sitting next to the rear side of the door. I grabbed it and held on. Two guys pulled me back into the car. I lay on that floor gagging as I realized how close I'd been. I would have bounced out against the wall of that bridge, and the bracing my foot hit would have forced me right onto the tracks beneath the train.

Buddha reached out and put his hand on my shoulder for a moment. "That was a close one. Stay in deep water."

Professor drove the rest of the afternoon. I felt hollow inside. Even Buddha sensed I wanted to be alone. It was strange how we hadn't seen the people shooting at us. We were being watched, otherwise how could the North Vietnamese adjust their ranges so quickly. That farmer; had he been in his field when I ran aground? It was strange how he didn't even look at us each time we passed—like we were invisible. Or he wanted us to not see him—like a tree, or a rock. That evening, after we were refueled and beached for the night, I mentioned it to Professor.

"You have to understand," Professor said. "He's part of the natural world. War is part of his natural world. He was behaving in a natural way—to continue his work. If he had run, or lay down in his paddy, he would have looked guilty. To remain working was the only choice he had."

Our crew consisted of two duty sections, three men each. Buddha said he didn't stand watches because as boat captain, he was on duty twenty-four hours a day. Weren't we all? One section always remained on the boat. Each man stood a four-hour watch monitoring the radio, checking in each hour with the duty officer of the division. We ran the diesel engines twenty minutes each hour to keep the batteries charged and the bilges pumped. Professor, Crow, and I had duty that night. I wasn't sleepy so I told them I'd stand the first watch.

I sat on top of the boat, resting on the corner of my cox'n flat canopy, watching the last LST of the day back into the turning basin and head out to sea. We had taken advantage of the amenities offered by the LST—hot fresh-water showers, clean clothes, hot food. After we returned to the boat, Snipe, Stonewall, and Dennis had gone to the LST then on to the beer hooch. I watched the stern of the departing ship glow in the setting sun until she rounded the sand dunes at the mouth of the channel.

9

Marine Chopper Down

4 March 1968

Two days later, a strange breeze kicked up dust devils along the riverbank at Cua Viet. Usually it blew in off the South China Sea but that evening it came from the west, from the Annamite Cordilleras, beyond Dong Ha, where the battle for Khe Sanh was being waged. For us, on the boats, it was a mysterious battle that we watched devour shiploads of supplies. A battle we couldn't hear or see, but caused the setting sun to appear as though it were filtered through a smoky haze. It reminded me of back on the farm when smoke from Canadian forest fires drifted south. We had smelled the faint hint of pine smoke but couldn't visualize the monster creating it.

A Huey gunship landed on the concrete staging area just east of us. The door gunners secured the M60 machine gun while the pilot powered down the helicopter. That surprised me. I thought there was only one gunner in those Hueys. Maybe he was training a new guy. From within the gunship I could see the pilot and co-pilot unbuckle and move back to the compartment the gunners were in. They jumped to the ground, one said something to another and the four of them walked toward the mess hall laughing. I wondered if they were the ones who had silenced the mortars the day I'd run aground.

Half an hour later the dredging barge, its thirty foot boom extended out over the concrete staging area, beached near us. The civilian workers jumped onto the ramp and headed toward the showers and the beer hooch.

The sun dropped over the horizon and disappeared into the western haze. I lay on my cox'n flat canopy and watched the stars come out. Settling in for the evening, I tuned our transistor radio to Hanoi Hannah, the communist propaganda station broadcast from Hanoi. The North Vietnamese station played a better assortment of music than our Armed Forces Network. "She'd Rather Be With Me" was just ending.

"Listen to that, you Marines at Khe Sanh. Do you miss your girl? Maybe she'd rather be with your friend back home. Warm, soft, safe, sitting under stars in a new Mustang convertible. Maybe she's forgotten all about you, burrowed into the sand like rats."

"Why do you listen to that bitch?" Crow said, from below me in the cox'n flat where he was sitting, trying to escape the subMarine-like confines of the well-deck. "She pisses me off. What does that bitch know? She probably just crawled out of a rice paddy from screwing half the gooks in Hanoi."

"I know my comrades have kept you Marines busy— maybe you didn't hear what your Walter Cronkite said— that your politicians are lying to you, that you have lost the war—nobody at home cares about you."

In the darkness, Professor climbed out of the well-deck. "She may say things that aren't true, but she's right about people wanting out of this war. Eugene McCarthy is show-ing strong for the Democratic primary in New Hampshire compared to Johnson. I guarantee you when they get to Or-egon and Wisconsin, McCarthy will win. People are sick of this war."

As if to support what Professor said, the radio droned on, "Are you boys excited about the presidential election? Oh, I forgot—most of you aren't old enough to vote. Do you wonder why you fight a war you have no voice in? Here's another song for you lovers beneath starry skies in your new Mustangs." "Thank The Lord For The Nighttime" echoed across the river as small ripples lapped our boat's stern. I pitched a concussion grenade into the river to thwart under-water swimmers then looked through the starlight scope at the fuzzy green world north of us.

I wondered about Marian. Why had she stopped writing? We'd had fun times over that summer I was in Bremerton. She'd never made any reference to opposing the war. Maybe she was with somebody else now. The wind shifted and a clean, cool breeze blew in off the South China Sea. It soon calmed and mosquitoes swarmed in.

Crow relieved me at 2200 hours. I went below but the foul odors drove me topside again. I slipped into a sweat-soured shirt, inflated my air mattress, and lay down above my cox'n flat with the melancholy tune of "Baby I need Your Lovin'" playing. I must have drifted off.

In my dream it was a sunny day on Whidbey Island. I was with a girl I thought was Marian but she kept her back to me. Marian's hair was auburn. This girl was shorter with raven black hair. She was waving to a sampan off the coast—be-yond the hedge of loganberry bushes we were hiding behind.

"Incoming! Incoming!" Crow's shout jolted me awake.

A blast nearby reinforced his warning and I was buffeted by concussion.

Crow climbed down his .50 caliber turret and into the cox'n flat. I jerked awake and heard the diesel engines cough to life. The boat surged back, stern ricocheting off another boat in the frenzy to escape the shelling.

"Bring the stern to starboard," I yelled down to Crow as I placed the starlight scope back in its case and snapped it shut.

"Is there anything I can do?" Professor called up from the cox'n flat.

"Get in the 20mm cannon turret. If we receive fire from the north bank—open up," I yelled down to him. "Crow, kick her ahead. You're clear of the other boats."

"How about if I take the helm, Crow get in the turret?" Professor asked.

"Whatever, just hold her mid-stream aimed toward the ramp, just in case we see Buddha and the others show up from the beer hooch."

We watched as NVA 122mm high-explosive projectiles slammed into the base. The staging area seemed to be the main target—it was uncanny how accurate the shooting was from eight miles away. It made me think again that some-body was watching—calling corrections. Maybe that flag man that had met us that first day had been right—the North Vietnamese did have a forward observer at the South Viet-namese naval base next to us. A pallet of ammo received a direct hit, scattering rounds which soon started cooking off in an impressive fireworks display. A petroleum bladder ig-nited, illuminating the waterfront. I caught glimpses of the dredging barge each time a shell detonated—boom extended skyward, the helicopter nestled nearby.

Three men emerged from the inferno. For an instant I thought it was part of our crew, but they jumped aboard the chopper. I watched the rotor turn as the pilot powered up. Then they were rising. A round detonated near them; almost where they had been parked. Was that a lucky shot? Concus-sion buffeted the chopper toward the extended dredge boom. The rotors smashed in a shower of sparks that blossomed into a fireball. The stricken chopper plummeted to earth as

I watched in horror from our safe haven in the river. Fire glowed white for a few minutes but quickly died to an amber shadow, flames licking at small mounds.

"Somebody needs to get in there," Professor shouted up to me. "There might be survivors."

"Everybody's in bunkers—they probably don't even know it crashed," I yelled back. Incoming artillery whistled over, now slamming down beyond the swale the hooches were nestled in. Our boat was closest to the crash site. "I think the shelling has shifted inland. Nose the boat up to the beach. I'll run over and see if anybody is alive."

"We should stay in the river," Crow called out from the turret where he'd been listening. "Buddha said when there was incoming to stay mid-stream."

"There might be somebody that needs help. We're the closest ones to them," Professor called back to Crow.

"Buddha's going to be pissed. Suppose there are gooks hiding on shore waiting for us."

"Professor's right. Shut the fuck up Crow. Suppose you were lying out there," I yelled. "Pull her in. Crow, grab me a shotgun and hand it up."

Crow mumbled something to Professor as he opened the small-arms locker.

"Load it, and put one in the chamber," I called down. "Professor, keep me in your view. If anybody comes toward me or if I start shooting, back out into the river."

I heard Crow chamber a round and a few seconds later felt the barrel bumping my leg. I grabbed the gun and a flashlight as Professor nudged the bow against the concrete ramp. I climbed down from above and moved forward along the catwalk. Pausing for a moment in the shadow of the ramp, I looked inland then dropped to the concrete, shotgun aimed at flickering shadows.

Ten meters from our boat lay the stricken chopper, now

a skeleton of twisted ribs and framework. I shined my flashlight about, hoping for a miracle. A smoldering mass hung out the opening where I'd watched the gunner a few hours earlier. I nudged it with the muzzle of my shotgun. The mass collapsed in a shower of sparks. It smelled like the cat a neighbor kid had thrown into a tire fire back home. A skull rolled out, bumped my feet, and came to a stop. Shards of skin dangled and I realized what the seared meat odor was as the flesh shriveled in a flare, like a candle just before it went out. I staggered back, stumbled and fell, spraying vomit across hot concrete. The skull I'd seen that day in the Tonkin Gulf over the side of the *Rogers* flashed across my mind—another pilot's skull.

This skull had a baseball-size hole on top of it. When I fell back I'd tripped over an M60 machine gun that had snapped loose in the explosion. It was the gun I'd watched the Huey gunner secure. On impulse, I picked it up and rushed back to our boat, threw it on the catwalk, then pulled myself up. The instant I was on board, the engines were thrown into reverse and the boat moved back into the river.

I picked up the M60 and went topside where I could see the other boats idling out in the boat basin in the fiery shadows cast from the burning base. "Idle over and blend with the other boats," I said to Professor as I kneeled outside the armor plate by the cox'n flat.

"What did you see out there," Crow asked.

"Nothing. There weren't any survivors."

"Did you see bodies?" He prompted.

"Let it rest Crow—he said there were no survivors. What do you want?" Good old Professor, I owed him for telling Crow to shut up.

They didn't know about the M60. I'd been in the shadows and I laid it on the catwalk before I climbed back up by the cox'n flat and the gun turrets. "I'm going to take a leak,"

I told Professor. I climbed down, picked up the machine gun and went to the stern where I opened the deck-hatch to a small compartment behind the engine room. I crawled in and stashed the M60 beneath the coiled towrope.

I knew Marines would be searching for the weapon at first light, concerned that it not fall into enemy hands. They'd tried to steal my revolver, I reasoned to myself, so I didn't see anything wrong with taking a weapon from them.

In the dawn, shells cooked-off sending black puffs skyward. Each time one exploded, everybody tensed and flinched. Our boat crew was safe. Again, I heard high-pitched, too-loud laughter as Buddha joked about their night in the bunker.

"Stonewall, I saw you in the corner praying. It must've worked. But then, you did have reinforcements. The Buddha was in there."

Stonewall looked at him and shook his head. Stonewall had been quiet lately—moody—so I didn't think much about it.

Dennis punched Snipe playfully on the arm and they giggled like young school girls who had been mooned.

"I wonder why they have divers coming," Buddha said, looking up the beach. I followed his gaze and saw two men with scuba tanks slung over their shoulder, carrying goggles and fins. Buddha had gone through diving school and considered himself an expert. He jumped off the boat and rushed over, Crow at his heels. I watched from the boat as the divers talked to some Marines, then strapped on their equipment and waded into the water. About twenty minutes later they came out and left.

"They were looking for an M60 that disappeared off that gunship. They think maybe an NVA gook snuck in here and got it—could have come along the shoreline. No one would've noticed him with all the shit falling," Buddha said, nodding toward the charred heap of wreckage the Marines were picking through. "Afe, I hear you pulled into the beach last night."

"We thought somebody should check for survivors on that chopper. The shelling had moved inland. It looked safe enough."

"I don't need heroes on this boat. I told you to stay out in the river."

I looked at Crow. "You asshole. Get over there and start chipping." Crow looked at Buddha for support but found none. That pissed me off. "Get the fuck going, suck-ass. Paint the whole side after you primer the rust spots. I want the scraped paint feathered—no rough edges or you can re-do it tonight with a flashlight."

"Well, you actually sounded like a boatswain's mate for a moment," Buddha grunted. "Why don't you speak up more often?"

I shook my head in disgust and motioned him to follow me to the stern of the boat. "I don't trust Crow. Last night, going in was the right thing to do. He argued against it."

I told Buddha about the M60 as we watched Marines shovel up charred remains and drop them into body bags. Professor yelled to us that it was time to get underway—to begin the run to Dong Ha. Flashing a conspiratorial grin at me, Buddha ordered us out into the river and we began another monotonous day of patrol.

Buddha spent the day playing with the M60. From the cox'n flat I could hear him down below, cocking it, the bolt slamming back and forth. It was an impressive gun. It weighted 23 lbs and could fire 500 rounds per minute. For army troops or Marines, assignment to an M60 was a point of distinction, recognition of superior ability. It took a strong man to handle the gun. Buddha was a big man so naturally, he should have an M60. Over time, the gun was to become his signature feature.

That evening, after topping off the fuel tanks, I headed for the beer hooch. As I crossed the staging area I noticed rubber tread marks from the forklift where the crashed Huey had been. Wreckage was cleaned away as if it had never happened; just an outline of burn marks they couldn't scrape off. I passed what was left of the supply pallets, so neatly stacked and lined up just twenty-four hours ago. Now there was a mass of C-rations, clothing, medical supplies, fuel bladders, sand bags, body bags, plywood, smoldering timbers, and ammunition—the small arms ammo still cooking-off occasionally. I flinched at a nearby explosion then laughed at myself. I could tell by the smell it was a can of lima beans and ham.

I recalled how, when I was a little boy, the grocery store in Bemidji had burned down. Several days after the fire, our family had made the weekly trip into town. We lined the sidewalk, awe-struck at the smoldering wreckage and the still-exploding cans buried in the rubble.

Normally LST's were out to sea this late in the evening but tonight, as I walked toward the mess hall, I noticed one being off-loaded, the pallets of ammo placed directly on to three LCM-8's.

It was a quiet night—not a round a fired.

10

A Body in the River—
Friendly Fire

5 March 1968

Fog hung low on the river the next morning. The LCM-8's were ordered to Dong Ha—Khe Sanh needed ammo. Buddha had returned late in the night and rolled over in his rack at the news that we were getting under way. I climbed topside and told Crow to drive; he was good on the helm. Boats' gurgling exhaust smoke blended with the fog as we backed into the river. Condensing droplets fell from the limp ensign as I peered into the gray cloud we were shrouded in. Thirty feet in front of me, the high bow of our boat seemed a shadowed apparition. Water beads, triggered by the vibrating engines, purled down the well-deck canopy onto the catwalk.

"Back down! Back down!" I yelled to Crow. We slammed into another boat. No harm done—we were only going about four miles an hour—but the shock of colliding in this dense fog was unsettling. What else might be out there? Where was the far bank? Where were the ever-present shifting sandbars?

"What the hell's going on up there? Afe, where the fuck are you? Where the hell did this fog come from?" yelled Buddha. I heard him climb the ladder from the well-deck to the cox'n flat. Then his face was at the crack looking up at me. "This shit's like soup. Why the hell are we under way?" I heard Professor explain the situation about the ammo—that we were ordered to make the first sweep ahead of the loaded boats.

By the time we reached the farmer's paddy the sun had done its magic. The fog was gone and the farmer was shuffling along behind his plow, the old water buffalo leaning into her yolk. It would be another hot day. Buddha stayed in the cox'n flat visiting with the crew. Everybody was in their positions except him and me. We were third in column. If there was a mine, the boats ahead of us would get it.

Buddha could be charming. It was hard to gauge him. He must have come out ahead with the cards last night, I thought. After the turn-around at Dong Ha he chuckled, looked up through the back of the cox'n flat at me and said, "You've got her this morning Afe—I need to rest up for a big game tonight." And down he went to curl up in his rack.

We had our section of the river memorized—the crew rotated turns at the helm, swinging around at the ends of our section without being told. On the west side of the river, just north of where we watched the farmer each day, laid the remains of a village called My Loc. I tried to imagine the horror that had happened there. Passing the ruins of a French Missionary Catholic Church, I recalled the story our guide had told us that first day.

About two years ago, so the story went, the NVA had positioned a Russian tank inside the church and annihilated an unsuspecting Marine patrol in an ambush. The NVA had overrun the platoon. The next day, Marines had retaken the village and discovered the lost platoon. Several had their hands tied behind their backs. They'd been executed, a bullet to the back of the head.

I thought of the Marine memorial service I had accidentally walked up on our first day at Cua Viet. The chaplain was leading the men in Psalms 23. The formation of empty boots, inverted rifles with helmets perched on them, left an empty feeling in my stomach as I recalled how I'd wanted to enlist in the Marine Corps. I sat back in the sun, between the gun turrets, feeling invincible, thankful the Marine recruiter hadn't been in his office that winter morning back in Bemidji.

It got hot that afternoon; so hot the farmer didn't return to his paddy. Barefoot, stripped down to cut-offs, I lay back in the sun. The steel got so hot I couldn't touch it for long. Over the months, the soles of my feet had toughened—like when I was a kid and we went barefoot all summer.

Snipe came up from below, complaining. "Buddha's snoring so loud I can't hear the diesels."

Stripping his shirt off, he sat on his folded flak jacket. I should have been used to it by then but I was still grossed out by his boil-covered back. He had said that it had started as acne one summer when he was working in a coal mine—coal dust had caused the problem. I couldn't help glancing over as he sat, his back to the broiling sun. The boils soon reached their breaking point, erupted, and yellow-green pus rivulets trickled down his back.

At the east end of our sector I could see out into the ocean. At Cua Viet, an LST was delivering cargo while beyond it, outside the channel, another waited her turn to off-load. Farther out, a destroyer moved slowly across the horizon. Fishermen began coming in for the day. I learned to recognize the lucky ones; heavy with fish, their sampan gunnels were near the waterline. Sometimes they returned my wave.

Late afternoon, Buddha came topside. I climbed down from my perch and went below for a nap. It seemed like I'd barely dozed off when the boat's radio woke me. I was sweat-drenched and clammy from lying against the rubber mattress.

"Tango one-one, this is Mike one, over." Mike one, a monitor, was the call-sign of the boat that overlapped the east end of our patrol sector.

"This is Tango one-one, go ahead," Professor answered.

"Tango one-one, this is Mike one, there's a body in the water near the north bank of the river, at the east end of your sector, over."

"This is Tango one-one. We're on our way, out."

"Everybody heard that," Buddha shouted. "Get to stations. Snipe, you get a .30 caliber in the well-deck trained north—if anything, I mean anything wiggles, you open up. Don't wait for an order. The same goes for the rest of you. Afe, you grab the body. Professor can drive. He must be the one missing from the boat that we heard about a few days ago when we were coming north on the LSD. They reported one missing. He must have gotten snagged on the river bottom or under the boat."

The sun had already dropped below the horizon. It would get dark quickly. I crawled out of the well-deck, onto the catwalk, and removed the wire mesh stretcher from where it hung below the starboard .50 caliber gun turret.

"Professor, hand Afe a couple of concussion grenades to toss near the body."

It was a classic VC set-up; the kind they'd talked about back in training. Booby trap or mine the body, set up an ambush on the riverbank, then get us while we recovered the body. Above me, gun barrels swung back and forth as we eased forward. If they fired I was only three feet below the muzzles. My ears would ring for a month.

The body was face-down, arms spread.

"Toss the grenades, Afe. Don't get too close, Professor. Kick her in reverse."

The engines revved and I watched sandy back-wash swirl in miniature whirlpools. I pulled the pin on a grenade and tossed it near the body. A few moments later, water mush-roomed with a low thump and pushed the body sideways.

"Get the next one closer Afe, on the other side of him."

I pulled the pin and pitched it underhand—like a soft-ball—past the body. With that thump he rolled over and moved toward the side of the boat.

"I think he's clean, Afe. If he was rigged something would've happened when he rolled. The boat hook—take the boat hook and pull him to you," Buddha said, looking down from his shelter between the .50 caliber gun turrets. Reaching out with the boat hook, gently at first, I tried to snag his pant leg. "Hurry Afe, he can't feel anything. Get him aboard. It's getting dark. We have to get the fuck away from the bank."

I took the hook then and snagged his rib, pushed down and pulled him to me. He was barefoot and shirtless but still wore jungle fatigue pants held on by a web belt. He was Caucasian male, couldn't really tell his age, about 180 lbs., brown hair. Birds or fish or water bugs had devoured his lips and eyes. I turned my face away when gas bubbled from his distended belly.

"Come on Afe—what's the hold-up. Get him on board."

I took a deep breath, held it and bent over the side with the stretcher. The west breeze and the river current held him against the boat and his outstretched fingers tapped the side. I tried to maneuver the stretcher beneath him but one of his legs was hanging low and I couldn't reach down far enough to get past it—the stretcher was too long and unwieldy.

"Hurry Afe—we've got to get away from this bank."

"I can't," I sobbed as I gasped air in, then sprayed vomit out over the body. "I can't."

"Get him the fuck out of the water. Now."

In desperation I flung the stretcher back on board then bent down, grabbed the body's belt, and pulled. A stiff leg—

the one that had been floating—rolled with him over the rail. I felt him slip back and threw my arms around his sticky waist, hugged him to me and rolled onto the deck where I lay beneath him. I think I screamed. Nothing coherent—I was being smothered, his bare chest against my face, water oozing into my mouth from his rancid body. I slipped out from beneath him and stood, gasping dry heaves. My lungs rebelled and I retched, unable to draw a breath. Something clung to the top of my head, hung down past my ear against my cheek. I wiped a hand across my face to push it off. Seaweed, I thought.

"How you doing, Afe?" Buddha said, directing a red-beamed flashlight on the body. The light gleamed on exposed bone that ran from elbow to hand. The mass sticking to my face was flesh.

"Oh," came out as I recoiled. My bare feet shot out from under me on the slick deck. The body's chest cushioned my elbow and forced a gurgling sigh to bubble from his throat. Decomposition and concussion grenades had weakened the body. The shard of flesh had the texture of raw lutefisk. It slapped me across the mouth when I ripped it from my head.

"Get a grip Afe. He can't hurt you." Buddha switched his light off and returned to his perch while in the new moon's glow I stared at the putrid flesh lying on deck. Curling my bare toes, I flicked it over the side.

Bile dribbled from my mouth as I stood on the fantail and scooped buckets of river water. I swallowed in an effort not to retch again as I scrubbed in the moonlight while the boat cruised toward base. Soapy water mixed with tears as I imagined myself lying there, falling apart. I glanced up and saw the lights of Cua Viet as our boat's engines changed pitch and we swung toward the beach.

"Crow, grab the other end of the stretcher—help carry

him over to the command hooch—they can take it from there," Buddha said. He stood in the sand holding a flashlight while Crow and I lifted the body into the stretcher then transferred it to dry land. As we crossed the staging area, I noticed that it was once again piled high with supplies.

Crow had the front of the stretcher. I watched the body's feet bounce and mosquitoes feasted on us as we carried him through sugar sand under a full moon. The breeze had died. Stench hovered and I wondered if the rancid smell attracted more pests.

The odor reminded me of three cows that had bloated when I was about five years old. It had been midsummer and my stepfather had dragged them out in the woods with the Farmall tractor. A few days later my two older brothers and I went to inspect them and discovered that they'd ballooned, their legs stiff, sticking out. I had snapped the top from a hazel brush shoot and brushed the maggots off a front hoof suspended three feet above the ground. Then I had sat on it and rode up and down like a spring-loaded teeter-totter. Maggots, blow flies, and thick-crusted beetles swarmed over the cows' mouths, eyes, and rear ends. With sharpened sticks, we had poked at the ballooned bellies and were rewarded with hissing gas. Greenish brown fluid had misted from the punctures.

At the command hooch we set the stretcher down and I stole a final look. A crowd had gathered. Two sailors—the dead man's friends I assumed—were swearing. I watched a column of scarab-like water beetles march from his mouth, across the lipless bare-toothed grin, and like lemmings, crawl in the direction of the river. Crow vomited. I was empty. I wondered if Crow was satisfied now. He'd seen a body up close.

Buddha told me to take the night off. "Run over to that LST, take a long hot shower and grab some chow before she pulls out."

I did that. I wasn't hungry but I went to the shower and scrubbed. I scrubbed until a lifer yelled at me for wasting *his* water—I told him to fuck off as I ripped the shower curtain open.

"What the fuck stinks in here?" he said, kicking at the wet, ragged cut-offs lying on deck. "You guys on the boats, you think you can get away with anything. I'm going to report you. What's your name? What boat are you on?"

I stood toweling myself. "Fuck off is my name. Fuck you is my boat. Now leave me the fuck alone." I pulled on some fresh cut-offs, threw a sleeveless fatigue shirt across my shoulders, and walked out barefoot—I had forgotten to bring my boots.

"Take your stinking rags with you," he yelled.

"Fuck off," I whispered.

The smoke-filled beer hooch was packed with Marines and sailors. The rough-cut wooden tables and narrow benches were full and a squad of Marines was tossing dice at the stand-up bar.

I bought several beers and went over to one of the stained plywood tables where some guys from other boats were sitting. I quickly drank three and opened a fourth, trying to drown the memory of the rancid taste.

"Here, take a shot of this." I looked over at Jimmy and recalled that he had given Buddha his nickname. He was a lifer—the captain of Mike one, the boat that had called us about the body. He took my half-emptied beer and poured Jack Daniels into it. "Buddha told me what happened. This'll help get rid of the taste." I liked Jimmy. He was good natured; always saw the light side of things. In another time, Jimmy would have been a great Santa.

When we were transported north on the LSD, Jimmy and I had been sitting on the fantail of the ship, visiting. We discovered we had something in common—he had served on the USS *Rogers* during the Korean Conflict, the same ship I had come to Vietnam on almost three years ago. Jimmy had laughed and said Korea wasn't a war either. Just a conflict. Jimmy had a Filipino wife back in the States he affectionately referred to as "The Huk," a pun on the Filipino communist rebels. And he was a very good card player. Rumor had it that he was into big-money games and sent several thousand dollars home each month. He was humble. He didn't flaunt his winnings—if somebody was short Jimmy would float a loan, interest-free. I shivered as the whiskey burned to my empty stomach.

Word had spread about the body I'd pulled from the river.

"Get used to it," said a sailor with whiskey bravado. "That's what we have to look forward to." He was from Tango 7, the kid who'd pulled me from the river the day I'd run aground.

"You never get used to that taste and smell. Next time there's a body in the water, you pull it out," I told him.

Incoming artillery rounds shrieked overhead. One detonated nearby and sent shrapnel through the back corner of the beer hooch—studs splintered and the roof corner dropped. Cigarette and cigar smoke was replaced by dust and cordite fumes. No one was wounded and I sat grinning at the mad rush for the door as everybody raced for bunkers. The rounds detonated on impact and sprayed a kill-zone about thirty meters across. Marines said not to worry. In this deep sand, shrapnel didn't reach out that far.

"Come on Afe. Let's get the fuck out of here," Jimmy shouted, running toward the door, bottle in hand.

I sat at the table, detached—a bit drunk—watching, wondering, who these people trying to kill us were. Who were these NVA gunners the pilot out in the gulf had never seen? The Huey crew that had died? The body I'd pulled from the river? I hadn't done anything to them. Rounds shook the empty beer hooch as they slammed into the neat rows of supplies on the staging area.

I grabbed four unopened beers from the bar, crawled under a table, and finished my whiskey. Puked it back out—thankful nobody was there to witness my moment of weakness—then rinsed my mouth with a cold beer. Another round fell nearby. Shrapnel ripped through the screen and ricocheted off the corrugated tin, like hail on a barn roof. I decided it was time to leave.

I was too far from the boat. Besides they were already out in the river and I'd have to pass the supply staging area to get to the river bank. The threat of friendly fire was a risk to be considered if I tried to race across the base. I stood in the sand at the foot of the beer hooch watching flares drift overhead. Why were the Marines lighting the target up, I wondered? A round detonated not far from me and I raced for the shallow crater. I recalled what an army guy had said back in the Delta. When you're in a hole it's just bad luck if a round falls directly on you—kind of like lightning striking twice in the same place. I realized I was terribly drunk.

I was struck from above.

"Man, get your ass down. There's room in here for us both." It was a black guy from his voice—he had jumped feet-first into the hole and hit me in the head with his boots.

For the next two hours we hugged the depression. I lay on my stomach, fingers locked onto fistfuls of sand as I tried to become one with the earth. Each time a round detonated we'd bounce up then back down with the air pushed from our lungs and sand raining down. I realized I was holding my breath waiting for the next round—the one that was sure to fall directly on me. Two rounds bracketed close and I dug a hole for my arm that I could rest my forehead on. At times we screamed; not for help—there was none.

Between explosions I listened to the Marine's story. He was from New Orleans. Enlisted when he was seventeen—his mother had signed for him, too. The night we laid there he was eighteen and a half and didn't think he'd see nineteen. He'd been in-country five months and already had two Purple Hearts. The first time he was wounded he spent three weeks in Japan in a naval hospital. The second time, they sent him to Danang for eight days. The guy was a little nuts, or very desperate. He rolled to his back and held one leg in the air. Said that with any luck he'd get wounded—three Hearts and you're on that Freedom Bird. Even to lose a leg was a small price to pay to get out of this cluster-fuck.

"Come on you friggin gooks, this way, a little closer," he shouted. Flames illuminated his waving jungle boot.

The shelling ended.

The Marine crawled out of our hole cussing. A pall of dense black smoke hung in the humid air. I walked back to the boat thinking about stories I'd heard and realized how lucky I was—I hadn't seen shit.

It was like an instant replay in the dawn. The staging area was littered with smoldering supplies. Buddha had a boat captain's meeting so I walked back to look at where I had spent those hours of darkness. Marines were busy cleaning up the damage. I saw body bags. Seagulls were picking at small bits in the sand and Marines were throwing rocks, cans, bits of wood at them.

I returned to our boat and found Dennis brooming soapy water across the catwalk where the body had been laying the night before. "I puked when I came up here this morning. Flies were swarming on puddles of jello-looking slime." He flipped an empty bucket into the river and retrieved it with the rope looped over his wrist. In one smooth motion he grabbed the bottom of the bucket, splashed water across the soap-covered deck and dropped it back in the river. Three pails later he grunted in satisfaction. "So much for that shit."

I shook my head and crawled into the well-deck to get ready for another day on the river.

At the west end of our patrol area, just past where I had run aground that first day, a sandbar reached out underwater and local kids would stand in the river shouting to us for food. Whenever I was on top of the boat I'd bring about a dozen cans of C-rations from our catch-all box—we didn't want them anyway. The kids were young, about five to twelve years old, boys and girls.

"Numba one, numba one," they'd call in unison as I tossed cans toward them. It reminded me of standing on the sidelines of the Fourth of July parade when I was a little kid, scampering for candy tossed by the rich, lucky people in the parade—the powerful people in our little town.

One day a man stood in the river as we approached. He looked harmless. He was naked above the waist and I could see both hands. As we got closer I saw scars on his back, chest, and arms—old shrapnel wounds probably—like a pack of dogs had ripped his flesh. He was leaning on a pine branch with a Y at the top that reminded me of a long-handled giant slingshot. I thought he was about my age but it was hard to tell because he was so skinny. I tossed a can of spaghetti and meatballs to him. The heavy cans sank. A little girl dived, toppling him. That's when I saw the stump. The little girl came up triumphantly waving the olive drab can. The crippled man struggled underwater for a moment, regained his foot, and stood up. I tossed a can of crackers, they floated. He reached out with his crutch, whacked the little girl, and raked the can to him. I tossed a few heavy cans far away from the cripple. The kids scampered away for them. Then I tossed a few more floaters to him. He rewarded me with a smile. After that I watched for him each afternoon and made certain that he retrieved a few cans. Once in a while I saved the ones we coveted; peaches, pound cake, fruit cocktail, beef steak and potatoes. Later, after we left Cua Viet, I wondered how he survived.

Our old routine from down south reasserted itself. After the first sweep of the morning Buddha ate breakfast then crawled back into his rack until the heat awakened him.

It was mid-morning, a few days after the shelling, we were at the west end of our sector—not far from the mouth of Jones Creek—where I could see out into the ocean. It was a typical morning, the fishermen had passed us traveling seaward, farmers were in their paddies, a company of Marines bivouacked along the river were packing up, getting ready to move out. Suddenly an A-4 Skyhawk screamed low over our boat from the north as he swept upward. I was topside, shirtless, without a helmet. A shower of hot 20mm cannon shell-casings showered our boat and threw up water geysers around us. In the first instant I thought we were being strafed. One shell casing hit my shoulder and knocked me off balance against a gun turret. I looked up at his smoking jet trail as he faded in the distance. It reminded me of the training jets that had flown over our house during the Korean Conflict.

In 1952 we had built a new barn with a shiny corrugated steel roof. The Air Force must have used it as a visual point for their flights to turn north to where they dropped bombs in the forests above Red Lake Indian Reservation. Those jets had screamed in low, rattling house windows, then were gone. My brothers and I would spend hours in the woods waiting for them in ambush. A few times we got lucky, emptying our .22 caliber rifles at the streaking planes.

"What was that?" Stonewall shouted from below in the cox'n flat. I told him and related my farm story. I was surprised—Buddha hadn't stirred.

About an hour later we were again at the north end, Professor at the helm. An artillery shell—an air burst—exploded near our boat. Miraculously, nobody was hit. Another round whistled past and exploded west of us.

"Follow the splashes," I screamed to Professor. He gave the boat full throttle and she leapt forward, upriver, at her full eight knots. Another round exploded behind us and as I looked back I saw muzzle flashes from a destroyer several miles out to sea.

"That's friendly fire," I screamed down to Professor. "Get on the radio, tell those fuckers to cease fire."

I was crouched down in Buddha's shelter between the gun turrets when I heard his voice from the cox'n flat. "What the fuck's going on up there, Afe?"

"I can see muzzle flashes from a destroyer outside the channel," I screamed as another round exploded to port. "Tell those idiots to cease fire."

I could hear Professor on the radio with our division commander—moments later the shelling stopped. Buddha stepped from the cox'n flat back to the starboard .50 caliber turret and climbed up through the top and stood by me, laughing.

"Why did you tell Professor to follow the splashes?"

"I remembered an old World War II movie where a destroyer captain did that when a Jap battlewagon was shelling him."

"You done good, Afe."

The shelling had shifted north of us. We could see the bursts. I knew it wasn't the *New Jersey's* sixteen inch guns—thank God—they would have flattened us. Later, I learned she hadn't arrived off the Vietnam coast until August 1968.

"When I was on the *Rogers* over here in '66 we did a lot of fire support and shore bombardment. It sure the hell is different being on the receiving end," I told Buddha as another flash and puff of smoke shot out of the ship on the horizon.

Aircraft circled. We watched them drop toward earth, fire their rockets, then sweep upward. Some jets plummeted like falcons fixed on prey, released bombs, then swept upward. They'd circle then return on long strafing runs. The distant cannon fire sounded like thunder peals.

"Shit must be stirring north on Jones Creek again," Buddha said.

11

Tango 7 Mined—
One Survivor

14 March 1968

Days passed. Blended—boring days, hot days. From the safety of the river we watched the Marine base get terribly damaged by NVA artillery about a week after we'd dodged the friendly fire.

Professor was receiving more mail than the rest of us put together—except Snipe. A network of former classmates was keeping him in the loop about opposition to the war. I was his sounding board when he read something that infuriated him. The presidential primaries were gearing up—50% of the population didn't approve of Johnson's handling of Vietnam. Eugene McCarthy, who opposed the war, did very well in the New Hampshire Primary.

"What do you think, Afe? Doesn't that tell you something?"

"It doesn't really make a shit to me. I'm not old enough to vote."

"That's not the point," he raged. "People are waking up."

A few days after Cua Viet was shelled, the morning didn't start well for Buddha. First run of the day to Dong Ha was still made by all boats. For the boat captains, it was a moment in the sun. Some coveted the spot, others hated it, but did it because it was their turn. It was our turn to lead the column on the north side of the river but the division commander switched our boat's position. Buddha returned from the boat captain meeting pissed off—Tango 7 had been selected to lead. There was heavy fighting along Jones Creek and the division commander believed we would have contact.

"You boys keep a sharp lookout. Did you hear those Marines talking in the mess hall this morning? It sounds like they're into some heavy shit. The NVA are being forced south, so we may get some shooting today," Buddha said, as we walked toward the boat. "Afe, close your side flaps this morning, but leave the front open. We'll be behind Tango 7, so keep a close eye on the bank he's alongside of."

"Are the gunners going in their turrets today or staying topside on the first run?" I asked.

"They'll stay topside—inboard, away from the riverbank. If the gooks do open up, it'll be at Tango 7 first and our crew will have time to get in position."

All boat engines were idling and diesel exhaust hung low in the thin mist. The thick fumes gave me heartburn and I burped Tabasco-drenched dehydrated eggs.

I backed our boat into the river and took position behind Tango 7. It was like the morning before and the morning before that. We patrolled west, past sampans chugging seaward, through the river narrows that were in our patrol sector, then turned south.

"I wonder where the farmer is this morning." I commented up to Buddha as we passed his paddy.

"Maybe got lucky last night and slept in this morning. Professor, run below and hand me up my M60."

Professor squeezed past me, went down the ladder to the well-deck and returned a few minutes later with the gun, passing it up through the opening behind the cox'n flat. Buddha was anxious to fire it but was worried about somebody spotting it. The Marines were still searching for it. They'd sent divers into the river several times. I was thankful I'd snatched it—my stock in Buddha's book had skyrocketed. He was like a kid with a new toy. At night when we had visitors onboard he'd pull it out from behind the spare rack and pass it around. It was a status symbol nobody else had.

I heard his knuckles tap on Crow's helmet. "Pass me up a box of ammo." Professor, standing behind me in the cox'n flat, heard the request and slid the small arms locker open to retrieve a box of 7.62mm belted ammo. Crow squatted below his turret, grabbed the box, and passed it to Buddha. I heard the hinged top snap down when he loaded the gun.

"Let those little fuckers stick their heads up now," he said with a devious chuckle. "Professor, Stonewall, Dennis, Crow, get below, throw your lifejackets on and get up on the port side of the boat—grab Snipe, too."

The river was predictable. I knew that as we swung west the haze would burn off. On cue, it disappeared and the river opened. One hundred meters ahead was Tango 7, stern-down, dragging her minesweeping gear.

"Close it up, Afe."

She was approaching the unusually high riverbank that jutted out into the river. Through the slits in my armor on the port side I watched the boat column sweeping the other side of the river. Beyond them, on the south bank, a company of Marines was breaking camp.

"Keep an eye out, Afe. I smell wood smoke but can't see anything," Buddha shouted down to me from his shelter.

I could smell it, too. Probably a cooking fire in the farmer's hooch we had just passed. We were on a straight stretch now, only that one narrow area where the sandbar angled out below the high bank.

"Stay out farther than Tango 7, Afe. I don't know why

he's so friggin close to the bank. I can see him kicking up sand. That bar must be working its way out."

I just nodded. I knew he often glanced down into the cox'n flat from where he sat behind me. He was right. I could see the wisps of sand swirling in the water behind Tango 7. "Should I call him on the radio?" I yelled up.

"No, he's the experienced boat captain. Let him figure it out."

We cleared that area. As we continued west I reflected on how patrolling was so deceptive. We spent countless hours watching the river and the banks for the smallest variation in foliage; anything, clumps of weed riding the river current, a mine camouflaged within, suspicious activity on sampans we shared the river with that would alert us to the presence of enemy forces lying in ambush. It must be difficult for the Vietnamese people, too. How would the old vets back home react to somebody—a foreigner, stopping them and searching their belongings? A sampan passed between the columns on its way toward the ocean.

"It's weird," I called up to Buddha. "I wonder what that gook thinks. One day he's stopped and searched, the next day he passes between ten of us and we wave."

"So, what about it?"

"If these gooks were patrolling our roads back home I don't think we'd be very happy about it."

"You're thinking too much. You're starting to sound like Professor. Just keep one little friggin thing in mind. They want us here to stop the commies from taking over."

"I've seen more dead Americans than gooks."

"That shit can change real fast. They're afraid to tangle with our boats."

It was a quiet morning and the droning engines lulled me. Outside my cox'n flat, below my field of vision, the crew sat, joking. Every once in a while I caught a waft of cigarette smoke and conversation. They were talking about R&R.

"I'm going to meet Nancy in Hawaii," Snipe said.

"I'm going to Kuala Lumpur," Crow said. "I'm going with the .50 caliber gunner from Mike one. Their cox'n went there and came back saying you could hire a girl for the week for eighty dollars. I saw his pictures. She was a beauty."

"What about Subic Bay—your girl there—you said you wanted to go back there when we were in Coronado," Snipe said.

"She's a pig compared to the girls in Kuala Lumpur."

Dennis stood up and yelled, "Afe, where're you going on R&R?"

I could see the top of Dennis' head through the slit in my armor. "I'm holding out for Sydney. I've been to about all the other ports out here. How about you?"

"I was thinking Hong Kong, but Australia sounds fun. My dad was there during the war."

"You better watch who you poke fun at down under, Dennis. It might be your long-lost sister," Crow said.

"Crow, your brain must be in your pecker-head," Buddha said. "You boys'll have a long wait for Australia—they don't let many go. Besides, we'll all be taking R&R the same week."

"Eight months should give us seniority on the R&R list." I looked back through the opening at Buddha. "What's the difference if we wait a little longer? We all have to put in twelve months anyway. That'll put us shorter when we get back."

"I kind of like that idea," Dennis said. "Have you signed up yet?"

"No, I suppose I should. Where're you going on R&R, Buddha?"

"I'm going to sunny Dong Tam—play cards and sip iced Jack Daniels Black Label with Jimmy."

"Stonewall, how about you?" Snipe asked. "You're kind

of quiet. Where're you planning to go?"

There was a pause, then Stonewall replied. "Me and some brothers are going to Hong Kong."

I thought about Stonewall's comment. He'd been hanging out less with us and more with other black guys. I'd noticed it at the beer hooch in the evening—I met his eyes once when he was deep in a story with some guys at his table and he had glanced away. Like he was guilty of something. But what would he be guilty of? He'd stopped going to Sunday church services.

I had to squint to see Tango 7 beyond the early morning sun reflected off the river. I kept station 50 meters behind and watched the riverbank and his wake for any sign of activity his minesweeping gear might snag.

I thought back to the *Rogers* and how the black sailors preferred to be together. They segregated by choice. They had their music. Hell, in EM clubs, ninety-nine percent of the time when fights started, it was over music. Maybe I didn't understand because we didn't have any blacks in school, but I wondered why they wanted to be with whites when all they did is hang out by themselves, anyway.

Suddenly Tango 7 was out of the water, sun glittering on the red-brown bottom of the wet hull, her propellers still spinning. A geyser of water shot skyward, the boat hidden for an instant. In a slow motion ballet, Tango 7 became visible as she flipped upside down, the bow lifting up over the stern, the capsized boat returning to earth, settling to the river bottom.

"Fuck!" I shouted. Buddha shouted. I think we all shouted in that first instant as spray from the blast misted our boat.

"Everybody to their guns. Now!" Buddha screamed. "Afe, pull into the bank. See if we can get anybody off the boat."

"Professor, pull up the sweep gear," I yelled out the side of the cox'n flat as I swung shoreward.

"Afe, did you see the guy taking a leak at the stern of

Tango 7? Did you see where he went?" shouted Buddha, hunched down at the side of my armor shield.

"Don't you think you should get between the turrets?" I yelled. "This is a perfect set-up for an ambush. I think he went out into the river. I lost sight of him in the blast."

"I thought I saw him sail toward the riverbank but I don't see him, "Buddha said. "Put your armor flaps down, you won't need them now."

I beached our boat, cut the engines, and rushed topside. I was only a few meters from the sunken hulk of Tango 7 and gazed down at the muddy river. Eddies swirled, drifted about the submerged well-deck searching for air pockets as the brown river claimed her.

"Buddha, I think I could swim into the well-deck behind the ramp and maybe get somebody," I said, remembering my pilot rescue training as I watched the medevac Tango boat pull in on the other side of Tango 7.

"You couldn't see in that shit-brown muck. Besides, it's too far back under the well-deck and up into the cox'n flat. You couldn't hold your breath that long. I'm guessing the concussion killed everybody. That asshole didn't have his crew topside like he was supposed to. Did you see? The one that was above deck got thrown off. You and the crew stay onboard while I go ashore to see if there's anything we can do."

Sun sparkled on dancing ripples as I looked across the river. It was fairly wide but shallow. What were the odds of passing directly over that tiny spot. Directly over that mine? Like that army guy had said back in the Delta—sometimes you just had bad fucking luck. I looked at the drying hull and couldn't imagine that on the other side of that rusted steel—maybe 3/8 of an inch—were six bodies. The explosion played again in my mind like a slow-motion movie. The geyser, climbing skyward, sun glistening on a billion water particles. The sudden splatters in the river around us, water and river-bottom returning to earth. I couldn't remember noise from the explosion, but the silence that followed.

Buddha returned to the boat and filled us in. The guy we'd seen thrown off was in critical condition with broken legs and internal injuries. We watched a medevac chopper settle down, load him, and take off in a dust cloud. "Those sneaky cocksuckers. Why don't they stand and fight?"

We stood on the walkway outside the .50 caliber turrets and watched another chopper arrive with Marine riverbank security and divers from Cua Viet to recover bodies and weapons. A halt had been ordered for all river traffic as a search commenced to determine how the mine had been detonated. Was it point detonated, the boat triggering it? Or command detonated; wires connected to a firing device, lying on the river bottom, triggered from a concealed position on the riverbank? A sampan with a man at the tiller hugged the far bank, making his way east, upriver. He pretended not to understand our demand to stop.

"There you go, turn him around," Buddha said, nodding toward the M16 I was holding. I shouted for him to stop but he continued on. His chest was in my rifle sight. I shouted again. He glanced toward me but continued east. With the hulk of Tango 7 in my peripheral vision, I flipped the safety to firing position. Burned explosive fumes from the detonated mine hung in the air. Nights cowering beneath incoming artillery flashed through my mind. That sampan, disobeying our order, must be our enemy.

"Do it Afe," Crow prompted from the catwalk at my feet.

I leaned against the 20mm cannon turret, steadying my aim, and gently brushed the trigger, rupturing the early morning calm. I raked the sampan, rounds impacting, wood disintegrating, boat crews cheering. Damaged but afloat, the sampan swung in the current and drifted down river. The sudden recoil, the sharp reports of the rifle, the pungent burned cordite fumes wafting the air jolted me back.

"You missed the gook Afe, put another clip into him."

I looked down at Crow. "You're a real killer aren't you? Real fucking tough."

I'd shifted aim at the last moment. I looked over at Buddha. He remained silent. I sat on my cox'n flat canopy and gazed down at Tango 7's rusty hull drying and crackling as the metal expanded in the morning heat.

We were ordered on to Dong Ha. There was no river traffic now and no people on the riverbanks. We passed the cemetery uneventfully, reached the bridge at Dong Ha, and swung around for our return journey.

A flurry of activity surrounded Tango 7. Two choppers rested on the riverbank. Marines had a perimeter set up and divers were inside the sunken boat. Demolition experts were analyzing the area for clues.

"Beach the boat, Afe. I want to see if I know any of those divers. You guys stay on board."

Four poncho-covered bodies lay high on the riverbank near the helicopters. Professor went to tell Buddha that we had received a radio call to proceed to our patrol sector. He came storming toward the boat with Professor at his heels.

"That useless bastard. He deserves what he got, but those kids laying up there on the bank—the divers cut two of them out of their bunks.

The stars shone with an unusual brightness that night. I had duty and, as had become my habit, I threw my air mattress across the canopy over the cox'n flat and lay staring into space, Tango 7 replaying in my head. I knew what I'd seen because I had been directly behind and, as fate would have it, I was looking at the kid peeing over the stern when the mine detonated. When the boat rose out of the water I had seen completely under it—sunshine and calm water on the far side—for just an instant. Like a sunbeam passing through the eye of a very slender needle. I knew what I had seen and like the star that raced across the sky in its death spiral, I realized it was us that should have been dead.

Thunder boomed from seaward and I sat up scanning the eastern horizon just as another salvo was fired from a ship far out to sea. Night firing was unusual, somebody must be in trouble. Or was it just H&I, harassment and interdiction—the same as the NVA sent our way. "Brown Eyed Girl" ended and Hanoi Hannah came on. "You sailors on the Cua Viet—that was for your friends that died today. They'll never see their brown-eyed girl again. Go home before the same thing happens to you. You black sailors. Listen to your leader, Martin Luther King. Go home. Refuse to fight. This is not your war. Your war is at home against the rich who control your life."

Two days later they found the boat captain and the cox'n at low tide. I was thankful they weren't in our sector. I recalled what the one sailor from Tango 7 had told me the night I'd pulled that other body from the river. "Get used to it," he'd said. "That's what we have to look forward to."

A Chinook helicopter dropped a bulldozer on the riverbank above Tango 7. We watched divers connect cables to the far side of the sunken boat and pull it shoreward. A section of bow tore loose and they dragged it up on the riverbank. The cables were reconnected to the hulk and slowly she rolled to her side. With a gush of water the boat righted itself, still settled on the riverbed. The river was at low tide and the cox'n flat and the three round turrets stuck above the water. When the boat turned over, debris bobbed up and slowly drifted seaward on the current. Papers—I couldn't believe the flood of papers that shot out of the hulk when it rolled. Life jackets bobbed up—a silent indictment against the dead boat captain for not having his crew in them, topside. Seagulls dove into the water around the hulk. For several days afterward they came in perching on the turrets, waiting for a feast.

12

Boat Race

18 March 1968

Early one morning I came topside to relieve Stonewall and found him with his eye against the starlight scope. It was rested on the edge of his 20mm cannon turret and aimed at the far side of the river. He didn't hear me because the engines on the boat next to us were running. I stood in the darkness watching, when suddenly the engines shut down and I heard a tape player. I stepped closer, assuming he was listening to a tape from home. As I eavesdropped, I realized it wasn't a family tape but a speech from Martin Luther King Jr. about why Americans shouldn't be in Vietnam. I listened as he spoke of the poverty of blacks and whites. He did make a legitimate argument about spending so much money on this war. But who would stop the communists if we didn't? He kept referring to the poor at home—black and white— and I recalled how my stepfather had felt quite proud the last time I talked to him—about a year ago. He said that for the first time, the farm had an income of twenty-nine hundred dollars for the year.

Before I went in the navy I never had a gauge to measure our standard of living. But by the time he told me that, I was earning more than he was. I decided—yes—I came from a family in poverty. I recalled the winters when the cows were dried up, no income at all for several weeks. I gave my trapping money for food. Homemade white bread smeared with lard and molasses was a staple on those winter days. When the cows began freshening, we ate the new-born bull calves. The meat was very pale and tasteless but with enough mustard it was edible. When King talked about seating white boys and black boys together at school I thought he didn't understand—the blacks preferred to be together. I made a noise then, hoping Stonewall would think I'd just arrived because I didn't know what to say about the tape. When he realized I was there, he shut it off.

"Nothing stirring across the river. The gooks took the night off," he said, handing me the scope. He picked up his tape player and went below.

Spring crept upon us. Hot day followed hot day as we patrolled the river. The crippled man stopped coming. Our dysfunctional family routine spiraled downward. Buddha kept a well-stocked liquor cabinet so our boat became a hangout when beached at Cua Viet in the evening.

The Tango 7 mining festered in Buddha's mind. After several drinks he'd begin chanting, gently shaking his cupped hand as though he were shaking dice, playing craps with an invisible opponent. "Seven come eleven. Seven fucking come eleven. Seven come eleven." His voice would begin low—almost a whisper—then rise slowly, then lower again. It seemed he was willing evil to our boat as retribution for his imagined guilt for not being in lead position the morning Tango 7 had been mined.

Buddha and his friends drank, played cards, and shouted each other down. It was impossible to sleep. Even topside where I had migrated, their voices echoed up in ridiculous, pointless arguments.

"Mitch, my boat will out-run your scow."

"I don't fuckin' think so."

"Afe, what do you think?" Buddha shouted up to me.

"I don't know—let's race tomorrow."

"Snipe, wake up. Get this thing ready," Buddha shouted, kicking the edge of Snipe's rack.

"What do you want me to do? It's as ready as it can be."

"Get your ass back there. I want those engines to shine. Grab another bottle of this rot-gut out of my locker on your way to the engine compartment." He was on a roll then and nothing could stop him. "Afe, get down here and join us for a drink. I want Mitch to see how a winning cox'n puts it away."

"I've got the watch," I called down from where I sat on top of the cox'n flat.

"Crow, wake up. Take over for Afe."

It had been four days since Tango 7 was mined and Buddha seemed obsessed with bad-mouthing the dead captain. "That useless son of a bitch. Letting those kids stay asleep. If I'd been leading the column like I was supposed to, that wouldn't have happened."

"No," Jimmy responded. "That would have been you and Afe they pulled out of the river."

I came below and through cigar smoke haze saw Jimmy sitting on the edge of a rack across from Buddha. Somewhere, Buddha had acquired a table—like a living room coffee table—and it sat in the passageway between the racks. Buddha sat across from Jimmy, their card game forgotten. Mitch was sitting on Buddha's side of the table so I sat down by Jimmy. Jimmy did have connections. He had brought a cooler full of ice. I scooped my tin cup full, held it out to Buddha for some whiskey, then topped it with Dr. Pepper, swirling it with my finger.

I glanced over at Buddha. He had gone silent with Jimmy's comment and was looking out from beneath those domed sockets with his head tilted down. I'd seen that look just before an explosion. He was drinking earlier in the day and drinking more since Tango 7. He upended his drink, let out a loud sigh, and slammed the tin cup on the table with a burst of laughter shaking his head beneath those hooded eye lids. That was the signal for the evening to end.

The next day, after the boat columns had separated to patrol their sectors, we raced Mitch's boat. Buddha tossed a grenade in the river between us. It detonated and the race was on. We were on a straight stretch and both captains positioned their crews on the fantail in hope that the bow would rise and not push as much water. Buddha and Mitch stood topside screaming as the old boats plowed water ten feet apart. Just outside my cox'n flat Buddha's tennis-shoed feet danced excitedly. Mitch was doing the same on his boat. They reminded me of Charlton Heston and Stephen Boyd in the chariot race scene in *Ben Hur*. Mitch's engines just had more power. We found out later they had gone through an overhaul a few weeks before we got to Vietnam. Our engines were a year past due.

Two days later we woke up to find Tango 11 had sunk during the night. The bow, resting on the riverbank, had kept the well-deck and our sleeping area above water. The old bilge pumps had given out. The boat wasn't far down in the water—the engines weren't damaged. The tide was going out so later in the morning we were high and dry. Buddha kicked Snipe off the boat.

"You useless fuck. Find yourself a new billet. I'm through carrying you," he shouted, throwing Snipe's clothes at him across the well-deck. "Get the fuck off my boat and take your greasy clothes with you."

Later in the day I found Snipe sitting in the shade of the mess hall with his clothes tucked under his arm. He was terrified about spending the night ashore. I told him to go to the division officer and request a transfer. When I listened to other boat captains, I'd come to the conclusion that Snipe was just as competent as most of them—it was Buddha who had the problem. It wasn't the enginemen's fault they were stuck with worn-out equipment. Buddha scammed Mitch's engineman into coming over and getting our pumps cleaned and running. When the tide came in we re-floated and backed off the beach.

Robert F. Kennedy announced his candidacy for President. Professor was ecstatic. Most of us didn't know what was happening in the world beyond our boat. Professor continued attending meetings with Buddha—at first that had bothered me; I should be the one going. But I came to respect the way Professor used the information he gleaned from meetings, placing it in context of the larger picture. He explained how Westmoreland had opened the base—Khe Sanh—not far from the Laotian border to hinder movement on the Ho Chi Minh Trail and block NVA reinforcements from coming south.

"Are you still reading that book I loaned you, *Hell In A Very Small Place?*" Professor asked.

It's a narrative written by Bernard B. Fall about the siege of Dien Bien Phu in 1954, the decisive battle won by the Viet Minh (North Vietnamese Army), ending French rule in Vietnam.

"I'm to the part where the Viet Minh have artillery on top of all the hills surrounding the base," I replied.

"There are some interesting parallels between Khe Sanh and Dien Bien Phu. The Khe Sanh battle started about the third week of January and it's still going. Right now that's about sixty days—that's about how long the French lasted."

"But we have a much better firepower and supply system," I said, in defense of the American position.

"I have to question that. Look how they pile supplies up

here and then let the NVA blow them away. You think they'd learn after the first time. And the fog—remember the fog at Dien Bien Phu? And those mornings it's foggy here on the river? It's worse up by Khe Sanh. Some days it never lifts."

I couldn't argue with Professor. He was right about the supplies being blown up. Why the navy kept piling them on the ramp, an invitation to get shelled, was beyond me.

The next day our engines started running hot and I told Buddha we needed Snipe back onboard. "Well where the fuck is he, on vacation?"

And that was it. Snipe returned. Buddha never acknowledged what happened. That evening Buddha returned from his meeting and said there would be a memorial service for Tango 7 the next day.

13

Memorial Service—
Tango 7 Crew

22 March 1968

Sand swirled around the small congregation as we gathered near the mouth of the Cua Viet River to bid farewell. The memorial service opened with "My Country 'tis of Thee" and I silently mouthed the words and wondered how many hundreds of times I'd sung that as a child after the flag raising and Pledge of Allegiance we all did in the little two room school I had attended. The boys from Tango 7 would never again roam the "woods and templed hills" the chaplain was so joyously belting out.

We followed along with the Chief Staff Officer of the division as he read the 23rd Psalm. The "Lord is my shepherd...."

I watched seagulls dip and dive and squawk in the turning basin, envying them their freedom, wondering if they had a sense of past and future. I didn't understand the line, "Surely goodness and mercy shall follow me all the days of my life and I will dwell in the house of the Lord forever." They were dead. How could mercy and goodness follow them all the days of their life anymore? I could see no mercy in having a sixty-six ton boat squash you, or in having to be cut in half to be recovered from the rack you died sleeping in—where was the mercy in that? He moved on then to Psalms 31 and I mumbled along as I studied the words of the smudged mimeographed copy. When he reached the line, "Pull me out of the net that they have laid privily for me," I remembered the discussion I had with the minister during my confirmation classes the year I was in 8th grade. I had questioned what "privily" meant and he had explained that it meant secretly. That the "net" was a metaphor for darkness—sin—and I thought, yeah, those NVA had netted Tango 7 privily. That line was more appropriate than the chaplain probably realized. Psalm 121 rang false. "He who watches over you will not slumber." That's bullshit I thought—He fell sound asleep on that Thursday morning. Maybe He had the mid-watch and dozed off when His relief didn't show up. Near the end, when it said, "The Lord will keep you from harm—He will watch over your life," I shook my head. He was too late.

The chaplain moved on to John 15: 12-17. When he got to the old cliché, "Greater love has no one than this, than to lay down one's life for his friends." I looked around at the others, then down at the sand. That was bullshit, too. The crew of Tango 7 didn't die voluntarily; they never saw it coming. When he ended with, "These things I command you, that you love one another," I felt like I was back in confirmation class sitting next to Shorty trying to suppress a giggle about a secret joke between us. That passage was a joke—we went out each day hunting fellow humans to kill—who were killing us. How could we be expected to love them?

The baton was passed to the chaplain who told us how important our mission was—how these men hadn't died in vain. I looked out over the sand dunes, out to the South China Sea, past the homebound fishermen in their low-riding sampans, past the warship silhouette, beyond the horizon and remembered how it was when I was little and terrified of burning in hell. The summer I was nine and my brother was six, a neighbor arranged for us to spend a week at a summer bible camp. We were assigned to a cabin which was managed by an apprentice preacher. In the evening, the campers gathered in a large, screened gazebo with a bonfire pit in the center and tiered seating around it. We learned of the fires of hell and the certainty of going there if we didn't take Jesus as our personal savior. At home we didn't attend church regularly. When we did, it was Lutheran. This Baptist version was a terrifying revelation. Each night we watched kids go from the bleachers down to the bonfire, kneel near the brim of the pit and beg forgiveness while flames cast shadows on their sob-racked little bodies as they made their vows in blubbering voices. Afterwards we returned to our cabins for the night. I lay on my upper bunk with the screen window a few inches from my face and watched the moon dance on waves as whippoorwills echoed and a loon called mournfully. I conjured up nine year old visions of eternal damnation. By week's end I couldn't sleep and on Friday evening my brother and I repented our sins and took Jesus as our personal savior.

A few years later I was in a foster home run by a devout Baptist couple who considered it their duty to save me. They sent me to bible camp—this one out in the sticks on the east side of upper Red Lake. They no doubt slept well knowing they were doing the Lord's bidding. The camp was programmed the same as the last one only more primitive. The evening bonfires were outdoors and after dark the mosquitoes moved in—an added motivator to be saved and sent to the cafeteria for a late-night chocolate Sunday reward. I'd been confirmed in the Lutheran Church the year before this camp and with the saving blessing I had received at Oak Hills I decided not to go through the charade a third time. On the last night of camp I was tag-teamed by three camp counselors until after midnight. They threw their hands up in disgust and left me. In the morning we all went home— three weeks later I was transferred to another foster home— couldn't have a heathen living among believers.

The chaplain finished his address and we recited the Apostles' Creed. This wasn't for the dead anymore; it was for us. "I believe in God the Father, Almighty, Maker of heaven and earth." That was of no use to the boys from Tango 7. It was fluff for our fears about eternity. I really hadn't come far since I was nine years old.

Then we recited the Lord's Prayer. I was comfortable with that because it was a plea for mercy. It acknowledged His omnipotence—we really didn't have shit to say about our fate—"Thy will be done." And it had been His will that the Tango 7 crew be killed.   Prayers for the Departed, "Almighty God, we remember before thee this day thy faithful servants Edward, Frankie, Earnest, Robert, Eugene, and Joseph," … "world without end." It had ended for all those guys on Tango 7. He chanted a prayer for the navy, said a blessing and ended with the Honor Roll, the full name and rank of each dead sailor. As he read names, their faces came alive for an instant. His conclusion, "May their souls, and the souls of all the faithful departed through the mercy of God, rest in peace." The chaplain's monotone voice told me that he would rather be in the officers' hooch sipping brandy or wine or whatever chaplains drank. The sentence was rubber-stamped into the bulletin, smudged—not straight. He was a lieutenant in the Navy Reserve attached to the Marine 1st AmTrac Battalion. The memorial service closed with the Navy Hymn. "Eternal Father, strong to save/Whose arm hath bound the restless wave…" I liked the melody of that hymn and hummed along—when it reached the "angry tumult cease" I recalled the green sheets of water washing over the *Rogers'* bridge, smashing at the inch-thick glass when we had been in the typhoon in the Formosa Straits during our WestPac cruise in 1966.

When the service ended everybody was thirsty and headed for the beer hooch. I returned to the boat—told Crow I'd cover for him. The service had stirred memories I wanted to explore. It was the first service I had attended in several years and I was troubled at my doubting. Was there truly a God? If there was—why did He allow bad things to happen?

We found out later the mine that had destroyed Tango 7 was of Russian manufacture. Buddha told us it was a 600 LB magnetic sensor mine—set to go off when the 22nd boat passed over it. We had passed over several times.

"Tango 7 just had bad fucking luck," Buddha concluded.

14

Man Overboard

24 March 1968

Two days after the memorial service we were going west, upriver, into the afternoon sun as a flight of jets passed over. I watched them disappear into the orange glow, knowing they were headed toward Khe Sanh. Sitting topside between the gun turrets, I could hear snippets of Dennis and Professor joking with Buddha below in the well-deck. Stonewall was at the helm and he yelled up, "Afe, what's that in the water up ahead?"

"It's a swimmer," I said, looking in the binoculars. "I wonder what he's doing in the middle of the river."

"Maybe it's a gook setting a mine. Let's waste the fucker," said Crow. He'd been lying on the fantail sunning and had climbed up by me when he heard Stonewall's shout.

"Let's take him prisoner. He can't put up much of a fight in the water. Hand me up a shotgun," I told Stonewall.

"What's going on up there?" I glanced down into the cox'n flat as Buddha came up the ladder and stood by Stonewall. We were quickly approaching the swimmer.

"It's Mitch. What the hell's he doing in the river?" I said, watching him tread water. "He must have fallen overboard."

"Slow down Stonewall, throw it in neutral—we'll coast up to him," I said. Buddha disappeared and a few moments later he climbed out to the catwalk. He reached out with the boat hook—the same one I'd retrieved the body with—and pulled Mitch to our boat.

Mitch was winded. He didn't have a life jacket on and when Buddha helped him over the bar armor rail he knelt on the catwalk gasping for breath while water poured off him. "Those bastards mutinied. They chased me with shotguns. I had to jump overboard. They were going to kill me. They wouldn't even throw me a life ring. They stood on the fantail laughing—flipped me the bird."

"What the fuck are you talking about?" Buddha said, as he helped Mitch to his feet.

"They mutinied. Those bastards mutinied. I'm the captain of that boat. Man your guns—break out grenades. I want to retake my boat."

He was drunk. Mitch was a career man and I think Buddha realized that the best thing to do was keep the whole thing quiet. "Come below. Get into some dry clothes and we'll have a drink to take the chill off and talk."

Two hours later, when we pulled into Cua Viet for the night, Mitch and Buddha were laughing up a grand time. Buddha went over to Mitch's boat but soon returned. "You pissed those boys off. We have an extra rack—stay here for the next few nights. They'll cool off." The next few nights turned into several weeks. Now Buddha had somebody to drink with all night. He wouldn't get roaring drunk, just a slow, steady buzz that increased as the evening lengthened.

Mitch knew he had screwed up and he tried to blend into our little family. He had the narrow, pointy face of a ferret. When he wiggled his bushy black eyebrows up and down, they looked like two caterpillars doing a mating dance. I was proficient as a cox'n but Mitch was a master. One afternoon

Buddha, Mitch, and I were sitting in the well-deck talking about boat handling and Mitch bragged how he could walk our boat up river, against the current, into an ebb tide.

"You're full of shit," Buddha said, pointing up to the hatch leading to the cox'n flat.

"Put your money where your mouth is," challenged Mitch.

"I've got an unopened bottle of Jim Beam with your name on it—Afe, is the tide going out yet?" Buddha probably felt safe risking it, knowing he'd get his share regardless.

I went topside and watched two clumps of vegetation pass. They seemed to be moving at a reasonably fast pace so I called down that yes, the tide was ebbing.

Buddha and I stood behind Mitch as he swung the boat so he was crossways in the river with the current pushing directly against the side of the boat plus the power of the out-going tide.

"See that gook hooch back there," he said, nodding toward a brown thatched hut on the far side of the rice paddy. "That's in line with the east dike of the paddy—line them up like a rifle sight to gauge our movement."

He began then. Shifting forward and back, swinging the rudder—he danced back and forth, laughing gleefully. "Buddha, old buddy—put it on ice; I'm working up a thirst." And he'd switch the helm and move the shift levers as he revved the engines. His foot work reminded me a bit of the Indian dancers at the Fourth of July Powwows we went to at home. Mitch was an expert cox'n. Buddha conceded without argument. After that, Mitch spent time with me in the cox'n flat, teaching me how he did it. Sometimes Buddha stood on the ladder with his head and shoulders above the deck, elbows rested on the edge of the hatch the same as I had seen him leaning against the bunks the first time I met him. He'd watch Mitch silently, then me as I repeated the maneuver. I came to realize that Buddha didn't know how to maneuver this boat—that's why he'd never come into the cox'n flat to show me.

15

Martin Luther King Assassinated

5 April 1968

Armed Forces Radio announced that President Johnson would halt bombing of North Vietnam at the end of March. It didn't change our lives. Johnson announced he would not seek reelection. That didn't change our lives. Mike 1 hit a mine—nobody killed but the boat was hauled down to Danang for repairs; there were no facilities in Cua Viet for performing maintenance so our enginemen struggled to make do with what they could scrounge. The scenery didn't change but the people did. One morning a Marine Amtrack—an amphibious armored troop carrier—got swamped while crossing the river and several Marines drowned. Another morning an Amtrack was stuck near the riverbank, bogged down in sand. Another towed it out.

On April 4th at 1801 hours, Martin Luther King Jr. was shot in Memphis, Tennessee and died about an hour later. That changed our lives.

At Cua Viet it was about twelve hours later. Dawn, April 5th. It must have happened after morning chow, after we'd pulled out into the river. I remember it as just another day on patrol. We didn't hear about the assassination until we'd topped of our fuel tanks then beached in the evening.

I was topside, on duty and Professor was in the well-deck reading. Dennis had gone to take a shower and the others were at the beer hooch. Snipe was the first one back—about 2130 hours and said something happened back home. A black man, civil rights preacher named King had been shot and the blacks at the beer hooch were mad. They figured the Ku Klux Klan did it. Dennis came back to the boat bloody nosed, covered in sand and shaking. He had been leaving the shower hooch the same time a black Marine came in the door. The guy was bigger than Dennis and grabbed him by the shirt, yanked him out the door and kicked him down in the sand. "Fucking honky," he had said and spit at Dennis, kicking him again.

"This is a powder keg ready to explode," Professor said. "He's not just a black preacher—he's the leader in the civil rights movement. If they've killed him there'll be hell to pay."

Crow and Buddha came back together. Buddha came topside and asked me where Stonewall was. I told him I hadn't seen him, it was his night off.

"I want the small arms locker secured tonight. I don't know what's going on but there was some pretty radical shit being talked. I think Stonewall is okay—he's not into that black equal rights bullshit—but keep it locked just in case."

I thought of the tape Stonewall had been listening to that night—about Martin Luther King saying we shouldn't be in Vietnam. I didn't tell Buddha because he was so unpredictable and besides, I liked Stonewall. He'd never done anything for me to doubt him. I went below and heard Crow talking.

"I remember him stirring up the locals in Birmingham in 1963. They pitched his ass in jail. Good riddance if they nailed him. He was pretty proud of himself at that bus protest in Montgomery. I was sixteen that year. I remember, because Pa told me not to play with Toby no more. He said them Niggers shouldn't be allowed on no buses."

"Crow, you don't know what you're talking about," Professor said. "King advocated nonviolence."

Buddha laughed. "Well, see where nonviolence got him."

Professor shook his head. "I don't think you guys understand. If he was killed you're going to see things here like back in the States—riots."

"Any friggin riots on this boat, I'll take care of them," Buddha said caressing the handle of the .38 caliber revolver he was wearing.

Stonewall showed up next morning just as we were ready to back out. He climbed on at the bow and crawled into the well-deck. I heard Buddha's voice but couldn't make out all they said, but the conversation might have gone something like this.

"Fuck topside—I'm staying down here. This ain't my fucking war no more."

"What the hell you talking about?" I heard Buddha say. I was surprised that he hadn't gone into a rage. I looked at Professor and he turned his palms upward and shrugged his shoulders.

"What am I talking about? Like one of the brothers said last night—ain't no gook ever called me Nigger."

"Nobody calls you that on this boat."

"No? Crow thinks it every day. I grew up around his kind. It's people like him and those assholes in Washington that killed King."

"What the fuck you talking about—people in Washington? What the hell do they have to do with anything?"

"You could never understand. Just let it be."

"No. I listened to some of the shit last night at the beer

hooch. Some of your 'brothers' saying they were done with this war. We got problems if that's your attitude."

I heard Stonewall's derisive laugh. "It's like the brothers said about them motherfuckers in Washington—white men sending black boys to kill yellow boys to keep the land they stole from the red men."

I drove and Professor stood behind me as we tried to listen above the diesel engine's rumble. Down in the well-deck Stonewall and Buddha talked while Snipe, Dennis, and Crow joked on the catwalk outside my cox'n flat. I didn't know who Martin Luther King Jr. was except for the tape I'd overheard. I realized he was important to Stonewall and now I wished Buddha knew about it.

"Listen," Buddha said. "Crow can be an asshole. I know that. I'll have a talk with him. You've always done a good job. Maybe I don't say it. You just do your job and if Crow or anybody gives you shit I want to hear about it. I remember back down in the Delta one night, Mays talking about King—I remember because Mays made him sound like a king—how so many people believed in him. And Mays don't talk bullshit. I'm sorry for your loss."

That was a side of Buddha I didn't think existed. Mays was a career black man. The captain of another boat, he was always friendly; kind of reminded me of Jimmy. He was the guy who had pissed off our interrogators at the POW training camp on Whidbey Island the past November. I laughed when I heard Buddha offer Stonewall a shot of Jim Beam. He didn't offer that to just anybody—it was his cure-all, the answer to weighty problems. They spent the rest of the run to Dong Ha in the well-deck. We were third boat in the column that morning—considered a very safe position. An hour later Buddha went back to the fantail and sent Dennis and Snipe forward while he talked with Crow. I couldn't hear their conversation as we passed the spot where Tango 7 had been mined.

The current had formed a small island of floating vegetation in the crook between the cox'n flat and the .50 caliber turret on the up-river side of the sunken hulk. A seagull
pecked and clawed at something nestled in it while another
perched on the lip of the 20mm cannon turret. I recalled again
the too-long-for-navy-regulations curly hair that hung down
over the kid's eyes as he reached over the side of Tango 7 and
pulled me aboard that first day on the river when I had run
aground. I wished I'd known his name. I didn't know where
he was from and wondered if he was in cold storage waiting
for the ground to thaw. That's what they did with bodies in
northern Minnesota—stored them until the frost broke. The
goal was to have the winter dead buried before Memorial
Day. It was a strange thought. That we had left the country
after the land had frozen for the season and the Tango 7 crew
returned before it thawed. Professor took over on the helm
and I went below just as Crow and Buddha climbed back
into the well-deck.

"Stonewall, I want you and Crow to shake hands—we're
stuck on this boat together for another seven months and I'm
not tolerating any bullshit. Crow, it's like I told you, Stonewall has never done anything against you."

"Shaking hands don't mean shit," Stonewall said. "It's
what's inside. I've lived with people like him all my life and
they don't change with the shake of a hand."

"I'm telling you both I will not tolerate this bullshit."
And so it was; an uneasy truce that left us all on edge.

A few evenings later I listened to Stonewall and Professor talking. Everybody else had gone to the beer hooch and
Dennis was topside on watch. The base was quiet. Business
at the beer hooch was back to normal though there seemed to
be more tolerance for soul music. I was still reading *Hell in a
Very Small Place*. Professor was reading a letter and Stonewall was heating a can of spaghetti. I heard Dennis climb

down through a gun turret and go to the cox'n flat to shut the engines off. I knew he was back topside when I heard him playing with the radio stations.

"I saw Martin Luther King once," Professor said. "My professor told us he was named prophetically and history would remember him as a symbol of freedom for Black people—the same as Martin Luther was in the sixteenth century for peasants persecuted by the nobility and the Catholic Church."

"Where did you see him?" Stonewall asked, looking up from where he squatted by his heating spaghetti.

"At Oberlin College, in October of 1964. My professor arranged a car pool for our class—he said we would witness history being made. We got there late and stood with the crowd outside the chapel, but his voice carried. I'd heard him on the radio and seen him on television, but to see him in person was very powerful. Fate placed him at this time in history."

"Maybe it wasn't fate," Stonewall said.

"His speech that day was *The Future of Integration*, and we dissected it for the next week during class. You know, Stonewall, his death is tragic, but in death he will be more powerful than he was in life."

"That's what some are saying—fuck, there goes my spaghetti," Stonewall said, grabbing at the bubbling-over can. "But it pisses me off. His was a voice of hope against all the fucking Crows of the world."

"I can't begin to imagine what you must think," Professor said. "But remember his message of non-violence. That's the legacy he left."

I sat listening to the conversation. I knew I felt closer to Stonewall than Crow as I recalled the southern boy in boot camp I had fought with. I didn't understand how Black people felt so I said nothing. How could I explain that I had spent three days in the brig for standing up for a Black kid? I recalled Stonewall's tape of King's speech. And there was Cassius Clay, changed his name to Muhammad Ali when he became a Muslim. He refused to go to Vietnam—had forfeited his heavyweight title and went to prison instead. You had to respect that. I didn't know any whites that had made a stand like Clay or King.

The Khe Sanh siege ended. The North Vietnamese had disappeared, back across the border into Laos and into the DMZ. We heard rumors that the area around Khe Sanh looked like a moonscape with B-52 bomb craters and the hundreds of thousands of other bombs and artillery rounds dropped during the battle. Patrols had discovered the bodies of thousands of North Vietnamese Army troops mired in the destruction.

We still made the first run to Dong Ha each morning past now-familiar points. The river had lost its importance as a conduit for supplies. Current and tidal action had flushed the tiny island from behind the Tango 7 gun turret—water was again chocolatey-brown as it swirled in little eddies through the bar armor. Leaking fuel from the submerged tanks formed an iridescent skin. Magically, small slicks formed and early morning sun played upon them as the current flowed. The leaking diesel reminded me of when I was a seaman apprentice standing fantail watch on the *Rogers* in Pearl Harbor. In dawn's stillness I watched fuel rise from the USS *Arizona*. The luminous colors hovered above the hulk. Rumors circulated that we would soon return to the Mekong Delta.

Incoming artillery became an irritant to be tolerated. Some nights were peaceful, others interrupted—no constant hammering like earlier—just a few rounds. Enough to keep everybody on edge. Enough to kill a few people. Buddha seemed to distance himself from life on the boat. As soon as we reached our patrol area in the morning he and Mitch went below, had breakfast, then visited or read. We often joined them. After a nap, Buddha would officially start happy hour with a low chuckle and an old cliché.

"What do you boys think? I'd say the sun's over the yardarm—somewhere." Then he'd growl a conspiratorial chuckle, lift a leg and fart, then step into the passageway beyond the ladder to the cox'n flat and pull a bottle from his locker.

Armed Forces Radio announced that the United States and North Vietnam were going to begin meeting in Paris for peace talks in early May. I was excited. We all were.

We drifted through May and June, hot days; dust from drying rice paddies powdered our boat in the summer wind as we waited for news from Paris.

Snipe talked as though we would be leaving within the month. "I'll be home before my daughter can roll over. In her last letter, Nancy said she smiles and is beginning to talk."

"I'm going to have to get on a diet," Buddha said. "I'm going back to diving school. Become a Master Diver. What are you going to do, Afe?"

I hadn't thought much about it. "I'm not sure. I read something about a Merchant Marine Academy out east. I might check that out."

"Merchant Marines? Why not stay in the Navy? Hell, when you reenlist they'll give you another stripe. You'll be the youngest chief I ever knew."

"I'm not sure what I want. I just like being outdoors. I love the ocean and traveling. I just don't know. Good thing I don't need to decide today."

Dennis was excited to go back to San Francisco. "Remember that weekend we went to Haight Asbury? I'm going back there on leave. I just felt right that afternoon."

"I don't want to piss on your parade," Professor said.

"But it took the politicians two years to reach an agreement during the Korean Conflict. Johnson and Big Business are in no hurry to end this police action. The economy is booming."

"This ain't no fucking police action. It's a war," Buddha said.

"No. To be classified as a war, war must be declared and authorized by the Congress and the President."

"Don't get professory on me—Crow, hand me the bottle—this bullshit's drying me out."

Stonewall and Crow didn't have an opinion and nobody asked them. Jimmy almost got in a fight at the beer hooch that night because he agreed with Professor—anybody that thought it was just about over was dreaming.

Weeks drifted by as politicians argued about the shape of the table—where the opposing sides would sit. No more sailors died or were injured on the Cua Viet River but Marines still held memorial services each week.

Robert F. Kennedy was shot on June 5th and died the next day.

That brought Professor and Stonewall closer. Professor said something about John Kennedy and the Peace Corps, how Robert would have continued in his brother's steps to help the downtrodden.

"Now the fuckers killed the only white man that gave a shit about us niggers," was Stonewall's comment.

Stonewall spent more time off the boat and was withdrawn during the day while on patrol. He stood his watches in silence, made short replies when spoken to, and sat on the fantail of the boat when not on watch—reading or listening to his tape player. There was a cold silence between him and Crow. Crow seemed to be drinking more. Pabst Blue Ribbon at the beer hooch wasn't enough for him. He was drinking more of Buddha's whiskey, which seemed to put him in a dark mood. Buddha ignored it. Snipe lived for his letters from Nancy. I think his daughter had been born about the time Khe Sanh was declared rescued. And there was an argument about that. The army had reopened Route 9 to Khe Sanh with Operation Pegasus and rescued the Marines. The Marines said they weren't in trouble—didn't need rescuing. Professor continued to read, offering me books he got in the mail. I thumbed through them but they were philosophical, often political and held no interest to me. He seemed to take a special interest in Henry Kissinger, a Harvard University professor and a consultant to President Johnson.

16

Farewell Cua Viet

2 July 1968

I watched the Cua Viet shoreline shrink below an overcast sky as we corkscrewed on swells awaiting our turn to enter the LSD. I could no longer see the bare pine branches that had been defoliated by North Vietnamese artillery shrapnel.

After our boat was secured inside the ship and the hold pumped out, I rushed topside and there it was, the ARVN flag at the Vietnamese base just west of the American base—they never had been shelled, just like our guide had predicted the day we'd arrived four months earlier.

No longer did my cox'n flat represent invincibility. South, in the Delta we were returning to, reports had made their way north of casualties; of rockets burning through armor plates and annihilating crews. I had seen a boat flipped like a child's tinker toy and left discarded on the river bottom. I think the rest of Tango 11 crew had changed, too—terrifying nights in bunkers, assassinations of the believers back in the world, boredom of days on edge, waiting for an explosion from the NVA or Buddha or Crow and Stonewall. The mythic camaraderie of brothers in war simply did not exist on our boat.

A few hours after leaving Cua Viet, the LSD passed a fishing trawler just off our starboard side. We could see the trawler crew eating their morning meal and Dennis commented on how it was a wonder they could survive on what they ate. "Remember how much weight we lost during SERE training? If I ate like those gooks I'd dry up and blow away. I'd starve anyway. I couldn't eat the shit they eat."

"You'd be surprised what you'd do when you're hungry," I told him. "Fish heads and rice don't look bad sometimes."

I told them more about the summer of 1964 when I was sixteen and bummed my way from Minnesota to Seattle, Washington. The day after I'd filled my duffle bag with food from a trash can, I hitched a ride with a guy that worked for the railroad in Helena, Montana. He put me on a train heading west. I met three guys in that box car and shared the food I had left.

"Weren't you scared?" Professor said. "I can't begin to imagine. I've seen those hobos when I drove by the railyard in Columbus."

"No, these guys were okay. They taught me a lot. The old one got killed when the train passed through a small town in Idaho. Friggin kids ambushed us—stood on both sides of the boxcar and threw fist-sized rocks in as the train passed through. They ricocheted around like ping pong balls. We curled up in the corners with our hands and arms shielding our heads. After we were past, one guy didn't get up. One of the rocks had gotten him in the back of the head. He was old. Somebody said he'd been in the First World War. Anyway, they were real happy to eat the food I scrounged. By then we had to wipe slime off the sausage and pick mold off the bread."

"Why'd you leave home?" Dennis asked. "Weren't your parents worried?"

I laughed and shook my head. "We were talking about

being hungry. I've glimpsed hunger, but I've seen the other side, too."

And I told them about when I was on the *Rogers* and we spent a week in Yokosuka, Japan. A shipmate and I took the train to Tokyo for a weekend. We got down there about noon on a Saturday and wandered around—went up in the Tokyo Tower, watched some sumo wrestlers butt bellies and bounce back like two bull buffalos slamming together in slow motion. Late in the afternoon we ate at the Tokyo Hilton.

It was early for the dinner hour so the place was empty except for a table of about ten Americans and an older Japanese couple. We were seated about twenty feet from the other table. There was an older American couple, very distinguished looking, and a younger couple with their kids. Our waiter bowed and asked if we'd like a drink. We were both eighteen that winter and had just come in from several weeks of patrolling up in the Tonkin Gulf. We had money to burn so we began drinking doubles of Scotch. After the second round our waiter bowed again and told us that the gentleman at the far table wanted to buy us a drink. I thanked him across the room and he nodded in reply. I knew they were watching so I felt a bit self-conscious when the food came. I had brook trout delivered on a portable brazier. The waiter stood turning the extra trout and vegetables, keeping them warm, and forking more onto my plate as I ate. I glanced up and saw the old woman watching me. My Granny had taught me table manners during my stays with her in Seattle, so I knew my etiquette was acceptable, even after several drinks. This old lady was watching me close so I took my fork, dug the eyes out of the trout heads, smiled and popped them in my mouth. She brought her hand to her mouth, turned away, and never looked back at me. When we finished eating, we had a double Cognac, smoked a cigarette, and asked for the bill.

Our little waiter bowed and said, "No, no. Gentleman

buy your dinner. I looked over again and saw they were done eating, just sitting around the table visiting. We couldn't believe our good fortune and we both went over to thank him. He smiled and nodded again—they were very gracious to two half-drunk sailors. I asked him his name and what he did in Japan. He just smiled again—said his name was Mr. Gillette.

One night, about a month later, we were back up in the Tonkin Gulf and I was standing bridge watch in the early morning hours when I realized the Captain was standing near me. You have to understand, the Captain of a ship is up near to God, not like Buddha. Anyway, he was a nice man. Sometimes he'd talk to you as an equal. I told him the story about Kip and me and Mr. Gillette in Tokyo and he chuckled.

"You know who that was?" he asked.

"No sir."

"Mr. Gillette is with the State Department. He was visiting the Japanese Ambassador. I received a letter from him recently commending me on what well-behaved sailors I have on my ship—that they were excellent ambassadors at large."

A helicopter passed low over us, heading toward the coast. Looking aft, at the receding fishing trawler, I said, "Anyway, when you look at these Vietnamese fishermen and what they eat, and how they farm, and how they live in dirt-floor hooches compared to the standard of living in Japan, you'd think that Americans should be able to help the Vietnamese. Just twenty years ago Japan was crawling out of the destruction of World War II. Without American help they'd probably be like Vietnam is today."

"Corruption," Professor said. "That South Vietnamese President and his cronies are getting wealthy while they string Americans along. Why do you think that ARVN base at Cua Viet never got shelled when we got hit damn near every night? Corruption."

Next morning we steamed into Vung Tau, off-loaded our boats, and took channels south to the Mekong River—not around the point through open sea like we had in the beginning of March when we went north.

Seaman Recruit Wendell Affield, San Diego, California March 1965.

Boatswains Mate 2nd Class Affield aboard armor troop carrier (ATC) 112-11 on the Mekong River, July 1968.

ATC 112-11 at Dong Tam in the Mekong Delta, beached for maintenance, scraping the hull, pumping and patching bilges below the well-deck that constantly leaked.

Second Brigade, Ninth Infantry Division troops return to ATC 112-11 after a search and destroy sweep.

Gunners Mate Seaman Stonewall in his 20 millimeter cannon turret aboard ATC 112-11.

Looking upriver from "Buddha" Ed Thomas's position between gun turrets. M-60 machine gun Wendell Affield retrieved from a downed Marine helicopter rests on roof of cox'n flat.

Cua Viet Naval Base at mouth of river, under NVA artillery bombardment. Note the small craft waiting off-shore and the LST seaward, outside the river, March 1968.

North side of Cua Viet River. Village destroyed in Tet 1968 battles.

Ed Thomas in position, sheltered by .50 caliber turrets on sides, 20 millimeter cannon turret aft, and cox'n flat in front.

RIVER ASSAULT SQUADRON ELEVEN
CUA VIET, REPUBLIC OF VIETNAM
22 March 1958

MEMORIAL SERVICE — 1930 HOURS

HYMN #14   "My Country, 'tis of thee"   p. 131

PSALMS 23, 31, 121   (unison)   pp. 55, 63

SCRIPTURE READING   (St. John 15:12-17)   LT C.J. Cox, USN
                                                Chief Staff Officer

ADDRESS   LT C.A. TEA, CHC, USNR
                                            Chaplain, 1stAmTracBn

THE APOSTLES' CREED   (unison)

THE LORD'S PRAYER   (unison)

PRAYERS FOR THE DEPARTED

PRAYERS FOR THE U.S.N.

THE BLESSING

HYMN #16   "The Navy Hymn"   p. 134

- -

H O N O R   R O L L

BM1 Edward J. HAGL, USN
EN3 Frankie R. JOHNSON, USN
BM3 Ernest W. WIGLESWORTH, Jr., USN
SN Robert W. CAWLEY, USN
FN Eugene NELSON, USN
SN Joseph S. PERYSIAN, USN

     This Memorial Service is being held in the honored memory of the above-named members of River Assault Squadron 11, who gave their lives in the defense of freedom on 14 March 1968 when their boat, an Armored Troop Carrier, ATC-112-7, was mined by the enemy while traversing the Cua Viet River.

         "MAY THEIR SOULS, AND THE SOULS OF ALL THE FAITHFUL DEPARTED, THROUGH THE MERCY OF GOD, REST IN PEACE"

PRAYERS FOR THE DEPARTED

     Almighty God, we remember before thee this day thy faithful servants Edward, Frankie, Ernest, Robert, Eugene, and Joseph. Grant them an entrance into the land of light and joy, in the fellowship of thy saints: through Jesus Christ our Lord. Amen.

     Almighty God, our heavenly Father, in whose hands are the living and the dead; We give thee thanks for all those thy servants who have laid down their lives in the service of our country. Grant to them thy mercy and the light of thy presence, that the good work which thou hast begun in them may be perfected; through Jesus Christ thy Son our Lord, who liveth and reigneth with Thee and the Holy Ghost ever, one God, world without end. Amen.

Memorial Service for ATC 112-7. Held at the mouth of the Cua Viet River, overlooking the South China Sea.

Wendell Affield, visiting Vietnamese children at a hamlet in the U Minh while they wait for the troops to return.

Mobile Riverine Force Division 112 boats enroute on Mekong River, to U Minh Forest, early August 1968.

Riverine Force boats getting underway after debarking troops in U Minh Forest.

Viet Cong suspect captured during U Minh operation. "Buddha" Ed Thomas stands guard, Affield looks on as Tango 11 transports him to army detention barge for interrogation.

ATC 112-11 on August 18, 1968. Three rockets detonate over well-deck loaded with troops from Second Brigade, on Hai Muoi Tam Canal, a few kilometers northwest of Cai Be. One soldier killed instantly, many seriously wounded.

B-40 rocket penetrates .50 caliber machine gun turret, severely wounds army sergeant manning the gun after sailor fled his post. Note bullet holes below gun turret and narrow canal, boats beached on far bank.

B-40 rocket strikes cox'n flat bar armor.

Second B-40 strikes in same area, burns through, sprays molten steel and shrapnel through compartment. Wendell Affield and radioman are wounded. Note rocket tail fins lodged in bar armor.

"Buddha" Ed Thomas in his cabin in the Upper Peninsula holding the flag from ATC 112-11. Autumn 1991.

CWO#3221

```
     VV   STN620
RTIEZYUW RUMUGKK0487 2311532-EEEE--RUYVSII.
ZNY EEEEE
R 181530Z AUG 68
FM CTF ONE ONE SEVEN
TO RUYVSII/TF ONE ONE SEVEN
INFO ZEN/CO SECOND BRIGADE NINTH INF DIV
RUYVSII/USS OKANOGAN
RUYVSII/USS INDRA
BT
UNCLAS E F T O
```

FOR OFFICIAL USE ONLY
DAILY INTERNAL INFO SUMMARY 28-19
    MOBILE RIVERINE GROUP ALPHA ELEMENTS RAN INTO SOME OF THE
MOST HEATED CONTACT IN MONTHS SUNDAY IN DAY-LONG FIGHTING ALONG
THE HAI MUOI TAM CANAL.
    WITH ARMY ELEMENTS STILL RECEIVING SPORADIC FIRE AT 2100, EIGHT
2ND BRIGADE COMPANIES CLAIMED TO HAVE AN ESTIMATED MAIN FORCE
BATTALION SURROUNDED ABOUT 17 KILOMETERS NORTHWEST OF CAI BE. AIR
FORCE PLANES RAINED THOUSANDS OF POUNDS OF ORDNANCE ON THE ENEMY
POSITIONS, WHICH HAD ALREADY BEEN SEVERLY POUNDED BY
ARTILLERY AND DOZENS OF HELICOPTER GUNSHIPS.
    AS OF 2100, NINE VIET CONG HAD BEEN CONFIRMED KILLED. U.S.

PAGE 2 RUMGUKK0487 UNCLAS E F T O
CASUALTIES WERE FOUR KILLED AND 82 WOUNDED, BUT THIS DID NOT INCLUDE
MANY OF THE LESS SERIOUS INJURIES SUSTAINED IN TWO DEVASTATING
AMBUSHES OF ASSAULT CRAFT OF RIVER DIVISION 112.
    THE RIV DIV 112 BOATS WERE FIRST HIT AT 1225 AS THEY MOVED UP
THE HAI MUOI TAM CANAL WITH 4/47 INFANTRY. IN THE WITHERING ROCKET,
RECOILLESS RIFLE AND AUTOMATIC WEAPONS FIRE, THREE NAVYMEN
WERE KILLED AND 15 WERE WOUNDED SERIOUSLY ENOUGH TO REQUIRE
MEDICAL EVACUATION. TWO OF THE KIA WERE CREWMEN OF ASPB-112-2, BUT THE
THIRD HAD NOT BEEN POSITIVELY IDENTIFIED BY EARLY SUNDAY EVENING.
MISSING IN ACTION WAS A BOAT CREWMAN OF ASPB 112-1 WHO DISAPPEARED
DURING THE AMBUSH AND WHO HAD NOT BEEN LOCATED AS OF SUNDOWN. TWELVE
ARMY PERSONNEL WERE ALSO MEDEVACED AND OTHERS WERE INJURED AS
THE ATC'S MOVED IN TO BEACH THE EMBARKED TROOPS. ALTHOUGH THE
GROUND ELEMENTS WERE ABLE TO ACHIEVE NO SIGNIFICANT CONTACT AS THEY
MANEUVERED IN THE AREA, DUSTOFF HELICOPTERS AND GUNSHIPS DREW ALMOST
CONTINUOUS AUTOMATIC WEAPONS FIRE FROM THE ENEMY POSITIONS. ONE
DUSTOFF HELO WAS SHOT DOWN BY GUNFIRE BUT THE CREW ALL ESCAPED
INJURY.
    WHEN THE SWEEP THROUGH THE AREA PROVED FRUITLESS, THE GROUND
FORCES WERE BACKLOADED TO BE MOVED SEVERAL KILOMETERS UP THE RIVER

After-action report excerpt from August 18, 1968. ATC 112-11 is not mentioned. Apparently nothing note-worthy happened.

17

Agent Orange

10 July 1968

We were transporting an army platoon to a tributary north of the Mekong River for a search and destroy sweep. Troops crowded the back of the well-deck beneath my armored cox'n flat because the forward section was a deathtrap. When enemy rockets detonated on the canopy over the forward part of the well-deck, shrapnel sprayed down. Everybody was braced for that first lump-in-the-throat contact. Our gunners scanned riverbanks, searching for that telltale warning that allowed a millisecond response before the Viet Cong fired—that heartbeat which made the difference between destroying the enemy or having a rocket burn through our one inch armor plating. Riverbank foliage hung into muddy water.

Buddha leaned forward, his face near the opening at the back of the cox'n flat. "Professor, tell Snipe to hand my canteen up, this sun feels like a heat lamp beating on my helmet."

Professor kneeled, stuck his head into the hatch near my feet and hollered, "Snipe, hey Snipe, Buddha wants his canteen. After a moment he continued, "He must be back in the engine room and can't hear me. I'll get it." He stepped into the deck hatch opening and down the ladder into the cool shadows of the compartment.

"They're packed underneath us," Professor said when he returned. "They must be expecting trouble." He tapped the metal canteen on the back wall of the cox'n flat to get Buddha's attention and passed it through the opening.

"Hey man, can I come above and see them machine guns?" asked a Black sergeant standing on the ladder. We were carrying a different platoon than usual. I hadn't met this guy before.

"Sure, but it's cooler below," I said.

He climbed the ladder and Professor directed him to Dennis. I looked back and glimpsed two sets of feet and legs—one tanned and bare, the other covered by baggy jungle fatigues tucked into canvas boots, laced tight and double-knotted. I caught snatches of conversation as I followed the stern of the boat in front of me, eyes slitted against the white-hot sun.

"That .50 caliber is a bad mother but I'd like to see the grenade launcher in action," the sergeant said.

"It can put out 250 rounds per minute but the belts only hold twenty-five—but yeah—it makes silage of the river-bank. Hey Buddha," Dennis yelled.

"What'd you want? Sarge, what the hell you doing in there?" I looked back through the opening behind the cox'n flat and saw Buddha leaning up and over the top of the starboard turret.

"Your gunner was showing me this grenade launcher—beats the shit out of that single shot M79 I carry. Any chance I can try it?"

"We're in a free-fire zone. See that movement over on the starboard bank? Dennis show him what to do."

I listened as Dennis explained. "It's loaded, so all you have to do is flip the safety off and start cranking. It's mounted to the top of the .50 caliber so just hold the gun handle to elevate the launcher with your left hand, and crank the launcher-handle with the right—the turret rotates so you can move back and forth. I'll get down so you have room to move." Dennis backed into the opening between the cox'n flat and the gun turrets.

Through the slits in my armor I watched the starboard bank get ripped by a series of explosions.

'Man, this is one wicked machine," Sarge laughed, cranking out another five rounds.

I heard Buddha shout down the turret, "Aim into the trees and see what happens." Above the riverbank, foliage shredded as grenades detonated in thick growth. "The shit sprays down—no escape."

"Tango one-one, Tango one-one, what are you firing on," the boat's radio blared.

"This is Tango one-one, we saw movement on the bank, over."

Tango one-one, cease fire."

"This is Tango one-one, roger, out."

"All boats be advised, we are in a populated area—the use of .50 calibers is restricted."

We already knew that. Because of the long range, we were forbidden to use the .50 caliber machine guns due to risk of injury to the Vietnamese locals.

"Hey Buddha, thanks a lot. You guys ever need a hand up here, just yell."

"Any time Sarge, I see the head of the column turning into the canal we're going to—we'll be dropping you guys in about twenty minutes."

"I best get below."

"Dennis, get a new belt into that Honeywell."

Landscape near the mouth of the narrow canal was a wasteland that reminded me of the swamps and hardwood forests of home in early spring—just after snow-melt— before it greened. The ground was covered with decomposing vegetation like the snow-flattened maple, oak, and bass leaves at home. Grass that should have been lush tendrils fluttering in the river current lay brittle brown. Wind gusts swept dry leaves into the water.

"I'm glad they sprayed this corner," the sergeant said, standing on the ladder, head above the deck hatch. "Friggin gooks got three of our guys here while you were up north— waited for two boats to get up around the corner then started shooting. The boats shot each other up while the gooks ducked down in their holes."

"Not going to happen today," Budda said. I heard his M60 barrel clank against the port .50 caliber turret. He was proud of his gun and let everybody know it. Now that we were back south he was safe to show it. "Yeah Afe, ya done good getting this little beauty. Maybe today I'll get a chance to really try it out. Watch that downed coconut tree."

I swung wide to miss the half submerged trunk of an ancient tree. Bare weathered roots reached skyward while at the bottom they still locked into the bank, holding the tree captive. On the lee side of the tree trunk I spotted an eddy pulling flotsam in from the passing current. A slow-moving whirlpool held the refuse, depositing it on the muddy bank as the tide ebbed and flowed. The wake created by the boat in front of us disrupted a flock of birds that I hadn't noticed behind the tree roots.

"Holy shit," Crow shouted from his turret. "Look at all those dead fish along the bank, they sure stink. There's a bird lying there, too. That spray must be some powerful shit."

"Maybe we'll see some belly-up gooks. Maybe that spray shit works on them, too," Dennis said.

"Send'em up here to collect those fish for *nuoc mam*," Buddha joked.

In the canal, I straightened the boat and looked back, catching a glimpse of dozens of small fish, their white bellies gleaming as they lay on the bank or turned slowly in the whirlpool. The black scavengers, overcoming their initial fear, flocked back, the breeze pushing stench and caws our way.

The radio ordered a recon by fire so the boats opened up with all guns as we approached the insertion area, shredding jungle on both sides of the riverbank. Two minutes later Buddha shouted, "Cease fire, cease fire. Afe, hard to starboard—take her straight in."

"Professor, stick your head below and remind Snipe to release the safety on the bow ramp," I said, as I spun the helm, turning the boat toward shore. We were traveling with the current so it moved quickly to the right as I revved the engines to push it against the riverbank. I released the ramp and watched the sergeant, at the head of his platoon, urging the troops off the boat before the bow ramp had descended all the way.

"Come on boys—let's get off this floating coffin." He waved his M16 above his head while he stood on the ramp and for an instant I recalled the story my sixth grade teacher told of her grandfather being with Teddy Roosevelt, rifle overhead, urging his boys forward up San Juan Hill. Mrs. Cheney said that her grandfather talked about Buffalo Soldiers—Black soldiers that fought that day but were never acknowledged in history books or paintings. Sarge jumped off the bow ramp and within two steps disappeared in the undergrowth followed by about thirty struggling soldiers.

"Kick that starboard engine ahead, Afe. She's broaching." I looked to the port side and saw the current had pushed the stern around in the few moments I'd been watching troops disembark.

"Okay, raise the ramp—this is our patrol area so just

back her out and hold her in the current while we see if they make contact."

It was a quiet day. We knew snakes hugged the shoreline, hidden beneath green leaves that left tiny wakes in the moving current. Birds dipped into water as they circled the boat in the narrow canal. We drifted down-river until reaching the next boat's area, then I kicked the engines forward and idled to the top of our section and began drifting down stream again. Buddha dozed topside. I looked through the opening at the back of my compartment and saw him scrunched down between the turrets, helmet tilted forward. His flak jacket pushed up on his cheeks making them bulge like nut-packed jowls of a red squirrel. The helmet absorbed the sun's heat and sweat dribbled down both jowls to form a tiny waterfall that dripped from the bottom of his chin. Professor and I looked at each other and laughed.

"What—what's so friggin funny," Buddha stammered, sitting up. His helmet tumbled forward over his face. "Fuck it's hot up here—Afe, drop the ramp. Let's go for a quick swim."

I lowered the ramp about half way to act as our diving board. Buddha, Professor, Crow, and Snipe stripped their clothes. I could see the top half of their bodies when they stood on the ramp. When they dove, their pale butts flashed in the sun. Half an hour later Professor came back to the cox'n flat and relieved me, "The water's great—even smells fresh—cleaner than the main river. Go jump in, I'll keep an eye on things."

I went below, kicked my shorts off. Setting a soap bar in a crack at the bottom of the ramp, I climbed to the top and dove in. It was brown and tasted a little mucky, but it was cool. Rising to the surface I spit water and swam around the boat several times before climbing back on board. I saw that Stonewall and Dennis had joined Buddha, who was still kicking around out in front of the ramp. I soaped down, lathered my hair and jumped back in for a rinse. The water was nice, I thought, as I paddled around the boat again. The chill after the hot sun reminded me of swimming at Nebish Lake with my brothers. After putting hay in the loft, after evening chores, we'd bike to the lake to wash away the sweat-caked itching chaff. Mosquitoes would feast on us when we came out of the water. When I was little, I'd cry in frustration as I tried to hold squiggling black bloodsuckers in my fingers so I could pull them off, while mosquitoes were driving me crazy.

The tide must be going out, I thought absently, as I pushed dead minnows away from my face—that little eddy must have lost its prize. I brushed soggy brown grass from my mouth, swam around one more time then grabbed the tire and pulled myself back on board as I heard the radio come to life.

"Hey Buddha," Professor shouted. "We're supposed to move up river and pick up our troops."

"You guys heard him, everybody back on board."

I pulled on clean cut-offs then went back to the cox'n flat. We cruised up out of the canal and back into the river. I watched the boat in front of me kicking up muck from the river bottom. "Tide's ebbing," I told Professor. "Damn good thing we re getting out of here."

Late afternoon the troops radioed in. They were close to the river and wanted us to pop purple smoke so they could find us. They'd pop yellow before they came out so nobody would get trigger-happy. Our smoke drifted into the brush when suddenly there was a low pop and yellow puffed skyward then drifted over to blend with the purple. Ten minutes later everybody was back on board.

The troops were thirsty and crusted with paddy muck. Several of them had run out of water because of the heat so Buddha gave them some of ours. "How'd it go out there Sarge," Buddha asked.

"Same old bullshit. That brown bar Lieutenant in the other platoon is gonna get somebody killed—I'd be tempted to leave the squirrelly little asshole out there. He's more dangerous than the VC."

18

Monsoons and Apparitions

14 July 1968

Summer waned—the rainy season dragged on. At times rain fell so hard the river surface seemed to churn. Cold, saturating, decaying. Clothes mildewed, nerves frayed, guns corroded. Hundreds more kilometers of rivers and canals became navigable with the higher water levels. Huge chunks of vegetation broke loose in the swift currents. Driving into ebb tide current with a platoon of troops on board, we barely made headway. And the rain poured down. The old Minnesota farmers had an expression for it: Raining pitchforks and hammer handles.

And so the days crept by—one operation much the same as the last.

"Wake up, Afe. It's your watch," Crow said, the red-lensed flashlight glowing on the bulkhead beyond my rack.

"What the fuck. I just laid down. Turn that friggin light off," I complained, rolling over.

"It's midnight. Time to get up," he persisted, poking my back with the flashlight.

"Yeah, yeah, I'm up." I found my flashlight on the ledge against the bulkhead, flicked it on and swung my feet to the tacky steel deck. I rummaged in a pile at the end of my rack and found a long-sleeved shirt and full-length pants. The mildew smell reminded me of our dirt floor basement at home. Maybe the mold would help ward off friggin mosquitoes, I thought. I waved the red-lensed light around the back of the well-deck. Everybody was burned out from the last three days. Buddha was on his back snoring with his mouth open and I wondered how many mosquitoes he inhaled. Crow and Snipe had netting over their racks and I could only see Stonewall's back. He mumbled in his sleep—something about coming home. There was an open book face-down near Professor's head and I had to smile. He still read, even at the expense of precious sleep, but now he was out to the world. Dennis had the rack above Stonewall and as I turned to leave the well-deck my light flicked across his face and again, like the first day I met him, he reminded me of my younger brother. The frown and clinched jaw of day replaced with closed-eyed innocence.

I crawled to the top of the cox'n flat and found Crow peering into the starlight scope at the far side of the river. He set the scope down, picked a concussion grenade out of the box, pulled the pin, and lobbed it twenty feet beyond the stern.

"That ought to take care of any little fuckers out for a midnight swim," he said, his voice an intrusion on the silent night. "Don't forget, there's troops just in front of us so don't fire forward—anything in the river or on the far bank is open season. I'm out of here." With that he went below.

It was a moonless night but the starlight scope captured light from the stars and illuminated the far bank in a green glow. I quickly scanned a complete circle to orient myself in the darkness. Then I repeated the circle, doing as I had been taught as a lookout on the *Rogers*—search five degrees, stop, watch for five seconds, then move another five degrees always overlapping the periphery—it took several minutes to scan a full circle. A flicker on the riverbank where we were beached, where troops were bivouacked, caught my attention. About every twenty seconds the flicker glowed—an army guy sneaking a smoke, I decided. Either dumb or feeling safe. The troops had set claymore mines to protect the land approaches. I tossed another concussion grenade into the river behind me, the theory being it would kill enemy swimmers in the vicinity. I wondered if I had ever injured one. I'd never know because the current would carry them away before daybreak.

I scanned the area again—I realized my mind was conjuring shadows when I held the scope on a leafy bush hanging in the river—the current was making it move, just like during the day. I tossed two grenades out the back of the boat and smiled to myself at my mind games.

It was like the time I'd tagged along with my brothers up to Redby, a small town on the Indian reservation to see the movie, *Dracula*. I think I was eight that summer. About midway through the movie I was so terrified I went out to the lobby and visited with the old Indian lady selling popcorn. I didn't have a nickel so she gave me a bag. On the way home my brothers heightened my terror by threatening to drop me off in the black rainy night along the dirt road fifteen miles from our house. Later that night in my bedroom, I had stood on tiptoes and peed out the upstairs window because I knew Count Dracula would capture me if I went to the outhouse. On this dark river, Viet Cong were my Dracula. They had phantom reputations—attack, fade away.

Illumination rounds fired from distant artillery positions streaked skyward and blossomed with dull thuds. Parachutes billowed and the flares swayed, casting an eerie twilight glow that created shadows in the jungle.

"Afe, Afe, it's me, Crow."

I swung the shotgun muzzle toward the voice. "Christ, you scared the shit out of me—what the hell you doing awake?" I recognized his voice and saw the dark shape standing below me on the catwalk. I heard him peeing into the river.

"Friggin mosquitoes woke me up—that net's a joke. I think it traps them inside it. Did Puff drop those flares?"

Puff the Magic Dragon was a twin engine cargo plane equipped with three six-barrel mini-guns capable of firing six thousand rounds per minute. Using night vision scopes and heat sensor equipment to locate enemy positions, Puff could annihilate a Viet Cong unit in seconds. They could also drop flares.

"I can hear small arms fire but I think the flares were fired from artillery. I didn't see Puff drop them." We watched the flares settle earthward below smoky trails. It felt safer just having another person awake, somebody to talk to.

"I can't wait for R&R," Crow said, climbing the bar armor toward me. "I'm going back to Subic Bay."

"You better come back—they'll throw the book at you."

"I don't really give a fuck. Sitting in the brig is safer than getting shot at. Man, am I thankful Buddha doesn't know I was a third class engineman before they busted me to seaman. Poor fucking Snipe—constantly getting ragged at—he's doing better than most enginemen could with these worn out engines."

"Why don't you help him? Give him a break?"

"Fuck that—what's in it for me? I hear a plane. Maybe it's Puff. There he is. Tuck your head in and pucker up, Charlie," Crow said to the unseen Viet Cong. "Puff's about to blow you a new asshole."

We had a grandstand view. Sitting on the edge of my cox'n canopy we watched the slow-motion drama unfold—almost hypnotizing as it danced across the night sky. Enemy tracers arced up toward Puff, Puff's orange hose of light rushing earthward. The tracers stopped rising toward Puff.

"Those little shits didn't have a prayer," Crow said. "Good riddance." A few seconds later Puff stopped firing. We could hear the plane circling the area. He must have thrown some flares because we saw a path of three heading our way. Suddenly green tracers reached skyward again and we heard Puff's engines change pitch as he veered away. It almost made me cheer—those little shits apparently did have a prayer I thought, as I tossed another concussion grenade into the river behind the boat.

About two hundred meters upriver a 20mm cannon roared and the radio came alive. "This is Mike one, I have movement on the east bank."

Without a word Crow climbed over the top of his gun turret and dropped inside. I yelled down to him, "Crow, wake up everybody, we'll probably be backing into the river." Then I rested the starlight scope on the 20mm cannon turret and focused on the far bank.

""What's all the excitement, Afe?" Buddha yelled, as he climbed topside. "Professor, are you down there?"

I caught a wisp of Professor responding to a radio message, "This is Tango one-one, out." Then he shouted up to Buddha, "We're supposed to get out in the river and patrol our sector—they think some VC are trying to sneak across the river."

"You want to stay up here, Afe? I think somebody just got spooked and shot up some bushes," Buddha said. "Man it stinks tonight. Friggin mosquitoes." And he coughed and spit.

Hot days, monsoon rains, and still nights hastened decomposition and made a perfect breeding ground. There was no escape—darkness brought them in full vengeance. Mosquito repellent, long sleeves, and netting offered scant protection. Even the stench in the well-deck living quarters didn't deter them—the diesel fuel fumes and exhaust; the cordite fumes and gun smoke; the moldy clothing and stale cigarette butts—nothing stopped them.

"You're getting close to the port bank Professor, swing her out a bit," Buddha said, looking ahead through the starlight scope.

"It's so dark down here I can't see the bar armor three feet in front of me."

"Okay, turn around. We'll pull into the bank when we get back to the troops. Here's the scope, Afe. I'm going below. Steer Professor to shore when we get down there."

"Must've been somebody imagining things when they opened fire earlier," I said.

"Yeah—kids—imaginations running wild."

"Swing to port, Professor. Take her forward easy, the current will carry us right to our old spot." I felt the bow nudge the bank. He revved the engines to push the boat up firmly, then shut them down and I heard him climb down the ladder to the well-deck.

"Friggin mosquitoes," followed a slap from Buddha. "I'm going to have a midnight snack and a nightcap—anybody else?"

I smelled steak grilling in the well-deck. A few days earlier we'd made a supply run. When we loaded the boat back at Dong Tam we'd liberated a sixty-pound case of frozen beef steaks. There was no refrigeration on the boat so like a pride of lions on a wildebeest carcass, we gorged ourselves before the meat rotted. It was beginning to have an off-odor so we rinsed each steak in the river then marinated it in Tabasco sauce.

"Hey Afe, you getting hungry up there?"

Why was Buddha in such a good mood? Oh well, enjoy it while it lasts. "Yeah, it sure smells good."

"Snipe, throw a tray together for him."

A few minutes later a red flashlight beam illuminated the hatch as Snipe came up the ladder from the well-deck. "Here you go; steak, canned crackers and a rum and coke."

"Thanks. This kind of service, I don't mind standing mid-watch," I joked as the drink burned down my throat.

I finished the meal and crawled between the turrets. Bending down to hide the glow, I flicked my lighter on to see my watch face—0300 hours—one hour to go. I held the starlight scope to my eye and made a 360 degree sweep, then sat down on the canopy. In ten days Dennis and I were scheduled to leave for R&R in Sydney. I looked forward to hot showers, clean sheets, sleep, and whatever adventure might be in store. I recalled places I'd visited on the *Rogers*, ports in the Orient. They were fun but I had no desire to return. I scanned the far bank once more then went down to wake Dennis.

"I never fell back to sleep," Dennis said. "Buddha's feet are so ripe you'd think that'd kill these damn mosquitoes."

"They're foul. Somebody should pitch those ratty-assed tennis shoes overboard—probably kill more fish than that shit they spray. Don't forget the troops in front of us. I've been watching the far bank." I handed Dennis the scope, went below and crawled into my rack. Brushing at the ever-present mosquitoes, I fell into a fitful sleep.

"Wake up Afe. You ain't on R&R yet. We're heading back to Dong Tam. Let's load the troops and get the fuck out of here." Peeking through a sleep-crusted eye lid, I watched Buddha pick at his ass and scratch as he blew on a mug of steaming coffee.

I rolled out of my rack, triced it to the bulkhead, then dug out a box of C- rations. Each meal was a surprise. That morning was a good morning; hot chocolate mix, strawberry jam, and white bread. I tossed a can of meat loaf—dog food we called it—into the catch-all box and rummaged for some fruit. Crow was finished with his can-stove and it was still burning so I borrowed it. I speared bread slices and toasted them over the open flame, then set a can of water on to warm up. Fifteen minutes later I was done eating, cleaned up, and ready for the day.

With troops loaded, tide high, but steering into the current, we made slow headway toward the big river. The droning engines mesmerized me as I squinted into the noon sun bouncing off the rolling brown wake of the boat ahead of me. Buddha was topside between the turrets dozing—I could hear him snoring. Professor and the gunners sat behind me visiting and Snipe was below deck with the troops. I fell asleep and ran full speed into the riverbank. Professor and the gunners were thrown forward into the cox'n flat, up against my legs. Buddha's helmet flew forward and clanged against the armor plate.

"What the fuck's going on? What are you doing in the trees, Afe? What the hell, did you fall asleep?" He demanded an answer, his red face against the slit at the back of my compartment.

The helm had caught me just below the ribs and knocked my wind out when I flew forward. The boat had hit the bank at an angle and bounced back into the river; broken branches hung from the top of the bow ramp. In the well-deck, the troops were laughing. Snipe climbed the ladder, stuck his head through the hatch near my feet and asked what happened.

"Is everything okay below?"

"Yeah, most of the troops were lying down. The ones that weren't were thrown down. I was in the engine compartment and fell against a hot manifold," Snipe said, holding his arm to show me a long red welt.

"Sorry." I said. "Yeah, I dozed off," I yelled up to Buddha. "How about somebody else driving for a while—I need sleep."

"You're the friggin cox'n. You stay at that helm."

"I don't want to hear a damn word if I fall asleep again. Your snoring was the only thing keeping me awake, and after five hours that quit working."

"Quit your whining and stay away from the banks," Buddha said, pulling his helmet over his ears, leaning back in the shade between the turrets. Fifteen minutes later he was snoring again.

"I'll drive for a while, Afe," said Dennis. I took my flak jacket off, folded it into a pillow and curled up on the warm deck.

The radio's sudden blare jerked me awake and I jumped to the helm. "Hold fire, there's a village beyond the tree line." We were almost to the main river and the lead boat was taking sniper fire. The setting sun was behind the trees along the riverbank.

"They ought to spray this whole fucking delta," Buddha said. "Get rid of those gook hiding places. You staying awake, Afe?"

"Yeah, I'm doing just friggin grand. Did you have a nice nap?"

"Quit your crying. You want to be paid boatswain's mate second class wages, you can earn them."

"Just like you, huh?" So that's what was bugging him again.

"Let it rest, Afe," Professor said in a low voice. "You won't accomplish anything."

"I know. It just gets old—he sleeps all day, keeps us awake half the night. We stand night-watches yet he expects us to function twenty-four hours a day while he really doesn't do shit—he knows it and doesn't care."

Moonlight danced on the wake ahead of me as the column turned into the Mekong. The mother ships—our destination—rose like rock formations in the still night. After off-loading troops on the *Benewah's* pontoon, we tied up.

The next morning Buddha returned from a boat captain's meeting. "Listen up everybody. They gave us a two day break to get ready for a big operation. We'll go into Dong Tam this morning. Snipe, get that friggin packing repaired. Afe, re-stock our supplies—you know what we need. Stonewall, I want new barrels on all the guns. Take Crow and Dennis up with you to get them. Do the .30 calibers in the well-deck, too. Afe, get the boat squared away then you all can go to the Club—one of my old diving buddies is here. I'm going to surprise him. Tomorrow we go out on BID patrol." With that, Buddha was gone for the day.

"Let's go up to the mess hall and get some decent break-fast," I said. "Then we'll come back, clean this thing up, and get the list done."

Buddha returned about noon, riding a loaded truck. "Afe, the *Benewah* needs these supplies. My buddy went up to Saigon for a week—there's no reason to stay in this dust bowl tonight—we'll just tie up out there once we're off-loaded." I glanced at Buddha—he winked and said, "Come on—let's hurry—this stuff is perishable."

We formed a working party and the driver passed boxes to us on the tailgate and we transferred them into the well-deck. From my cox'n flat, while backing into the boat basin, I heard Buddha laughing. "Another box of steaks. Crow, you go onto the *Benewah* and get ice. While you're at it, hit the mess deck and nab some Tabasco sauce—I noticed they left bottles on the tables. We'll eat good for the next week. Snipe, pass me my bottle—sun's over the yardarm somewhere."

I glanced west, upriver, as we approached the *Benewah*, and spotted three clumps of vegetation drifting our way. I recalled the warnings of hidden mines as I ploughed through one—those instructors had cried wolf.

Very early, before sun broke the horizon, Buddha returned to the boat from an all-night card game and told us to get under way to relieve the boat on BID patrol. He was in a jolly mood. "I won five big ones last night—I'm on a roll."

The sun crept up out of the river as the night breeze died. Soon after we pulled away from *Benewah*, the smell of grilling steaks drifted to the cox'n flat. Brown waves chopped against the bow, making dull thuds as I pushed through them. I swung west near the south riverbank and watched a man mount the seat on his irrigation pump. It was built into the bank and reminded me of a water-wheel on a grist mill. Small cupped paddles attached to a chain lifted water up about five feet and spilled over the dike into the rice paddy.

Professor climbed into the cox'n flat to take the helm and I went below for a break. Buddha was already snoring so I quietly collected my stove, steak, and a box of C-rations and joined the rest of the crew on the fantail. By mid morning the coolness of the night was gone and the armor plating clicked as it expanded. The crew rotated through their turns at the helm. Mid-afternoon I came into the cox'n flat and found Professor driving.

"Look at that little guy pedaling, I wonder how many miles a week he goes?" I joked. He moved slowly, lifting water from the river—flooding several acres—a quart at a time. "You have to give him credit. I don't know anybody back home with that kind of patience."

"Remember that farmer up north?" Professor said. "How I told you these people don't want us here? They've been living with the seasons for thousands of years—those straight canals we see? The Funan dynasty started digging them about the time Christ was born. They were completed by the Angkor Kingdom around 1100 AD—almost four hundred years before Columbus sailed to America."

I recalled my last two months in school—the beginning of eleventh grade—how the history teacher rambled on about Chinese dynasties that lasted for thousands of years. How I'd been so bored that I walked out of school and never looked back. I watched the peasants now. They reminded me a little bit of the Indians back home who still hunted and fished for a living. The old ones still spoke Ojibwa. On Sunday mornings there was a radio church service in the old language. But the younger ones, the ones my little brother played baseball with, they all spoke English. We passed near the man pedaling his water-wheel and I stared at him.

"I wonder what he's thinking," I said to Professor. "Look at him. We're right in front of him and it's as though we're invisible.

"See that flattened swath of rice in his paddy?" The day before, we'd watched a hovercraft speed across the rice paddy, Vietnamese workers fleeing toward dikes as the loud machine swept past. "He's probably wondering how he's going to feed his family because of the damaged crop. Remember that farmer up north that kept working even when there was shit going on around him? They've lived with war for so long in this country that we're just another obstacle—like bad weather—that they have to deal with. Like I said, their lives cycle with the seasons. Down here their survival is dependent on the Mekong and they've developed livelihoods in harmony with the river—not invading armies."

The sun settled upriver, and in the dusk, on one of our countless circles, I noticed the man was gone. Where did he go at night? He never stopped to eat. The contracting armor clicked in the cool evening. Did he ever get a day off? It had to be very boring—spending days just sitting—pedaling to nowhere, watching life float by. I tossed a concussion grenade into the river. Our instructors had said they couldn't be trusted.

"The VC own the nights," they'd said.

19

U Minh Forest

2 August 1968

Our riverine assault boat division made a six hour run west on the Mekong River through monsoon drizzle carrying a full platoon of army troops on each Tango boat. We were moving deep into the U Minh Forest, located near the southwestern tip of South Vietnam. There had been no outsiders since the French departure in 1954. The American war had missed these people—predominantly farmers—in this remote area until now. Buddha had returned from a boat captain's meeting and told us that the VC had training camps, hospitals, and POW camps in the vast jungle swamp. He said they even came there on R&R.

At dusk our boat column received sniper fire when we turned south into a smaller river and passed through the large town of Can Tho. We were ordered not to return fire; speed up, get past. It was a common tactic of the VC to fire on us from populated areas—if we returned fire and wounded villagers, it provided them propaganda.

I drove into the night; the boat quieted—the well-deck packed with sleeping troops, our gunners lying on the deck between their turrets behind me in the cox'n flat, Buddha topside between the turrets trying to stay awake. Professor sat in the corner behind me dozing. I followed the colored lights mounted above the boat ahead of me as we snaked slowly south on narrow dark rivers. Sometime during the night fog set in low, about a foot above the water.

In the early morning hours I must have hallucinated. Mixed diesel fumes and fog hugged the river, hung in the still air, and drifted me back to the train I'd ridden through the Cascade Mountains of Washington when I was sixteen. It had been dawn as the locomotives crawled toward the summit tunnel and diesel fumes hovered, sucked into the open-doored boxcar. The rising sun had illuminated the white peaks of the mountains across the valley. Looking down at the fog bed resting in the valley, I seemed in another world— above the clouds.

"Afe, back down, back down," Buddha yelled. I grabbed the throttles, threw them into reverse, and revved the engines. I barely missed the boat in front of me—somehow I'd crept up on him when my mind had drifted. "You been driving all night—why the hell didn't you wake somebody up to take over?"

Troops were stirring in the well-deck. The smell of heating C-rations wafted up from below through the hatch near my feet. A sergeant climbed the ladder, stuck his head through the hatch. "They just called on my radio—we're about half an hour from our insertion point."

"Did you hear that, Buddha?" Professor called up from behind me.

"Yeah, after they're dropped we'll move south to wait for them—we can eat then. Everybody get your flak jackets and brain buckets on and get in position."

"I'll be glad when this operation is over," the sergeant said, slapping a mosquito. "We didn't get no sleep last night. This is my second tour in the Delta and I never seen mosquitoes this bad."

Our radio came to life with last minute instructions and the sergeant went below. I raised my armor shields while the gunners climbed into their turrets.

"Swing her in Afe. Drop the ramp."

I pulled up toward the shoulder-high grass on the river-bank and pushed water inland. I dropped the ramp and Snipe stuck his head up through the hatch and said the troops were stepping off into a foot of water. I watched them move toward a tree line on the far side of the paddy—at least they'd be on high ground when they reach it, I thought. From my cox'n flat I watched an officer, the sergeant, and the radio-man come together in the tall grass talking and pointing across the rice paddy. A moment later the officer picked up the radio handset and spoke into it.

The army had 105mm howitzers mounted on barges—towed by LCM-8s—for mobile artillery support. When operations stretched beyond the range of stationary artillery, these units accompanied our boats to support the troops. Upon reaching the area of operations, they were anchored securely to the riverbank and could instantly respond to fire mission requests. I knew they brought up the rear of the column because several times during the night I'd heard the radio checking on them, urging them to keep up. From around the river bend, about five hundred meters behind us, I heard a blast followed by an explosion thirty meters short of the tree line. The officer spoke into the handset again followed a moment later by another blast and explosion—this time on target. I could almost read his lips the third time—fire for effect—a moment later the tree line erupted as we watched from the safety of our boat. Five minutes later the artillery barrage stopped and the troops advanced.

"Crank her up, Afe. Let's move upriver," Buddha said, repeating the radioed orders.

I beached the boat at our troop pick-up location near a fisherman's hooch, shut the engines down and climbed topside. Buzzing flies, the sing-song chatter of children trying to get our attention, and the distant thud of artillery filled the morning air. The children seemed different—inquisitive but not begging.

"Afe, take Crow and Dennis with you. Check the area—search that hooch behind Papason—make sure there aren't any surprises."

I loaded a 12 gauge shotgun, filled my pockets with extra rounds, then strapped a .38 caliber revolver to my waist. Dennis and Crow took M16s and extra clips of ammo. We jumped off the boat onto the sandy riverbank.

An ancient Vietnamese man squatted in the sand, sun shining on his leathery face. Arms extended, elbows resting on knees, his hands hung limp, like bats in a cave. One eye closed, the other at half-mast, his wispy goatee was stained with betel nut juice. Flies crawled undisturbed as they explored his wrinkled face. He was barefoot, wore baggy black pants and a ragged shirt. Faded scars laced his bony hands. He remained motionless when I approached—made no hint of my existence. It was disconcerting. For a moment, anger flashed at his impertinence.

Back home, on the Indian reservation near our farm in northern Minnesota, there had been an Indian man who sat on the ground, cross-legged on a blanket and listened to the powwow drums—they said he was over one hundred years old. He couldn't hear anymore, never spoke, but loved the rhythm. When I was a child he fascinated me—his white-filmed eyes staring into the sky while his fingers tapped light cadence to the drums. "He feels music through the air," an elder told me. My older brothers and I had Mohawk haircuts that summer and played cowboys and Indians—they always made me the Indian.

"Is the old fuck dead?" Crow asked, waving his hand a few inches from the old Papason's face.

"Let him be. He's not going to hurt anybody. I'm going into the hooch. You guys keep an eye out back. Buddha can see the front if anything happens."

"I want to go in," said Crow. "Maybe I'll find a souvenir."

I looked at him and motioned with a wave of my gun barrel to move around to the back. The front yard was bare dirt—sugar sand and black delta silt. Flies rose sluggishly as I approached the little house.

It was a one-room hut—no door—constructed of vertical small posts, covered with bamboo-and-grass-thatch walls and roof, with a hard packed dirt floor. The dominant feature was an ornate brass bed frame. Ten scrawny chickens perched on the bare springs—each tied by the leg. The brass was green-hued and caked with generations of chicken manure. I watched a fresh-laid egg bounce from the hen's puckering butt, down through the springs, to the shit-crusted floor. They were small black chickens—like bantams—and reminded me a bit of snakes when their heads shot forward, snapping at flies. Manure ammonia blended with fish smell. Flies swarmed in protest at my invasion of their sanctuary. Near the hooch doorway, against the wall, a large dented copper pot simmered on a low charcoal brazier. I realized that was the source of the fish smell. I hooked the lid of the simmering pot with the shotgun muzzle and peeked. Fish heads and entrails rolled lazily in bubbling broth, flies hovering just beyond the heat halo.

"What the hell stinks in there?" Crow asked, sticking his head in the back door. "Fuck, how can you breathe?"

"Lunch cooking—are you hungry."

"I'm glad it's you in there, not me."

Near the brazier stood a long, low cabinet, doors askew

on broken hinges. Gallon jugs of *nuoc mam*, Vietnamese fish sauce, rested in a corner. On the floor near the brazier lay an assortment of vegetable greens and roots—stock to be added to the fish head broth, I assumed.

An oil lamp covered in spider webs and fly scat hung from a bare overhead roof brace in the dim windowless interior. In the far corner, a pile of bedding lay wadded on the floor.

Retreating from the hooch, I shouted to Buddha that the people were just farmers and fishermen—no sign of them supporting the Viet Cong. Crow, Dennis and I returned to the boat. Several young children, standoffish when we first arrived, now trailed us. They'd never seen Caucasians or Black men in their lives. We gave them C-rations, showed them how to open the cans and packets, and quickly gained their confidence. I glanced shoreward—the old papason hadn't moved.

We must have fascinated the children. Vietnamese have no body hair. One child rubbed my arm, pulled the hair on it then began rubbing my tattoo. When it wouldn't rub off he spit on it and rubbed harder. I laughed, pushed him away, rumpling his hair in a playful gesture. He frowned and jumped back and I realized I had committed a taboo. Vietnamese culture frowned on touching the top of another's head. Stonewall was surrounded by children. The boys, more bold, stroked his black skin, like petting a puppy. The little girls looked on in silence. I snapped a picture and several children darted from our boat back to the riverbank. I'd committed another taboo. In snapping the picture, I captured their spirit. On the main river, people were beyond such superstitions.

Late afternoon, out of boredom, Crow, Dennis, and I extended our search to the surrounding area. Along the sandy riverbank, fish nets hung drying in the sun—cleaned of debris, repaired, ready to set out again. A weathered sampan rested on the bank above the high tide mark. Mounted on the stern was a single cylinder outboard with a small propeller attached to the end of a long shaft. Flies swarmed above juices at the bottom of the boat.

Patrolling north, inland of the hooch, I spotted an abandoned French fort with six-foot-high dried mud walls. Corner guard towers had collapsed and aged timbers jutted skyward. Grass and trees flourished in the once-packed parade ground. I recalled a story Professor had told me of how—late in their war—the French government had abandoned troops in remote areas and I wondered at the tales of terror this fort could tell. Horror of being left behind; families back in France left to wonder about the fate of their loved ones.

We circled inland from the river and discovered a cemetery entrance guarded by a small shrine. Beneath a stone canopy were two statues—Buddha and the Virgin Mary. I thought again of how Professor said the Vietnamese were a blend of many cultures—Buddha, the ancestral god, Virgin Mary, the French god, left by missionaries a generation ago.

"Hey, a souvenir—that's what I've been looking for," Crow said, reaching into the shrine for the Buddha statue.

I looked at him and shrugged.

"I'm going back to the boat. Fucking gooks could pick us off here. We wouldn't have a chance."

"Go ahead. I'll be along," I replied. Dennis followed Crow back to the boat and I listened to the silence as the breeze rustled above me.

The cemetery was shaded by mangrove and nipa palm. Leaves whispered of agonies endured in an unfriendly environment; of torment inflicted by invaders. Professor had talked of different cultures trying to force their ways—Angkor, Mongolian, Chinese, French, Japanese, now Americans. The

Vietnamese endured, like the palms above me, battered and damaged in typhoons, yet surviving, sprouting new growth, new generations.

Like the elder sensing drum rhythms, I sensed Vietnamese ancestors watching me and thought again of the Indians at home. They had family plots at each homestead and what, I had thought as a child, were above-ground crypts for their dead. Here, even though I was unable to read the inscriptions, I studied headstones that afternoon in the shaded jungle cemetery—history embedded in the lichen-covered characters. No enemy here.

I returned to the riverbank and found another boat crew lounging in the shade of coconut trees. They had enticed the children into climbing trees, cutting the large nuts, and tossing them down. I was amazed how kids scampered up the trunks and danced around the crown like small monkeys. It was a happy afternoon as we lazed in the shade, hacking through thick husks to the coconuts, savoring the sweet juice and white meat, playing with the children. That evening the army troops bivouacked near the riverbank. Sarge came aboard and told us it had been a quiet day but he expected to see shit the next day. Before dawn, the troops boarded the boat and we moved south, deeper into the U Minh Forest.

20

POW and
Can Tho Ambush

10 August 1968

Drizzling clouds enshrouded dawn. Along the riverbank palm leaves shimmered limp and rice paddies lay abandoned. Enraged hands slapped vampire mosquitoes and blood trickled down the exposed skin of men who sat tensely in the well-deck this eighth morning of the operation.

Two hours later, steam rising on riverbanks, Buddha shouted down, "Swing to port Afe. Yell down to Snipe to get ready to drop the ramp."

I watched troops climb up over the steep bank—not high, more like a paddy dike; I could see beyond to where two tree lines came together in an L. Friendly rounds hissed over us and detonated in the tree line. The sergeant stood atop the bank and reached down with a helping hand to the heavily loaded troops. The last one out was a green replacement. He looked completely worn out. Sarge stretched, grasped his hand, and pulled him up. The kid's canteen snagged in a thicket and his helmet slipped off and rolled into the river. The sergeant released his hand, said something I couldn't hear, and the kid retrieved it. Again the sergeant grabbed his hand, this time jerking him up. They stood for an instant, silhouetted. The sergeant looked disgusted as he reached out, closed the kid's flak jacket and pushed pouches of M16 clips back, behind his shoulders. The clips of ammo had swung to the front when he had slipped. Then he pointed toward the platoon, now out into the paddy.

"Spread out," I heard him shout to the troops. "Come on kid, pick your feet up," he said over his shoulder as he rushed past the tired soldier to catch up with his platoon. From the safety of my cox'n flat I watched through slits in my one inch armor as the kid struggled through the muck-bottomed paddy. Artillery went silent and the tree line smoldered as the sergeant caught up with his troops.

That night we patrolled a narrow section of river. About midnight, drizzle started. The starlight scope was useless because rain fogged the lens. In the blackness the scope showed only fuzzy green static.

I sat alone topside, scrunched between the turrets, water dripping from my soggy hat, my mind conjuring horrors. With only five feet of water separating us from the riverbank, I imagined how easily Viet Cong swimmers could reach our boat, pull themselves on board, and throw grenades into the turrets and down into the well-deck—or they might overrun us and cut our throats after skinning us alive like instructors had warned during our training.

"Ease to starboard, Dennis. You're almost on the bank," I whispered down to the cox'n flat. Then I laughed, "Why am I whispering, they know we're here."

"Who does?" Dennis whispered up to me.

I wasn't the only one paranoid, I thought, as I pitched a concussion grenade off each side of the boat.

"Swing her around Dennis. I see Tango 9 just ahead."

The army troops were bivouacked several hundred meters inland from us. Flares illuminated their perimeter. Small arms fire was exchanged intermittently; deep reports of

AK47s and the swift replies of M16s muffled through the wet night.

Buddha had said that at dawn the troops would sweep toward us, hopefully trapping the VC between the river and the infantrymen. We were the anvil—the army, the hammer, with the Viet Cong caught between. Back on the farm my brothers and I could sneak through our woods at night and I wondered what was to stop the VC from doing the same— they knew this terrain.

"What the hell," I shouted, as a white specter sailed past, less than ten feet above us and flashed orange-red on the riverbank about twenty feet beyond the boat. I thought it was an ambush and instinctively threw grenades up on the riverbank even as I realized what had happened. A burned up illumination round had drifted earthward, the white parachute passing above our boat, flaring for an instant when it struck earth.

"What's going on?" Buddha shouted, scrambling up the ladder into the cox'n flat. "Are you sure that's all it was?"

"Yeah, when it flared up I glimpsed the parachute caught on a bush."

"Well, shit, I'm up now. Can't sleep with those friggin mosquitoes. You want me to sit topside for a while?"

"I won't argue—come on. Pass up a couple of cases of grenades," I said. "There's only about a half left. You can't see shit up here so I've been tossing quite a few." He passed them to me then crawled up through Crow's turret. I handed him the starlight scope then went below. The mosquitoes were horrid. I felt along the ledge behind my sweat-sour rack, found a bottle of repellent, and drenched myself, adding to the dampness. They buzzed into my nostrils and ears as I brushed in frustration, trying to sleep.

Back on the farm they'd been a nightly torment. We kept the windows open in our upstairs bedrooms to air out the baking heat of the day's sun. Rusted screens bulged out from generations of kids pushing heads against them. My little brother and I shared a bed, and in the darkness of the well-deck I smiled as I recalled a trick I loved to play on him he fell for. I'd release a massive, silent fart—best after a bean soup supper and blackstrap-covered white bread—then spit into the air. He'd whip the sheet up over his head, only to be gassed.

Early morning the army began its sweep. My armor was up, the gunners were in their turrets, and Buddha was top-side sheltered between the gun mounts, his M60 loaded and ready.

"Those hot shell casings fell on me last time you were shooting," Crow complained to Buddha.

"Stop crying and keep your eyes peeled."

About noon the army called. They had a prisoner and wanted us to transport him down to an army barge that had ARVN interpreters and a holding cell. They popped purple smoke as they neared the river. Professor was driving the boat and he eased up to the bank. Two troopers appeared, followed by two more holding a blindfolded man by the arms, his hands tied behind him. It was the first close-up, live enemy I'd seen—any of us had seen. The troops handed him up to Buddha and me and we each grabbed an arm and lifted him onto our boat. We tied him to the bar armor just below the cox'n flat.

"His buddies'll see him there, "Buddha said. "If they want to shoot at us, they'll drop him first."

I recalled the sense of helplessness I'd felt during our training when I was a blindfolded POW. Did this guy feel terror? Being passed through the air, bare feet skidding along our steel catwalk, body tied, trussed up against abrasive iron bars, engines rumbling beneath him. He was tall for a Vietnamese—looked well-fed. He wasn't wearing the black pajama Viet Cong uniform, but a blue silk shirt with khaki pants. I was surprised how small he was. The top of his head was below Buddha's shoulder and as Crow snapped a picture I couldn't help but think the guy looked harmless.

Professor pulled into shore alongside the holding barge and Buddha and I lifted the prisoner from our boat across to it. An army trooper grabbed his foot when we swung him out and for a moment the prisoner was stretched between our boat and the barge.

"Let him go," the trooper said. Buddha and I released the prisoner's shoulders and he swung head-down against the side of the barge. The soldier pulled the VC suspect up and laughed as blood trickled down the prisoner's forehead into the dirty rag tied over his eyes. "That might soften the little shit up."

We jumped across and followed them to the shade of a canopy on the barge. He tied the prisoner to a post against the front wall of the holding pen. "You," the trooper pointed at Buddha. "Put your face close to this guy—you are all I want him to see when I pull the blindfold off."

Buddha stepped up to the prisoner, bent forward, his face two feet from the blindfold.

"Closer," the man said. Buddha leaned forward and the prisoner's blindfold was ripped off. The Vietnamese man's eyes opened wide and he began chattering rapidly. "Slow down, slow down, what the hell's he saying?"

Five South Vietnamese Army soldiers loafing nearby burst into laughter. One stepped forward. "He thought he was face to face with the Buddha."

Professor called from our boat just then. He'd received a radio message ordering us to get back on station. I heard a sharp crack and looked back as the South Vietnamese interrogator slapped the prisoner a second time. He glared defiantly, his head twisted to the side as the ARVN soldier secured a rope around his neck. Blood dripped from his nose onto his blue silk shirt.

The U Minh Forest operation was over. Huge caches of enemy food, weapons, ammunition, medical supplies, and clothing had been destroyed. Everybody was exhausted. Miraculously, the army had taken no casualties and our boats remained unharmed.

"We can expect some shit today. They know we're down here—there's only one way out—and they've had ten days to get ready. Crow, Dennis, make sure you have plenty of Honeywell rounds belted. They don't want you firing the .50 calibers because of all the civilian gooks down here. Afe, keep your armor flaps up today," Buddha said, from where he sat between the gun turrets. "Tell Snipe to stick his head up here."

I kneeled down by the hatch leading to the well-deck and called out, "Hey Snipe, Buddha wants you."

"What does he want?"

"Stick your head up here and ask him."

The engineman came over to the ladder, climbed three rungs toward the cox'n flat, stuck his head through the deck hatch. "What do you want?"

"Those boys are caked with mud. Last time we made a long run they laid in my rack and got it all full of shit—tell them to stay the fuck out of it."

"Yeah, mine too," I said.

"I told them not to—they don't listen to me."

"What the fuck good are you?" Buddha mumbled. Snipe took that as a dismissal and disappeared below.

Early morning sun warmed us as the troops boarded. I raised the ramp, swung into column, and we began the run north. It had taken all night to travel down here and this morning I was driving into flood current, which slowed our progress.

"There's where the flare landed the other night that scared the hell out of me," I told Professor, pointing to the charred spot on the riverbank. "I wonder where the little parachute disappeared to."

"I'm just glad to get away from the mosquitoes," he replied, looking out the slit as he scratched the bite scabs on his arms. "You want coffee?" He kept a canteen of water, a C-ration stove, and a supply of coffee packets tucked away in the cox'n flat. I nodded yes and he kneeled to make it.

"Remember the day we came aboard?" I said. "The coffee spilled across my gauges and Buddha bitched about it to the old boat captain—said the cox'n shouldn't be drinking coffee and driving? We sure had a thing or two to learn."

The boat settled down for the long run back to the main river—crew at battle stations, army troops in the well-deck, searching for comfortable positions. Usually they hated being on the open river, away from solid ground. From the comments filtering up through the hatch they sounded happy now.

"....feel like I have web fucking feet."

"...two pints low thanks to the friggin leaches and mosquitoes."

"...quit your crying ladies—you get an extra sixty-five a month for the inconvenience."

I was mid-column when we were ambushed at a bend in the river. In the first moments, boats often returned fire and shot across the curve—across the flat terrain, hitting boats on the other side. Eyes didn't penetrate jungle but iron did.

"Use your Honeywells—both of you. Get both sides of the river." I stole a glance up behind me at Buddha. He was scrunched down between the turrets and it always amazed me how that much bulk could squeeze into such a small space.

Ambushes were instant chaos—the first millisecond of panic as adrenaline spiked, followed by return fire, the cacophony of incoming and outgoing heavy weapons, rounds ricocheting off armor. Driving the boat was a maddening job. Instinct screamed for me to shoot back. Instead, I had to concentrate helplessly on the internal voice of training that demanded, "Hold position. Don't broach. Don't bunch up. Maintain distance." The boat in front of me slowed. Through the smoke I could see he was stopped because of a backup ahead of him. I threw our engines into neutral.

"What the fuck you stopping for, Afe?" Buddha yelled down to me. I glanced back as rounds slammed against my armor plate. He couldn't see the back-up because he had to keep his head down.

"They're backed up ahead of me," I screamed. All fire had been coming from the west bank. Rounds slammed against my starboard armor. I peeked through the slits and saw foliage move and smoke rising from the muzzle of a machine gun. I was surprised to glimpse two enemy helmets. It was very unusual to see our tormentors.

"Your .50 caliber, Dennis. Use your .50. See them over there," I shouted.

Dennis opened up and I watched trees and earth and foliage disintegrate. The bunker was silenced. When I looked out my front slit, I saw the boat ahead of me move forward. The ambush was over as suddenly as it had started. We listened to radio calls for damage and casualty reports. The boats had taken several hits but no casualties. Two minutes of insanity left us on edge, adrenaline rushing, everybody shouting, laughing, re-telling what everybody knew. Not a word was said about using the .50 caliber machine guns we had been forbidden to fire.

About 1400 hours we passed out of the narrow river and into a wider one—about two hundred meters across. I glanced back as I made the turn and saw the army artillery barges bringing up the rear of the column. We moved into a straight stretch; troops climbed out of the well-deck and removed boots and socks. They rolled up trousers and sunned legs and feet. I put my armor flaps down and watched the men on the catwalks outside the well-deck. Their skin was chalky and spotted with gray sores—wrinkled—like from being in a bathtub too long. Ulcerated blisters drained from infected leach bites. The decaying flesh smell wafted into my cox'n flat.

We were cruising full speed—about six knots—when mortar rounds bracketed the lead boat. We maintained column cruising north, not responding. Army troops shouted obscenities and flipped a finger at the invisible enemy. Suddenly, rumbling like a fast-moving freight train, a rocket thundered past, just above my canopy. I didn't see it but thought I smelled the faint odor of burned propellant. Troops scurried for cover as several boats were fired upon. The barge-mounted 105mm howitzers roared and I saw explosions beyond the tree line bordering the river. I couldn't see the barges, but Buddha stood up and looked behind us as the firing increased.

"All four barges are shooting." he shouted, "Eight guns—fuck, the barges go sideways each time they fire a salvo. There's a spotter plane directing them—that's how they know where the little shits are hiding."

I looked over and saw the Cessna—nicknamed Bird Dog—just as he fired a set of rockets. The little plane jerked backward in the air when the rockets left their pods. I heard chatter on the army radio, ordering the barges to cease fire. No more mortar rounds or rockets came our way. No time to go ashore for a body count, our goal was to reach the Mekong River before darkness. By late afternoon the river continued to widen, and with it, our sense of security.

"Professor, tell Snipe to send up a box of C-rats. The rest of you can eat now, too. I think we can relax," Buddha said.

The gunners slipped out of their turrets, sat down in the area below them and ate. I dropped my armor flaps again and felt my stomach growl when I smelled the simmering food.

"Take a break Afe. Grab something to eat," Dennis said, standing at my elbow, holding his dessert—a mug of hot chocolate and a can of pound cake.

I ate a lunch of spaghetti and meatballs—flavor enhanced with Tabasco sauce—and pecan cake washed down with steaming coffee. After a cigarette, I folded my flak jacket into a pillow and lay on the steel deck below Crow's gun mount and watched fluffy clouds through the open top of his turret. Dennis woke me with a light kick on my bare foot.

"Get up, Afe. There's lights ahead. Buddha wants us in our turrets." I jerked awake. The breeze had cooled and it was dark. I stood beside him for a few minutes while my night vision adjusted. Colored masthead lights of the boats ahead of us came into focus. Beyond them, Vietnamese cooking fires twinkled on the riverbanks.

Our boat was fourth in column as we approached Can Tho—we anticipated sniper fire again. Sewage, wood smoke, decaying vegetation, and fish smell hung low on the water in the moist evening air as we steamed toward the town.

"Hey Buddha," I shouted up. "Don't you find it strange—all the lights and boats but nobody moving on shore?" Beached sampans and junks looked like a ghost fleet bobbing in the waves of our wake. Enemy rockets, mortars, and automatic weapon tracer rounds pierced the darkness.

"Hold fire, hold fire," the radio blared. "Speed up—I say again—do not return fire."

A boat behind us was hit. He returned fire. In an instant, all boats were firing from their port side. Smoke filled my cox'n flat and blended with the smells of the river. I focused on the boat's identification lights ahead of me. Our starboard guns opened up, replying to the enemy fire from the west bank. A petroleum tank on shore exploded. I caught wisps of radio chatter demanding all boats to cease fire.

Buddha was screaming down into the turrets. "Cease fire—God-fucking-damn-it, I said stop shooting." Suddenly the boat ahead of me swerved to port. "Stay in column Afe, stay in column, hold your course."

A sampan, night fishing, was directly in front of me. Again Buddha shouted, "Stay in column, stay in column, run him down if he doesn't *di di*."

The Viet Cong were suicidal in their dedication. They were known to lob grenades from their sampans onto our patrol boats. As our blunt high bow approached the sampan, it disappeared from my view. I braced for impact even as I knew the fragile ten-foot wooden boat was no obstruction for the sixty-six ton monster I was driving. Over the months I'd ploughed through clumps of vegetation bigger and heavier than he was.

"Watch him, watch him—hold your course," Buddha shouted.

It was then I glimpsed the sampan. In the suddenness of the shooting I had forgotten to put my armor up so I had a full view of the firefight. It was exhilarating—the green tracers crossing the river. I felt safe inside my dark cox'n flat watching the madness. Our blunt bow created a swell as it ploughed through the water and had shunted the sampan aside. It was obvious the man and boy were only peasants out night-fishing.

In the glow created by burning fuel, waterfront structures, and firing weapons, I stared at the terror-filled faces shining in the darkness. The look of helplessness—the awareness that they had no control of their destiny was evident. It was as if they'd been caught in a time warp. A 17th century setting for the fishermen in their fragile sampan, run afoul 20th century steel and firepower. For an instant I felt our eyes lock and I thought of the shrine honoring the different gods back in that swampy cemetery and wondered which deity these fishermen called upon. As they slid astern, I recalled how they'd looked up at our boat. I'd seen them, but knew they couldn't see me.

Out of the kill zone, our guns fell silent but the battle continued as the tail of the column passed through the town. I turned east on to the Mekong River and watched the flash of the barge-mounted artillery fire into Can Tho. Later, they said it was beehive rounds—rounds filled with thousands of little darts.

"Crow, Dennis, why didn't you stop shooting when I told you to?"

"I didn't hear you. Before, you always said to open up if the other boats did," Crow told him.

"That's bullshit—I know you heard me. Why'd you start shooting Dennis?

"I saw where those green tracers were coming from— that was the only place I shot."

I heard Buddha stand up and knew he was looking down into Stonewall's 20mm turret. "Why didn't you start shooting when everybody else did?"

"I saw kids running around by those sampans pulled up on the riverbank—I ain't shooting at kids."

"What a fucked up deal—how do you know those "kids" weren't VC?" Buddha said. I heard him climb over the turret and step to the side of my cox'n flat. "Afe, come topside for a while. I need a break—I been wedged in that little hole all day."

In the well-deck, I listened to Buddha and Sarge while I warmed my coffee water.

"Those little fuckers got more than they bargained for

back there," Buddha said.

"One of the artillery barges reported a rocket—wounded two men—that's why they opened up with beehive rounds."

"I hear they rip a new asshole on whatever they hit."

"You don't want to see what they do," Sarge said.

"I'm going to sack out for a while. Do you boys need anything?" Buddha said to the troops in the dark well-deck.

"How about a shot of Jack Daniels?"

"How about a medium rare rib-eye steak with all the trimmings?" a voice drawled.

"How about a real rare piece of meat laid out without all the trimmings?" another voice mocked to laughter.

"Sorry. Fresh out. How about some C-rations—made fresh in '56," Buddha told them, as he unlashed his rack and let it flop down.

I went topside and crawled between the gun mounts above and behind the cox'n flat and set out my coffee, crackers, and cheese spread on the canopy in front of me. Professor, Crow, and Stonewall were sleeping on the deck between their gun mounts. Dennis was driving, and Buddha and Snipe were in their racks in the well-deck. I'd slept most of the afternoon and was wide awake. The firefight and that sampan kept playing over in my mind. Stars danced on the phosphorescent wake of the boat ahead of us. Professor relieved Dennis. The low hypnotic hum of diesel engines, the gentle breeze created by the boat's motion, and no mosquitoes as we moved along lulled me. Darkness was my friend—nobody could see me.

I huddled in the cloak of safeness and drifted back to childhood—to a bright spring day. Randy was a toddler and I was about seven and we were playing in the woods. Partridge were drumming late that year and we lay behind a log peeking under it, watching one strut, then fan its tail. Randy got bored and jumped up and ran toward it yelling and laughing as it burst into the air. Then we went down to the swamp and chased bullfrogs and cupped pollywogs in our hands, watching as they swam in circles. Wild strawberries were ripening on the south side of pasture hills and after playing in the swamp, we wandered over and sat among them stuffing our mouths. I laughed at Randy because he looked like a clown with the big red strawberry juice stain covering his chin, cheeks, and nose. Rosy, an old cow, came up behind us, nuzzling our heads in curiosity.

A cloud drifted over—darkening the day. I jerked awake. The engines had changed pitch. I climbed down to the fantail, opened the engine compartment hatch, and shined my flashlight down. The compartment was flooded and water was near the air intakes. The boat's stern was almost submerged.

"We're sinking," I shouted. "Swing to starboard, run up on the bank." I could see the shoreline in the full moon. The chance of VC being there was slim, I thought. "Professor, get on the radio, tell them we're beaching before the engines get flooded. We need the portable pump, too." I could hear Professor on the radio when Buddha climbed up beside me.

"What the fuck's going on, Afe?"

"I was sitting here when the engines changed pitch. I stuck the flashlight down and saw they were flooded."

"Did you check them every hour like you're supposed to?"

"Yeah, matter of fact I checked about twenty minutes ago—I had to pee so I looked in when I went back."

"That sounds like bullshit. It couldn't flood that fast."

"One of those mortar rounds back in Can Tho exploded near the stern. I felt the concussion on the rudder. Maybe it knocked the packing loose." I knew he'd accept that story, and it would grow as he retold it in smoky well-decks over card games and whiskey.

"Yeah, that could be. Professor, what's going on—is the pump coming?"

"Two boats are staying with us. The rest of the column is continuing on. One of the boats has the pump."

"Stonewall, get on the helm. You won't be able to fire forward anyway. Crow, Dennis, get on your .50 calibers. Don't shoot unless I tell you. I'm going to talk to Sarge—probably put them ashore at least until the engineroom is pumped out." Then Buddha turned to me and said, "Scared shit out of me—I heard you yelling. I jumped out of my rack into about a foot of water. The bank's coming up. Get up front and guide Stonewall in—at least the moon's out so we can see."

"Dennis, hand me up a shotgun," I said, talking down into his dark turret. I heard him slip down out of his turret, move into the cox'n flat and open the small-arms locker. A few moments later he was back and handed me the gun and two handfuls of shells.

"It's loaded with one in the chamber."

I moved up the catwalk to the bow and held onto the raised ramp with one hand, gun in the other. From what I could see, the riverbank was low and grass-covered without trees or brush—probably mucky, I thought. The boat slid onto the bank and I jumped ashore, surprised to find solid footing. "Buddha," I called. "Drop the ramp. There's just grass and sand out here."

I heard Snipe release the ramp safety latch. A few moments later I watched it cast a shadow coming down. A Tango boat pulled up on each side of us.

"What the hell's going on, Buddha?" I recognized the boat captain's voice from Tango 4.

"Friggin mortar round detonated behind our stern. Must've knocked our packing loose. I saw them fire it. Thought for sure we'd get hit. I yelled to Afe to swerve. It missed us by about six inches."

I smiled in the darkness—another war story born.

"Here's the pump. Where do you want it?" said the engineman from the other Tango boat.

"Hey, Snipe," I yelled as the troops passed me, stepping ashore from the downed ramp. "Where do you want the pump?"

"Take it back to the fantail. The water'll drain aft from the well-deck as it's siphoned out."

I handed Buddha the shotgun and helped wrestle the pump up onto our catwalk. The engineman unwound the suction hose, dropped it into the engine compartment through the hatch, and started the motor. The instant it was primed, water shot over our stern back into the river. Below, I watched Snipe wade to the rear of the compartment through oil-covered water and lean down, feeling the area where the propeller shafts passed through the hull.

"Water's gushing in around the port shaft. I'll have to pack rags in just to stop it or we'll never get drained."

Buddha had come back to the fantail unnoticed and said, "You'll have to stay back there—keep an eye on things. I don't want to sink in the middle of the river."

With screwdriver in one hand and rag in the other, Snipe leaned into the armpit-deep slurry and felt around the flooding shaft, forcing material into the ruptured seam. As he strained forward, his boil-covered bare back oozed pink puss in my red-lensed flashlight beam.

"Okay, I think I've got it," he said straightening up, leaning back to stretch his cramped muscles as the water receded. I heard Buddha tell the sergeant to get his men back on board. The Tango boats nestled near each side of us, hooked on and we were pulled back into the river. Lines were snugged up and we proceeded east toward Dong Tam as dawn crept up over the horizon.

I spotted the *Benewah* between me and the blinding red glare of the new sun. I was in my cox'n flat and heard the sergeant rouse his troops.

"Come on boys, get up. There's hot chow and fresh coffee half an hour ahead."

We were the last boats to arrive. As we approached, one of our towboats cast off allowing the other to push us against the pontoon where a sailor grabbed the forward mooring line. Our tow boat kicked his starboard engine into reverse and slowly eased our stern in. Troops emerged from our well-deck onto the pontoon where another sailor sprayed them with a high-pressure fire hose—removing the worst of the encrusted mud before they went aboard ship.

After breakfast Buddha climbed onto the boat. "Mail call. Jesus Christ, are you starting a library? Here's another pack of books," he complained, tossing a box to Professor. Then he called out names for the handful of letters. "Snipe, Afe, Snipe, Snipe, Crow, Stonewall, Snipe, Professor. That's it. I guess you and me are orphans again Dennis."

Dennis shrugged, "Mail don't mean shit."

Snipe sat on his rack with a wide grin as he opened a thick manila envelope and pulled out several pictures. "She can roll over—look," he said passing me a picture. "She's three months old and can already roll over."

Buddha snorted. "Wait until she's sixteen and rolls over—you won't be so happy then."

Snipe looked at him, then clipped the picture to the bulkhead at the back of his rack. It looked like a refrigerator door with dozens of pictures of Nancy and the baby pinned up. Buddha's snide remarks no longer bothered him.

Professor shook his head as he read a letter. "Now Johnson has this guy Henry Kissinger working on the Paris Peace Talks. I studied a book he wrote while I was in college. I'll guarantee you, if he's involved this war will go on for years."

"You don't know what the fuck you're talking about," Buddha said. "We're killing these little turds faster than they can reproduce. Eventually Uncle Ho will run out of recruits."

"You just don't get it. They fought the French for eighty years. What makes you think they'll stop fighting us?"

Buddha shrugged, "Like I said, they'll run out of gooks."

We cleaned from bow to stern then got towed to the *Askari* where a huge crane lifted the boat from the river and set it on skids. The bilge pump, propeller shafts, bearings, and packing were replaced. Late afternoon, back in the water, we pulled into Dong Tam, topped off our fuel, and replenished supplies. Early evening we went back out to the *Benewah* and tied up for the night.

After the U Minh Forest operation, we had several days of down time. It was the middle of the Northeast Monsoon Season—periods of heavy rain, drizzle, incredibly hot days, and mosquito-filled nights. We took our turn patrolling around our mother ships, carrying supplies, restocking our supplies. Most days and nights found us tied to the pontoon along side the *Benewah* with the rest of the boat division.

A pet monkey lived on the boat tied next to us. He'd silently creep onto other boats and snatch food, cigarettes, lighters—any small object grabbing his fancy. He loved to eat and had gotten quite plump. "Hi, Ti Ti," I said, as he perched on our well-deck bulkhead just below the canopy. "You're getting fat—almost ready to eat."

"That's not funny," the owner said, from the boat next door. "Friggin ARVNs tried to buy him—when I wouldn't sell, they tried to steal him."

I coaxed the little monkey into our well-deck. He sat on the ledge for a moment scratching himself, chattering, then jumped down, grabbed the crackers I'd thrown, left a little turd, and jumped back to the other boat. Dennis, Stonewall, and I stood laughing. He was fun to play with but his shit stunk.

We'd missed beer call on the pontoon that afternoon but didn't really care. Tied alongside *Benewah*, nobody needed to stand watch, so we relaxed and had a few drinks from our own stash. Evening drifted along. Radios and cassettes blared music across the dark water as sailors moved from boat to boat, visiting.

About midnight Buddha climbed aboard with four friends and turned on the overhead lights in the crew living space. "What the fuck you boys sleeping for? It's Saturday night. Wake up. Afe, I got some ice, get my bottle. Professor, I was telling Mays what you said the other day about that kraut Kissinger—what was it again? It sounds like he agrees with you. Afe, grab that Dr. Pepper."

I was surprised to find the wind had kicked up and was blowing rain sideway into the well-deck, dripping off the canopy. Professor rolled over in his rack and rubbed his eyes. "Forget it. You'll argue anyway."

"Try me," Mays said. "This is my third tour and I don't see things getting any better."

"Okay. Can I get some of that pop and ice?"

"Hell yes," Buddha said. "You want a little flavoring?" he added, waving the bottle. Professor nodded yes, and Buddha poured, mixing it half and half.

"Well," Professor began. "First of all, Kissinger is Jewish, not German." And the conversation progressed along this line.

"Yeah, whatever the fuck," Buddha grunted. "Get on with the story."

"I had to do a paper for a political science class my senior year. A friend who was an intern in the U.S. Senate had met Henry Kissinger and told me to watch him. I went to my college library and looked him up and discovered that he had written a book in 1957 titled *Nuclear Weapons and Foreign Policy*. In the book he argued against all-out nuclear war to battle communism because a nuclear holocaust would destroy U.S. industry. Instead, he argued in favor of limited conventional war. A war to be fought in third world countries. A war in which the U.S. industrial base could grind an opponent to bankruptcy through attrition—a war like Vietnam. Kissinger has been preaching his sermon for so long that he got Johnson's ear—now I hear he's sucking up to Nixon behind Johnson's back."

"That's bullshit," Buddha said. "If we don't stop these friggin commies here they'll end up in Australia."

"They call that the Domino Theory. But let me finish. Scholars and government policymakers think Kissinger is the authority on alternatives to a direct confrontation with the USSR and Khrushchev."

"Jesus Christ, Professor. You sound like a professor—I guess I named you right. Speak English to us common folks. Have another drink."

"In 1962 Kennedy pulled Kissinger in as a consultant. That's where the whole concept of Special Forces like the Green Berets started from—how to fight in these backward third world countries. Truth be known, it was probably his recommendation that created the Bay of Pigs fiasco. He was able to construct the model on which to test his theory—the Vietnam conflict."

"This is a war—not a fucking conflict," Buddha snarled.

"Kissinger's school of thought became doctrine for the Kennedy and Johnson Administrations. And if Nixon becomes president, Kissinger will continue. He can never admit he's wrong—so if he gets involved in the Paris Peace Talks he'll drag them along for years just to test his theory."

Professor finished as though Buddha hadn't spoken.

"That's academic bullshit. Nobody has the power to manipulate government," Buddha said, finger swirling his drink. "Besides, people wouldn't let politicians pull that kind of shit."

The lights began to dim. Dennis went up to the cox'n flat and started the engines. Above the drone of the diesels, in the pulsating glow of the brightening lights, Professor said, "What do you think is happening right now? When Johnson won the last election it was with the promise of getting out of Vietnam, but his pride got in the way. He doesn't want to be the first U.S. President to lose a war. And Kissinger—Kissinger's a product of Harvard. An academic—a political scientist. With his East European background and intellectual mindset he's totally insulated from the American working class. He has no more empathy for you and me than he does for the North Vietnamese."

"Remember what our instructor said about empathy and the Vietnamese," Buddha piped in again. "That a bullet was the best cure for empathy. Just give me my M60 and some gooks. I'll give them empathy."

"I don't know," Mays said, shaking his head. "Things have gone downhill since '64, the first year I spent over here. I went home to L.A. after the riot in my old neighborhood in '65 and saw how the government didn't do shit to fix things. Then it happened in Detroit in '67 and DC after King was murdered. All The Man did is send in troops. I'm beginning to wonder if we shouldn't just be taking care of business at home."

"Amen to that," Stonewall said from his bunk.

Crow sat up listening. "You'll see shit straighten up fast when George Wallace gets elected."

"That redneck motherfucker'll never see the White House," Mays said. "It's people like him and you that cause the problem."

Crow smirked.

Mays left.

Rain poured—canopy-vibrating sheets of water sloshed onto the catwalk and splashed into the well-deck.

21

Hai Muoi Tam Canal

18 August 1968

Sunday dawned drizzly with wet earth smell hugging the river. Like the rank odor of a wet dog, the musty-mold smell of monsoon season saturated the well-deck. A crewman from another boat was discovered drowned—wedged between two boats like an old tire. Probably got up to pee over the stern, slipped and lost his balance. They wrapped him in a poncho and a motor-launch came out from Dong Tam and took him to the morgue. During the night, Army Intelligence received information about a battalion of Viet Cong north of Cai Be, a large town just northwest of us.

"Afe, Dennis, next Monday you boys head out for Sydney," Buddha said, when he returned from the boat captain's meeting. "We're getting underway in one hour; hopefully catch those little shits with their black pajamas down." He was in high spirits and laughed at his clever play on words.

I looked at my calendar. Another day crossed off. We'd been in-country 208 days; 157 left to go. For an instant I paused and thought about being discharged. My four years would be up and the Navy was all I knew. What would I do? Surely not return to the farm. We loaded our platoon and headed up river. Sarge asked if he could come up.

"Hey Sarge, we going to see some shit today?" Buddha said, his face against the opening.

"I hope not. Can I drive this thing?"

"Well I don't know. Afe, can he drive?"

"Be my guest—you have 157 days to practice. Just follow the boat ahead of you."

"You already counting? It's best to wait until you're under a hundred otherwise it drags—me I'm down to thirty-three and a wake-up. Man, this thing turns slow."

Two hours later the radio ordered armor shields closed.

"Okay Afe, get your flaps up. The rest of you get in your turrets—lock and load. They must think we'll see Charlie today. Keep your head down, Sarge."

I took the helm and Sarge crawled down the ladder to his troops.

"Professor, stick your head below. Tell Snipe to have all four .30 calibers loaded and ready," Buddha said.

By 1100 hours the sky was clear and heat waves miraged from the canopy over our well-deck. The lead boat swung north from the Mekong River into the mouth of Hai Muoi Tam Canal. Sampans scurried toward the town of Cai Be and when I swung our boat around the headland and into the canal, an easterly breeze blew the town smells into my cox'n flat—one inch armor couldn't block those. Sampans tied to the bamboo wharf bobbed in the wake pushed out from our boats.

"Close it up Afe—thirty meters," Buddha said. "Get your flak jacket on and fastened—does everybody have their's on?"

"It's hot, we don't need them," Crow said, from his turret.

"Shut the fuck up and get it on. Is your Honeywell loaded?"

"Why so close?" I asked, cocking my helmet back. I was

fifth in column as I watched the lead boat approach a busy bridge.

"They don't want the troops too spread out when we off-load them."

Fighting the current and an ebbing tide, the lead boat broached against a piling under the bridge. "Are you watching him, Afe? Kind of like when we went into the LSD. Take it at an angle, directly into the current; don't let it get you on the side.

The sun was directly over the boat. With the armor up, my cox'n flat was stifling. Sweat trickled from beneath my helmet and dripped onto the smooth metal helm. It seeped from my armpits, down beneath my flak jacket, and soaked into my cutoffs, eventually saturating them, dripping on to my bare feet.

"Okay Afe, take her under. Show'em how it's done." For a moment I was in the shadow of the bridge. I looked through my slits, up at the underside timbers and realized the French might have built it. Maybe the same ones who built the mud fort down in the U Minh Forest.

"Close it up Afe. Look at all the shit in the water." The wakes of the four boats ahead of us had pushed most of the clumps toward the densely covered banks. Dark green foliage hung into the water, completely obstructing the riverbanks. The tide continued to ebb and the canal narrowed, making our progress drudgingly slow with the heavy load we carried.

"I don't like it. There's not a gook on the river," Buddha said. I glanced back and saw him place his hand on the top of his helmet and wiggle it back and forth—almost like he was trying to screw it on. Then he scrunched down farther between the gun mounts. "You guys get your finger on the trigger. I can feel it. Afe, you know what to do."

Yes, I did know. In the event of an ambush we were to

assault directly on to the enemy position. Our reinforced bow ramp protected the troops from incoming fire as we approached the riverbank. I was to drop the ramp and disembark the troops so they could spread out, flank, and overrun the enemy. I grabbed a T-shirt rag and ran it around the sweat-slick helm. The lead boat—Mays's boat—lurched sideways in an explosion of smoke and debris as machine gun fire and rockets ripped into her port side.

22

In the Kill Zone

18 August 1968

Fire erupted along the riverbank. We—all the boats in the column—returned fire. Tango 11 was in the heart of the kill zone. She shuddered under the onslaught of machine gun rounds as I spun my helm to port and threw the left engine into reverse. Within seconds a pall of smoke hung over the river. I saw spurts from an enemy machine gun coming from the riverbank directly in front of me. Kicking both engines ahead full, I straightened the helm and rammed the bunker.

"The ramp, Afe. Drop the ramp." I glanced back. Buddha's face was against the opening at the back of the cox'n flat, his eyes wide.

"I did. It didn't go down."

"Professor, tell that useless friggin Snipe to release the safety latch," Buddha shouted.

The safety latch was to prevent the ramp from dropping accidently, and the boat swamping in case the cable I controlled for lowering and raising it from the cox'n flat snapped. It seemed incongruous, but I recalled the time Snipe hadn't released the safety latch back in California. Buddha had yelled at him that time, too. But then, the latch had been welded closed. Now, if he didn't release it, the troops were trapped.

Through the slit in my port side armor I glimpsed a flash, a rocket fired, from the riverbank, followed by an explosion in the middle of our well-deck canopy. Flames shot skyward.

"Tango one-one, report damage, over," requested the command boat from farther back in the column. Automatic weapon fire raked us port and starboard.

Professor knelt at the hatch and looked down into the well-deck. "I don't see Snipe," he yelled up to Buddha.

I glanced back, saw Buddha's mouth move but didn't hear because another rocket slammed into the canopy over the troops. I leaned forward over the helm, face against armor and peered through the slits as I shouted to Professor. "Two rockets detonated on our canopy. Go see how bad it fucked the troops up. Tell Snipe I need to get the ramp down." Face against sun-warmed steel, I stared, mesmerized by the shredded canopy—like a gigantic razor-clawed paw had reached down and scooped sections from it.

A third rocket hit the bar armor directly in front of the cox'n flat—about three feet from my face. I slammed off the bulkhead onto the deck. Thick smoke burned my lungs and white stars flashed through blackness as I struggled up. "I can't see. I can't see," I screamed, hands clawing at my face, digging at my eyes.

Fingers wrapped around my wrists and pulled my hands away. "Look at me," Professor shouted. "Look at me." I saw him then, blood trickling down his cheek. His face and bare arms sooty from the flash.

"I couldn't see," I said, quietly. We locked eyes for an instant. I reached for the helm trying to steady myself as the world exploded outside our steel crypt. My ears rang and when I knuckled smoke from my eyes, flashes—like lightening—shot through blackness.

"Back off. Back off," shouted Sarge, standing on the ladder near my feet. "We're all fucked up. Nobody left to go ashore."

"What's going on down there?" Buddha shouted. Concussion from the last rocket blast had blown smoke out through the opening. Buddha had a soot band, like the Lone Ranger's mask.

"Sarge said we should back off. All his troops are fucked up," Professor shouted to Buddha.

"Back down, Afe."

I threw both engines in reverse, full rpm's, but went nowhere. I glanced out my side slit and was surprised to see exploding jungle a few feet from the side of the boat. Stonewall and Crow were firing into the bank, cutting swaths like an invisible buzz saw. Between the tide and the current, the boat had broached when I was knocked down. I spun the helm hard to starboard as engines screamed in reverse and I watched liquid mud churn forward through the propellers and up against the bank. The boat shuddered with the impact of in-coming rounds and the recoil of thousands of rounds fired from our boat. A rocket detonated somewhere aft on the boat—on the bar armor, I thought—it didn't penetrate, but it jarred us loose from the mud suction.

Crow stepped into the cox'n flat and looked at me. "My .50's not working. I'm going below," he said.

I wondered why he didn't switch to his grenade launcher as he'd been taught. His pale balding head was the last I saw him as he descended the ladder.

"Move up river, Afe. We got to get the fuck out of here," Buddha screamed down to me. "Crow, Crow, why the fuck aren't you shooting?"

"He went below," Professor shouted.

"Afe, swing the boat upriver—to starboard," Buddha

yelled.

I looked through my slits, surprised to see that we were still pointed toward the smoky bank.

"Morphine syrettes, we need morphine." I glanced down at the army medic standing on the ladder. He'd lost his helmet and his bare arms and hands were slick with blood. He was splattered across the face with shrapnel. He climbed a few steps toward the cox'n flat. "I said I need morphine— you guys must have some."

I knew Buddha had it in his locker. I looked at Professor and he yelled up to Buddha, "The key. The army needs our morphine." I glanced back and saw Buddha lean back, digging in his pocket while trying to stay below the tops of the turrets. He passed the key down, dropping it to the steel deck. "Tell that fucking Crow to get back up here."

"Go down and get the morphine for him," I yelled to Professor. "He doesn't know which locker is Buddha's. Tell Crow to get the fuck up here." I envied Professor his moment of respite as his head disappeared down the ladder. He'd lost a lot of hair since I'd met him. He needed to get his helmet back on. I glanced down and saw it on the deck below his boat's radio and kicked it over near the hatch coaming so he'd see it when he returned.

Above the din I heard shouting and glanced down. Professor was standing at the base of the ladder looking and yelling at somebody toward the engine compartment. Then he climbed the steps, grabbed his helmet, and pulled himself up into the cox'n flat.

Buddha's masked face was against the opening. "Where the fuck is Crow?" he shouted.

"Between the lockers in front of the engineroom with Snipe," Professor yelled back.

"Tell that cowardly son-of-a-bitch to get up here before I kill him," Buddha screamed. It was an idle threat. If he stood up to go below, enemy fire would immediately rip him.

"He said he's not getting shot-up for a bunch of gooks," Professor screamed back over the roaring guns.

"Do you need help up here?" It was the black army sergeant, standing on the ladder.

"There's no one in that .50 caliber gun mount," I yelled, waving toward the turret. Without hesitation, he was up the ladder, into the gun mount, and firing the grenade launcher. Smoke and cordite fumes from the machine guns made it difficult to breathe.

An explosion on the starboard shield knocked me against the radio. Hot smoke clouded the compartment. Professor pulled himself to his feet then helped me up. I grabbed the helm and tasted blood as it dripped onto the instrument panel. My jaw ached. I tongued broken teeth and realized that my face had hit the bulkhead when I was blown back.

"Afe, turn the boat—turn the boat. The current is swinging it down river," Buddha bellowed through the smoke and noise.

"Tango one-one, send damage report, over," demanded the radio.

"Afe. Swing the boat. We're dead in the water right in front of their rockets."

I watched muzzle flashes through smoke rising on the riverbank as my hand reached instinctively to shift the starboard engine into reverse so the boat would swing back into the current. My fingers closed around the cool, sweat-polished brass shift lever and a rocket penetrated the armor a few inches above my hand.

Seared flesh and burned hair smell filled the compartment; a stench like the white hot docking iron we'd used to sever lambs' tails in the spring. I heard high-pitched plaintive bleats. Lying on the deck, looking up through smoke and flames at the armor, I focused on the hole not there moments before.

I begged God, beseeching Him to save me—though I knew He had no reason to. I looked toward the hatch to the well-deck. I could go below. I was wounded. I'd done my share. Let somebody else take over, worry about the boat and crew. But there was nobody to take my place. I was trapped. My universe had narrowed to a small steel compartment. I curled fetal.

Soft light enveloped me. Time and fear and pain ceased to exist. I was in Peace. Yet I knew pain, tasted cordite, felt seared flesh. I was conscious of incoming and out-going rounds. My fingers traced paths through blood trickling across the warm deck. Our radio squawked, screaming in the smoky distance. I was conscious but beyond that mundane world. I was safe within my bright cocoon. In that moment I knew God. But the moment of eternity was not to last.

Why wouldn't the radio stop?

"......Tango one-one...Mike one pull alongside. They must be dead."

That's us, we're not dead.

"Tango one-one, back down, back down, back down," the radio shrieked.

Unconsciously, my hand reached up but refused to do what it was told. I stared at it—the top—blackened oozing flesh. I grasped the helm with my other hand and pulled myself up.

"Tango one-one, if you hear me, back down, back down, back down," the radio shrieked again.

It happened from a great distance. I pulled the port shift into reverse—reached up with my right hand but it refused to obey—the left reached across the console, pulled the starboard shift into reverse and opened the throttle. I was on a plane outside this insanity and like an impartial observer, watched the scene unfold, comfortable with the knowledge that I would leave honorably. I braced for the next rocket, terrified yet at peace, knowing I had done my best. I placed my face against the armor slits in front of me.

Artillery rounds detonated on the riverbank. Blast concussion pushed smoke back and revealed why the radio was trying to contact us. We had turned 180 degrees and were drifting downriver into the line of fire from Mike 1's 40mm cannon. Because of smoke and the restricted view in their gun turret, I knew they wouldn't see us. If they put rounds into our bow it would annihilate our already wounded troops. With my left hand, I grasped my right and tucked it inside the stirrup of the brass throttle. Both throttles full speed reverse. I watched the 40mm cannon rounds slam into the riverbank. Thirty feet and they would be hitting us. We began slowing, slowing, twenty feet, ten, five, stopped, moving back. Throw port engine ahead, full throttle. Swing helm hard starboard. The boat quivered. Turned. Engines at full throttle, enemy machine gun fire savaging our boat. Cobra helicopter gunships screamed in, releasing rockets ten feet above us, decimating the riverbank. Friendly-fire shrapnel slapped against our armor. Turned into the current I saw the stern of the boat ahead of me—shift starboard engine forward—open both throttles. I looked toward the bank on my port side—surprised to see we were still abreast of the spot I'd run ashore just a few minutes earlier.

"Afe, Afe, are you okay?" I looked back and saw Buddha's face in the opening, his voice distant.

Blood dripped onto shattered gauges. I looked at the hole in my armor then down at my numb hand. I touched the still-hot scorched paint where molten iron from the warhead had ricocheted around inside the compartment. My leg hurt—blood oozed from several holes. I looked at Professor. At the blood trickling down his face and from his arm, and realized how incredibly lucky we were. When a rocket penetrated the cox'n flat it always killed or maimed the people inside.

"How you doing, Afe? You want me to drive?" Professor shouted.

A rocket penetrated the port .50 caliber gun mount. The explosion buckled my legs but I clutched the helm and stayed on my feet. Sarge was blown out of the turret and into the cox'n flat where he lay on his back screaming, clawing at the hurt on his chest. He reminded me of a bobcat I'd caught years ago in a #4 wolf trap. The screams began deep in his throat and rose from a low hiss to a high squeal as his hands clawed my bare legs. His chest was a mass of shredded purple flesh, black skin, bits of broken shield pieces and nylon from his flak jacket.

"Get away. Get away," I screamed. His stump fingers sprayed my legs. I grasped the helm, my bare feet sliding on the wet deck. He squirmed between my legs. Trying to escape this new horror, I pushed him over to the hatch with my blood-crusted feet. Arms reached up and pulled him down into the well-deck. It was then I spotted Dennis, blood splattered, laying on the deck below his turret squeezing his leg and staring at me.

"My leg, my leg. I'm hit. Oh fuck, it hurts—help me," he pleaded. There was a look of wild-eyed panic in his eyes.

I looked at Professor, then at Dennis, then back at Professor. "Take the helm, I'll look at Dennis."

He had both hands around his leg—high on his thigh—squeezing tightly and I realized why he was panicked. He hadn't actually looked at the wound—thought he was hit in the groin. Below his fingers a dark stain spread on his faded green pants. I pulled my knife and slit the pant leg open.

"Look Dennis, it's in your leg—it's not bad." He looked down at the dark, silver-dollar-size bulge and the blood leaking from the hole and began screaming. Not words—just screams. The blood splatters were from Sarge—he'd sprayed Dennis, too.

I took his head between my hands and shook him. "Dennis, it's not bad. Stop. Stop screaming. Get the fuck up and start shooting. Get up and put out rounds." I dropped my hands. I was tired. He looked at me, at my damaged hand and my blood-covered legs. He stood up and began firing his grenade launcher. I moved back to the helm.

I looked through the slit at the port riverbank, braced for another rocket. I was surprised to see we were still near the spot I'd originally landed—friggin ebbing tide, I thought.

"Here, Afe." I looked at Professor. He wrapped a battle dressing around my hand and wrist. Then he took the T-shirt I'd wiped the sweat-soaked helm with back in Cai Be, poured canteen water—wasting good coffee water, I thought—on it and wiped my face. I was surprised that I could see better. "Go below Afe, I'll drive."

"I'm okay." I looked at the destroyed instrument panel in front of me. The fouled deck I stood on. I started laughing. "Look at this fucking mess. Buddha's going to be pissed. No sleep until we clean up tonight."

Professor started laughing, too. I laughed until tears stung my blistered cheeks.

"What the fuck? You guys having a party down there?" We looked back and saw Buddha's masked face and laughed harder.

"Afe's worried about the mess," Professor said.

"You guys are nuts. Professor, get a bandage on your arm."

I looked over then and saw where a piece of shrapnel had ripped a gash in his upper arm.

"It's okay—it doesn't hurt."

We moved north through the pall of smoke. The lead boat was dead-in-the-water, another alongside connecting a tow rope. I could see two men hunched down, as though leaning into a storm, securing the line. A rocket detonated and one of the crouching figures disappeared.

The riverbanks were a twisted mass of splintered trees and bunkers. Close-in artillery support sprayed us with shrapnel—but it forced the VC firing rockets at us to stay down, allowing us to escape. Our port .50 caliber machine gun was silent—the rocket that hit the sergeant had also destroyed the gun, but Dennis and Stonewall continued to shoot. A continuous stream of fire sprayed from the guns in the well-deck. The troops couldn't all be dead or wounded, I thought.

I watched Mays's crippled boat move forward. She was an Alpha boat—lightly armored and faster than our Tango boats, with an enclosed twin .50 caliber turret forward and a single .50 caliber turret mounted above and behind the cox'n flat. Instead of slits in the armor surrounding the gun mounts she had thick blocks of Plexiglas for the gunners to look through. I always wondered if they would actually stop a bullet. I could never understand the logic of putting those lightly protected boats in the most dangerous position.

"Watch the west bank, watch the west bank," blared the radio. I recognized the voice of the radioman on Mike one, the boat behind us.

I looked out my side slit into the mouth of a three-meter-wide canal. About fifty meters up, a sampan—almost bridging the canal—ferried four khaki-clad soldiers across. One leveled his shoulder-fired rocket launcher at us and fired. In his haste he fired high—over our canopy. Stonewall was focused on the bank downriver of the canal mouth and hadn't spotted the sampan. The soldier was reloading his rocket launcher as they nosed the south bank of the canal. Mike one fired their 40mm cannon at the same instant Stonewall spotted them. Watery debris and smoke shot skyward—like Tango 7 the day she hit a mine—then settled in stillness. In another instant we were past the canal and jungle blocked my view.

An explosion ripped our port side, aft. I regained my feet and saw that the boat had swung to port, angling toward the bank. I spun the helm and got back in column.

"Tango one-one, do you have fires under control?" the radio asked. I'd blocked radio chatter out but our call-sign caught my attention.

I heard Professor respond. "….it's in the well-deck. Under control, out."

I put my face to my armor slits and saw the fire—smoldering in supplies stored in the bracing above the well-deck, beneath the canopy. Gunfire eased as we moved north out of the kill zone. Stonewall and Dennis stopped firing and in the sudden silence I heard shouts from below in the well-deck.

"Go below, Afe," Professor said. "I think we're out of it. Have that army medic look at you."

"He should patch you up," I said. Blood oozed from his arm and countless tiny spots—like somebody had thrown a handful of small pebbles—speckled his body.

"Afe, go below." I glanced back and saw Buddha staring down at us.

I looked at Professor and remembered the first time I'd seen him—the quiet assurance he'd exhibited in the face of Buddha's diatribe. He looked back at me and reached for the helm. "Go ahead Afe."

I released the helm and again worried about how they'd repair the shattered gauges. My legs ached. I looked down, surprised to see dozens of small shrapnel wounds, with one larger wound on my shinbone. Blood trickled. I had forgotten about it. The small ones had cauterized shut.

Sounds echoed. I looked out my side armor, bewildered at flowers glowing in the pure sun as they swayed in the breeze, trellised on branches that dipped to the water.

"Go below Afe. I'll take care of it," Professor repeated.

I looked at him, confused. Why was he there? I had

slipped back into the light.

He held my arm as I stepped onto the ladder. I looked at the soft sunbeam coming through the jagged hole in my side armor as I wrapped bare toes around the steel rung and stepped down. Sniper rounds slammed against armor. Stonewall and Dennis opened fire, followed by staccato bursts from the well-deck.

I stood on the ladder, chest level with the cox'n flat deck. Broken glass, shell casings, and trails where my toes had skidded, intrigued me. My injured hand reached out and crusted fingers traced ever-changing designs through the blood puddle.

"Afe, what are you doing?" I looked up, surprised to see Professor standing above me, driving the boat. Blood oozed from small holes in his legs, too. I looked up at him, shook my head no, and stepped down the ladder into the well-deck.

"More ammo, more ammo," shouted an army gunner firing one of our .30 caliber machine guns. A trooper with a bloody bandaged head scampered up with another case. At the forward gun, two men were changing a barrel which had no doubt overheated. Several men crouched along the sides of the well-deck, firing their rifles and M79 grenade launchers at the riverbanks. The overhead awning, shredded from earlier rocket hits, hung flapping from the ribs it had been recently stretched across. Mold, cigarette butts, diesel fuel, and exhaust fumes were overpowered by scorched flesh, blood, cordite, and fear.

Men wrestled smoldering cases of ammunition from the twisted bar armor above the well-deck in front of the cox'n flat and threw them overboard. One man, hugging a case of smoldering grenades against his stomach, slipped and fell.

"Jesus Christ, if that blows, we all go," said another, passing him with a case of smoking ammo. As he struggled up I looked down at where he'd fallen.

The once army-green deck was now a jumble of empty shell casings, ammo crates, discarded weapons, and shredded clothing. Blood, caught in the steel rib foot-grips of the deck, trickled in rivulets to the center, then aft—downhill. It was beginning to coagulate. It was mostly from the first few seconds—when those first three rockets had struck. I watched in fascination. Blood coursed down the deck and formed a dark pool at my bare feet. I recalled how on butchering day in the winter our mutts would fight for the steaming blood that gushed from a pig's severed throat, licking the hog's face, head, not missing any. My bare toes squished in the puddle.

Recoiling, I stepped back, eyes now adjusted to the dim interior. I moved toward my bunk. I wanted to lie down and close my eyes. The black sergeant moaned in the bloody snarled mess that had been my pillow and blanket. That surprised me—I was certain he was dead. He was heavily bandaged and sedated but low gasps escaped as twitches convulsed his body. On the bunk below mine a small body lay, still, eyes open, bloody—Mexican or Puerto Rican or Indian. I couldn't tell.

"Hang in there, we're out of the shit, you'll be on a dust-off real quick. Do you hear me?" The army medic, though wounded himself, attempted to keep the wounded conscious. The seriously wounded were silent—probably sedated by Buddha's morphine.

"More ammo, more ammo," a gunner demanded.

One of the troopers throwing damaged cases over the side looked at me and kicked at a case of .30 caliber ammo. "Don't just fuckin stand there, bring it to him." I picked it up, cradled it in my arms and carried it forward. The trooper had removed the empty box so I pulled the lid off and hung the full one in its place. The riverbank seemed silent.

"Why are you shooting?" I asked.

Everything seemed distant—I felt detached.

"So those little fuckers keep their heads down—there's open land on the other side of this jungle along the river—they're probably following right along with us."

I moved toward the back of the well-deck, but stopped at Snipe's rack. There was an army guy in it who was wounded in the head and neck. Blood spray speckled the wall of pictures Snipe had taped against the bulkhead. Some of them had been knocked off. One lay face-down at my feet. I picked it up—couldn't really see anything because of the blood coated on it. I wiped it against the side of my cutoffs. Nancy was holding the baby. She was cute in a mousy sort of way with her cropped hair and freckled face. The baby was smiling. I hoped she wouldn't grow up looking like Snipe.

Where were Snipe and Crow I wondered? I reached out to set the picture on a ledge when crisp new pain sliced into my foot. Imbedded in my heel was a twisted pair of glasses. I bent down—my body was stiffening—and retrieved them. One lens and bow were missing and the other side dangled, held by electrical tape. Glancing around, I wondered who they belonged to. They must be important if he taped them. Then I saw the strap on the back had been severed. I gently set them on the ledge next to the picture just in case the owner came looking for them.

Several wounded men huddled in the rear of the well-deck. I crossed over to our small table. All seats were occupied by wounded troops who were visiting, smoking, joking about the *Playboy* centerfold laid out across the top of the table. A bloody finger had traced an outline of her breasts with a blood smudge over each nipple. They were bantering back and forth, some angry others happy, about getting wounded. The discussion went something like this.

"I'm out of this motherfucker for awhile," said one with

a bandaged leg.

"Man, I got thirty-seven days and a wake-up. I ain't never climbing back onto one of these fuckin boats. My arm starts healing, I'll whack it—break it open. I'm done with this bullshit. It's somebody else's war now," said one with his arm in a sling, bandaged from wrist to elbow.

"Poor friggin Sarge. He was getting short. Now his wife won't even recognize him," said a small guy laying in Dennis' rack with an I.V. tube stuck in his arm and a bandage over his stomach. He talked slow and dreamy with a southern drawl. "I'm going home, he said, his eyes closed. "I hear the catfish leaping. I'm gonna fill a stringer."

"Hang in there," the medic said, feeling the man's pulse. "You're going to be skying on a dust-off real quick."

My fingers wrapped around ladder rungs and I pulled myself back up to the cox'n flat. Professor looked at me. Silently I shook my head "no" as I reached for my helm. The shooting had stopped now—only explosions behind us. The sky beyond the slits was clear, the sun hard. A cold draft pierced the cox'n flat, sending a chill through me.

"Buddha, I think Afe is going into shock," Professor called.

"What the hell's he doing back up here? I sent him below."

"He just came back—took the helm."

"Afe, why aren't you below?"

"I'd rather be up here. It's a mess down there."

"Are you okay?"

"Yeah, I just got a chill."

"Well it's hotter than fuck up here."

The medic came up the ladder and said, "I've got 12 men I need medevaced, four critical. We have a dust-off chopper on its way. If you beach near the medevac boat we'll get our wounded over to it."

The medevac boat—the Tango boat with the helicopter pad—was beached about thirty meters north of us. I nudged our boat into the riverbank against jungle brush and lowered the ramp. Bandaged troops climbed off our boat and disappeared into thick vegetation ahead of men carrying stretcher cases. Not one man was without a battle dressing. The shrapnel from the overhead rocket explosions had definitely caused havoc. I recalled the sergeant's words from several months ago about hating the boats—about being defenseless.

During those minutes beached, Stonewall went down to the well-deck and passed several cases of 20mm ammo up the hatch to the cox'n flat. Professor slid them back between the .50 caliber mounts. Dennis, kneeling, pushed them back to the step-up by the 20mm turret.

"Send up some .50 caliber ammo," Dennis called down.

Stonewall passed four cases up to Professor then came back up the ladder. I watched him as he climbed into view. He had lost his helmet and his tight black curls were matted with grime from the oil that he misted over his ammo to keep the gun from jamming. Sweat had run down through the oily grime and left wide streaks on his dark skin. There were several small wounds clotted over on his lower legs where shrapnel from the rocket that had injured the sergeant must have sprayed him. He looked at me, then reached forward and poked his thumb into the rocket hole in my armor.

"Close, huh," he said, glancing at my bandaged hand and down at my legs. Then he stepped aft and climbed into his turret where I could hear him reloading his cannon.

Shots rang out. VC were attempting to isolate the army troops on the riverbank between boats.

"Motherfuckers!" Buddha screamed. "Hold your fire. Dennis, Stonewall, we have men out there. Don't shoot."

The troops returned to the boat, stretcher-bearers first. Then I saw a muddy trooper wave from the ramp that all were back on board. It had been a short, sharp exchange but there were no new casualties. I raised the ramp and backed into the river. Stonewall opened fire and the bank erupted. Below, troops in the well-deck were shooting, too. It had only been a few snipers this time, not bunkers dug into the bank firing rockets. As we moved up river the army began transferring the wounded in a skimmer—a 12 foot fiberglass boat with an outboard motor. On the second trip, a wounded man in the boat was hit by sniper fire. We moved about three hundred meters north and again beached near the medevac boat. The riverbank appeared secure and other boats were soon strung out along both banks while the skimmer shuttled wounded to helicopters as they took turns landing on the medevac boat.

"Afe, we need to get you back to the *Benewah*," Buddha said, looking down through the opening at me. "I don't want you in that skimmer—it's too open. Those gooks are going to catch up with us again. I think it's safer to get off the boat and go along the bank. I can cover you."

I looked out the slit in my armor above the rocket hole. It did look safe but brush hung into the river.

I heard a noise; a round being pumped into the chamber of the shotgun. I looked behind me at Professor. "Here, Afe, just in case. I'll pass it down to you." I glanced around the cox'n flat—at the empty ammo and grenade boxes, the bloody skid marks, the blistered paint from the smeltering metal that had miraculously ricocheted in a circle around Professor and me.

"My ears are ringing," I said

"Doesn't surprise me. There's blood trickling from them," Professor said. He reached forward and wiped a finger up the side of my neck and held it out, shiny wet. "Get down the ladder and I'll hand this to you." I climbed down, he handed me the 12 gauge and said, "See you back at the *Benewah*."

Moving forward, up the blood-crusted deck to the front corner by the ramp, I pulled myself up out of the well-deck, onto the catwalk. Buddha climbed down from between the turrets and came forward on the catwalk. "Stay along the bank where I can see you. Professor radioed the guys on the medevac boat—they'll watch for you."

I looked across the water between the two boats. It wasn't very far—about thirty meters. Buddha held the shotgun in one hand and my hand in the other as I stretched my foot out toward the bank to test the footing.

"Okay, let go," I said, and swung the other foot from the boat to the bank.

He handed me the gun. "Stay low," he said, then walked aft, climbed up between the turrets, and picked up his M60. For an instant we made eye contact, then he gave a slight nod and I moved forward.

It was impossible to climb through vegetation that hung over the riverbank. Moving inland and north, I tried to keep the river in sight. New growth laced through dead vines and branches like a loosely woven mat. Crouched low, I pushed forward, at times crawled beneath low canopies—like the sumac maze I'd played cowboys and Indians in when I was a kid. Battle dressings snagged on thorny vines. I looked down and discovered that I'd already lost the bandages on my leg—they were wadded around my ankle, ties trailing between my toes. My injured hand was coated with dirt and bits of brown leaf. When I paused, ants licked trickling juices. I was mid-way between the boats when shots rang out. Single shots increased to long bursts. I crawled back toward the river.

Inching forward on my stomach, I glimpsed brown water and heard Vietnamese voices behind me. The voices seemed far behind—but still I worried about giving my position away. Shots moved closer, fired from my side of the river. Fear of capture spurred me forward.

During our POW training, when I was being interrogated—when the guard shaved my tattoo—he'd threatened to cut it off. Laughed when he read it—Death before Dishonor—and assured me I would tell him anything when he carved it off my arm. I wished I had a long-sleeved shirt, now.

Shots rang closer. Suppose our boats fired on me—they couldn't see me in the thick growth. I hugged the ground and angled toward the river. A chopper was approaching the medevac boat.

The jungle floor moved less than two meters in front of me. The nose of a B-40 rocket slowly rose. It rested on the Viet Cong soldier's right shoulder—between us—shielding me from his vision. In a smooth motion, he rose to a crouching position in his spider hole, rocket launcher and head above ground; then, with his launcher, melted back down.

Lying flat, I raised my shotgun. Slowly the helmet came up—by the tilt of it, I knew he'd look directly at me when his eyes came into view. I had one chance. The helmet paused and I began to panic. Maybe I should try to ease back out of sight. No. He'd hear me. I wished I had a grenade. I was afraid he'd hear my teeth chattering. My neck and hand and leg throbbed. Why had I agreed to go along the riverbank?

The chopper drew nearer. The helmet went down. Moments later the rocket warhead reappeared. He planned to fire at the chopper. Closer, closer, the rotors came. Leaves shivered—I felt the thumping vibration. The helmet rose. He didn't sense me—he was focused on the chopper. Raising my shotgun, I aimed at his ear. There was a spider on his ear lobe—was that why they called it a spider hole? The side of his head was squarely in my sight. Gently I caressed the trigger. Stupid, the safety was on. Friggin right-handed gun—my finger slipped out of the trigger guard, around and under, silently moving the safety to firing position.

He turned toward me then, stared into my eyes over the top of the launcher—an instant, a lifetime—my brain had already triggered the signal to my finger. The shotgun recoiled and he disappeared in the blur. Blow-back splattered my face. I dropped the gun, grabbed a fistful of leaves, and smeared bloody tissue fragments from my eyes. Retrieving the gun, I jerked forward and wormed past the spider hole. Beyond it was a rip of fresh dark earth; something gleamed in the pungent soil—a bone fragment, teeth intact. Red dripped down from the low-ceilinged foliage. An eye hung—like a Christmas tree ornament—from a tendon that had twirled itself around a bare twig. I hurried past without looking in—the B-40 rocket warhead angled up at the back of the hole.

I heard the chopper land on the boat deck. Boats started shooting inland—over my head. I lay flat for a moment then moved forward, slithering along the ground. The chopper flared skyward again. Glancing up I glimpsed it through the leaves—shots fired from behind, at the chopper, I thought.

Crawling the last three meters, I slid into muddy water.

"Hurry. Hurry. Come on," shouted a sailor from the well-deck of the medevac boat as he trained his .30 caliber machine gun on me.

Good thing he wasn't trigger-happy, I thought. I looked up beyond him and saw the boat captain crouched between his turrets. I picked my way through the maze of snaky roots at the bottom of the river—through burning nettles, thorny brush, and vines as my bare feet felt their way.

"What the fuck are you doing on the bank? There's a battalion of VC regulars along here," the sailor said, pulling me aboard.

I picked up my shotgun, crawled into the well-deck, and crouched in a shadowed corner—gun between my legs, barrel still warm.

Five of us waited in the well-deck. The more critically wounded had been medevaced, leaving behind bloody bandages, plasma bags, morphine syrettes, shredded clothing.

"You got a couple little visitors," said a soldier pointing at my legs. He was naked above the waist with bandages covering a back wound.

"Little fuckers," I said, squeezing my fingers together, pulling the leeches from my ankle. First one, then the other flew across the well-deck—blood trickled down and disappeared beneath my arch.

Three of us were walking wounded, two on stretchers. My feet were caked with mud from crawling in the river. Pink-tinted marl oozed up between my toes from this new deck—like two colors of Play Doh mixed together. Viet Cong were firing from both riverbanks—not heavy like in the kill zone, no rockets and machine guns—but the 20mm cannons and Honeywells kept firing.

"Incoming chopper," a sailor shouted down to us from the cox'n flat. "Get ready to move above."

I heard it coming—saw it skim the river surface toward us at high speed, swerving from bank to bank as it approached. Near the boat it flared up then settled on the tiny landing pad. I hunched on the catwalk below the pad, ready to rush the chopper.

"You three go first, then we'll get these stretchers passed up. Keep your ...," one of the sailors shouted to us, his voice lost in the cacophony of rotor wash and machine gun fire.

We pulled ourselves up to the landing pad between the bow ramp and the canopy and raced to the helicopter. I was first in, and sat against the wall, shotgun cradled between my legs. As the others rushed forward, I saw another boat cox'n approaching—I hadn't noticed him in the well-deck. He grinned as he drew near, cradling his right wrist with his left hand. His right hand dangled from a tendon. He stumbled pulling himself aboard. I reached forward and when he stretched his good hand toward me, the injured one waved in the rotor wash.

A childhood winter memory came unbidden as the hand flopped—of a goldfinch, skewered through the breast by the sharp end of a dangling piece of wire we hung chickens from when we butchered them. The little bird must have flown into it while flying through our woodshed. I recalled how the finch had swayed in the winter wind, frozen stiff. In the rotor wash, the almost-severed hand flapped like the little bird.

The wounded cox'n jumped in, sat next to me, and began yelling incoherently over the shrill screech of the chopper's turbine as he scratched at the tourniquet above his wrist. "Fuckin gooks." Blood seeped from his bandaged wrist, misting through the wind-washed compartment. "Little cock-suckers." He was sedated—apparently felt no pain. The third wounded man jumped aboard, then crewmen rushed across with the two stretcher cases, ducking low as they ran. Sharp slaps, like an open hand smacking the side of an empty tin pail, whacked the chopper.

From where I sat, I faced the medevac boat captain—a ruddy-faced German. Like Buddha, he crouched down between the gun turrets. I'd listened to him that first day at Coronado complaining about "friggin kids not having a clue." Now we were about thirty feet apart. The eyes beneath his helmet surprised me. They were open wide and his mouth formed a silent "oh" as he watched the chopper quiver with impacting bullets.

The turbine whined and we lurched upward. I glimpsed our battle-damaged boat—canopy shredded, armor on the starboard side of the cox'n flat a distorted mass of steel, paint blistered, bullet holes in the catwalk surrounding the gun turrets. Empty ammo crates littered the catwalk on both sides of the boat. Buddha was hunched between the gun mounts, firing toward the riverbank with his M60 machine gun. We plummeted down toward the river and shot forward, passing back through the kill zone at water level. The chopper flitted from bank to bank attempting to elude hostile fire, reeling convulsively as it took hits. The engine screamed and we swerved up over the riverbank, spinning in a tight curve back down to the river. One of the crewmen flinched, made the sign of the cross, flipped a finger toward the riverbank, then winked at me. A soldier screamed from a stretcher, then vomited, spraying it through the wind-whipped compartment.

Smoke rose and muzzle flashes blinked from damaged bunkers along the riverbanks as we flew south. Bombs, napalm, rockets, strafing, and thousands of rounds from our boats had not silenced the Viet Cong. Hugging the river placed us closer to enemy fire but shortened the window of opportunity for them to shoot.

"This is my fourth trip this afternoon," shouted the crewman. He pointed at a smoldering chopper resting in a rice paddy. "They went down about an hour ago but we pulled everybody out." Soaring skyward I sensed we were safe and looked over to the crewman who raised his hands palm-up, indicating no sweat.

Flying south toward the big river I reflected on the scenery below, wondering if the Viet Cong soldier in the spider hole had been raised in the Delta—if, as a child, he had played in these forests and fished and swam in the rivers. Wondering if he was in the light I had experienced earlier as I lay on the deck of my cox'n flat.

23

Medevaced to USS *Colleton*

18 August 1968

Afternoon sun was still high in the cloudless sky when the *Benewah* came into view. I pointed toward it and the crewman shook his head. "We've been taking casualties to the *Colleton*," he shouted.

How would Buddha find me? He and Professor said they'd see me back at the *Benewah*. I rubbed my eyes—wind made them burn. I felt strange—detached from this sudden shift in my life. I seemed like a fly on the wall, watching. Small details blossomed to great significance.

Men stood in the shadows of the landing pad on the *Colleton* as our chopper raced in, dodging masts, radio antennas, and cables. The instant we landed, they ran forward, crouched beneath the still turning rotors, unstrapped stretchers, grabbed the ends, and ran toward the entry way.

A sailor dressed in blue dungarees and a blood-smeared white T-shirt helped me out of the chopper and across the landing deck, then reached for my shotgun. I pulled back. It belonged on Tango 11. Buddha would give me hell if I lost it. Besides I needed it. The sailor pointed to a pile of weapons; grenades, canteens, ammo pouches and belts, rifles, helmets—thrown haphazardly, covered with mud, some damaged, all discarded from the wounded that had come before me. There were even a few claymore mines tossed on it. The pile was a shock to the senses. It was so—unmilitary.

"Just bandage me up," I argued. "I'll catch a ride over to the *Benewah*."

"You still have to give me that gun," the sailor replied.

A sharp stab, like a wasp sting, pierced my butt through my damp cutoffs. "Tetanus shot," a medic said.

"Cocksucker," I whirled and kicked at him, dropped my gun and fell. My legs had stiffened and didn't obey. I was tired of being hurt.

"Everybody gets one," the sailor said, picking up my gun, setting it against the bulkhead behind the pile. As he guided me away by the arm, I looked back at the pile and wondered who would answer for such flagrant neglect.

We moved through a passageway, down a ramp, and into a large open area under a roof. It was the triage area; we were sorted according to the severity of our wounds. I sat on the warm deck and leaned back against the bulkhead. I heard another medevac chopper approaching. Two stretcher-bearers rushed in carrying a raging soldier, his leg shattered midway between knee and hip. He was covered with blood, convulsing uncontrollably. Men struggled to hold the tourniquet in place as the ruined leg flailed erratically, jerked by the stump it was still attached to. When he was moved from stretcher to gurney, the damaged leg slipped between and snapped free, the weight ripping it loose from strands still connecting it to his body. It hit the floor with a dull splat, splashing me with blood.

Calf muscles spasmed. It reminded me of butchering back on the farm—after skinning, the carcass hung on the crosstree to chill. My brothers and I would poke the steaming mass and watch small muscles quiver, as if they lived independently.

The jagged femur bone glistened above the severed leg, shards of tissue oozing blood across the deck. Flies gathered on the puddling juices. A medic scooped the leg up and carried it away.

I was tired and nodded off. Through hooded eyes I counted seven flies nibbling at a seeping hole on my leg while several crawled across my toes. It reminded me of the old papa-son down in the U Minh Forest that we had laughed at who squatted motionless in the sun while flies crawled across his face. Now I understood. Why waste energy brushing them away?

Another chopper came in. Dennis limped in and sat down next to me, his leg bare, his wound swathed in a stained battle dressing. My mind drifted back to the moment he was wounded, how he had conquered his fear and crawled back into his gun mount.

I wondered about Crow. Why had he deserted his gun? That sergeant wouldn't have been wounded if Crow hadn't run. And what about Snipe? Why hadn't he released the ramp safety latch? It was strange. I hadn't seen either of them when I went down to the well-deck. Were they hiding in the engine compartment? Buddha had threatened to shoot anybody who abandoned their position during a firefight. I wondered if he'd do it. I wondered if Crow felt guilty that he was uninjured and the man who'd taken his place was horribly maimed. I couldn't imagine carrying that guilt.

We sat in silence, Dennis and me, as chopper exhaust fumes wafted down the passageway from the helo deck, across our open compartment, and out over the river. Flies seemed to fidget at the mucky pungence and av-gas odor disturbing their bloody feast.

I watched the brown river flow seaward. At times, a Tango boat passed on BID patrol or a sampan or patches of vegetation floated past. On the distant riverbank the waterwheel sat idle and ripening grain waved in the paddy beyond the dike. A shaft of afternoon sun angled off the river softening the blood speckled pistachio green walls of the open compartment we sat in.

"I have to puke," I told a passing medic.

"Out the compartment door," he said, helping me to my feet. "It stinks enough in here. "How long have you been waiting?"

"I'm not sure—a long time. My ears are ringing."

He guided me across the walkway to the lifeline and held my shoulders as I leaned over the side. Thin bile dribbled down my chin and I watched it disappear into the brown river four decks below.

"I'll clean you up and you can lie down. It'll be a few hours before we get to you." I held the lifeline as he began cleaning. "How'd you get these leeches on you?"

I twisted painfully and looked at the back of my legs. "I was in the river."

"This'll take care of them." With an alcohol drenched cottonball he dabbed each one and they fell twisting to the deck.

"I pulled two off my ankle," I told him absently, as the leeches spiraled on the warm green deck.

He washed my wounds with brown antiseptic, put fresh bandages on, scrubbed crusted filth from my body, then helped me down the ladder to a berthing compartment. He gave me a shot. "For pain—we'll come and get you," he said, pulling the sheet to my chest. My body had stiffened while sitting against the bulkhead. Rubbing my blurry eyes with the clean sheet, I pulled it up over my bare shoulders and shivered as I drifted off, wondering at the incongruity of white sheets and air conditioning.

I woke slowly, naked beneath a bright light—back in that other light, I thought contentedly. Then I heard a metallic ping. Slowly my eyes focused through the mist. I was on an operating table. There was a dull tingling sensation in my neck and I realized I'd been given a spinal. I was floating. I watched a doctor's green eyes.

"It's a gear off a wristwatch," the masked face said. Then I heard another ping. I turned my head to the right and saw an arm and hand extended out. The pings were bits of iron dropped into a steel dish. I watched in fascination as the doctor worked. Blood seeped around wrist bones as he probed in the open joint. With a grunt of satisfaction he recovered a half-moon shaped piece of glass from my wrist—it didn't ping, it echoed with a dull thud. Black bits of iron mixed with jagged purple flesh. Bones sparkled in the overhead light as the scalpel moved quickly, cleaning damaged areas, slicing out embedded shards, straightening broken bones. A medic pulled a curtain across my shoulder, blocking my view. I closed my eyes.

The ringing in my ears blurred outside noises as I stared at the overhead—I was ten years old again, out in the woods in my secret place, shadowing deer at the salt-lick near Horseshoe Lake.

Like a leaf on a gently flowing current, I drifted. I lay trying to remember. Air-conditioning, iodine smell, ears ringing, body throbbing, it all washed over me as I rose from the depths of anesthesia.

Low sobs penetrated my calm from a bed nearby. "Where's my hand? I can't find my hand. I want my fucking hand."

"Lie still, you'll rip your stitches and start bleeding again. Don't move. I'm giving you a shot," said a medic. Sobs trickled to sniffles.

Memories swamped the calm as I recalled the day's events. I opened my eyes and saw a medic standing nearby. "What time is it?" I said, struggling up. "I've got to get back to my boat."

"What are you doing?"

"I'm going to the head," I told him, before I realized I was connected to a tube. "I've got to pee. My eyes hurt."

"You can't get up. I'll bring you a bedpan."

"I can't go in this thing with you watching."

"Call me when you're done."

I lay there about to burst, nothing coming out. I worked my way out of bed, removed the I.V. bottle from its hook and shuffled toward the head.

In the bathroom, I looked in the mirror. Watering eyes stared at a bruised, puffy face with burned-off eye brows. My gown fell open and I looked down. I was peppered with hundreds of small bits of shrapnel just below the skin. A few larger pieces had been lodged in my left leg and right arm. Those had been removed along with bone chips and damaged tissue. The fifth rocket, the one that had penetrated the armor two inches above my right hand had caused the most damage. The back of my head and neck hurt where several small pieces had entered when the molten steel had ricocheted around inside the cox'n flat. I was covered with a burning, itchy rash from crawling along the riverbank, sliding through large patches of brush that burned like nettles. The right side of my face was sore. I tongued my mouth and discovered several broken teeth. Pink fluid drained from my ears and everything had a haze to it.

My eyes felt as though somebody had thrown a handful of ashes into them. I took stock of my surroundings as I returned to my rack. I was in a large compartment on the ship, a small hospital ward, filled to capacity.

"Why are you out of bed—let me help you back." It was the medic who'd given me the bedpan.

"I'm hungry. What time is it? My eyes hurt."

"Evening chow is in two hours. Your eyes are burned, we

need to get you looked at."

"How can it be suppertime? What day is it?"

"It's Monday afternoon—you've been sleeping since they brought you back from surgery early this morning."

"I need to get back to my boat. Buddha's going to be pissed if I don't get my shotgun back."

"Who's Buddha?"

"My boat captain, he said he'd see me back at the *Benewah*."

"You're on the *Colleton*." The medic helped me onto a gurney then rolled me out of the compartment. "Don't worry about Buddha."

The room looked familiar—the table—the bright light. A medic removed my bandages and a doctor debrided the wounds, scraping the tissue raw.

I lifted my head and watched another medic scrub me with brown solution using a soft brush, working out bits of shrapnel near the surface. "You'll be picking bits of iron out for the rest of your life," he said.

I surveyed my injuries and again realized how fortunate I was. A hole in my right shin was swollen with infection. More bone chips were discovered and removed then the hole was packed with iodized gauze string. It hurt to turn my head—deep in my neck—and I recalled the spinal I'd gotten two years earlier to numb my body when my appendix had ruptured and I needed emergency surgery. It felt like that now.

The dreams began that night, my last night on the river. Dreams of the Viet Cong soldier. Noises, shadow movements, pain kept me awake—I thought I was awake. Ringing in my ears was distracting. When I closed my eyes *he* stared at me and I wondered if he was in the bright light. I wanted him to know I was sorry. And I drifted. I was alone, being chased through jungle, thorned vines snagging tattered fatigues, slowing me. My pursuer crashed through jungle. I threw myself behind a tree as *he* loomed over me. He grabbed my shoulder and I lashed out.

"You were yelling last night, something about worms getting you," said a medic, standing beyond my reach. "You're being transferred this morning,"

It was like looking through an aquarium. I knuckled my eyes and the pressure burst as liquid streamed down my cheeks. Gently I ran fingertips over eyebrow stubble and recalled the flash from that third rocket, when my face was against the armor slits—when I was looking at the shredded canopy.

24

Army 3rd Field Hospital-Tan Son Nhut

20 August 1968

Four of us were loaded into the chopper. We lifted off the *Colleton's* flight deck and flew northeast toward Saigon. As I looked down at early morning fog concealing the waterways, I recalled my last ride. Wind dried my eyes and they felt scratchy. I flinched when large raindrops pelted the helicopter. The fog disappeared and I searched the tree lines, expecting to see muzzle flashes. I closed my eyes as we vibrated north—when I looked down again it was with curiosity, not fear. That realization startled me and I lay exploring it—the longing for that bright sheltering light.

At 3rd Field Hospital we were carried into a sandbagged quonset hut. A medic rolled me past what must have been the main nursing station at the head of the ward, down a long aisle, and slid me from the gurney to a bed. The building reminded me of a neighbor's hog barn back home. Long and narrow, beds lined outside walls with a double row—head to head—down the center. Just like farrowing crates. Nurses and medics hurried about. It seemed to be a catch-all ward, ranging from soldiers recuperating from jungle rot to amputees awaiting flights home. The more serious cases were closest to the nurse's station. The ward was brightly lighted by a string of bare bulbs down the center. The quietness surprised me, and the smell—it was antiseptic—sterile.

I smelled her first, then heard the soothing voice with a Texas lilt. She redressed my wounds, then rubbed ointment on my body to relieve the itching caused by the burning bushes I'd crawled through along the riverbank. She was blond, the first woman I'd been near in months, and she was beautiful.

"Where are you from?" she asked, as she wiped my crusted eyes with a damp cloth.

"Minnesota."

"How'd you burn your eyes?"

I told her and she said she'd have somebody look at them.

Late afternoon a doctor examined me while the nurse observed. "His eyes are trying to form blisters but apparently he's rubbing them. Apply ointment then wrap them."

"This is routine for burned eyes," she said, standing close as she wrapped my eyes. It keeps bacteria out."

I could smell her perfume and her sweat and her minty breath.

"Your perfume reminds me of the lilacs at home when they're blooming," I told her, desperately searching for a lifeline—something to keep me afloat in my blindness.

"It's made from flowers. You'll be fine—next spring you'll be home to see those lilacs bloom." She laid her hand on my chest for a moment, then was gone.

Sounds terrified me. I felt vulnerable, lying in the middle of the ward, unable to identify strange noises. Night and day no longer existed. The nurse often paused with a few words and a touch.

Morning. I thought it was morning. They fed me juice and jello because my jaw was so swollen. Not broken, just badly bruised. The doctor decided I should be transferred to an Army hospital in Japan later in the day. My dressings were changed, pulled loose from crusted flesh. Irrigating, they called it. Keep the wounds open and draining so dirt and other foreign matter would come out. I was guided to the bathroom one last time, then placed on a stretcher.

I heard the nurse's voice as she bid each patient fare-well. "You'll be fine. Remember those lilacs next spring," she said, her cool hand on my forehead. Then we were out on the hot August afternoon tarmac.

"Rotten fucking smell," a voice near me said, as they carried us to the medevac plane.

I could taste the decay he was talking about, the rot— like that night we had landed here seven months earlier. But I also smelled tarry heat rising from asphalt. Nobody an-swered the voice as we were loaded into the shaded belly.

"What the fuck you bringing those coffins on for? I ain't riding with no fucking corpses." It was the voice again, and through my ringing ears I heard forklift tractors drop their loads and back out.

"Calm down," said another voice. "Be thankful you're not in one of those boxes."

"Fuck you man—you fly in here, pick up a load, and you're back in Japan for happy hour. Don't fucking tell me to be thankful. Those sorry dead fuckers are probably the lucky ones."

Taxiing down the runway, I felt lost, aware that I'd left something in this world we were leaving. How were the guys on the boat? What happened two days ago? It seemed much longer. I knew other boats had taken casualties. Were any of them on this plane—on stretchers or in coffins? I recalled what Professor had told me one night when he was trying to convince me that we should get out of Vietnam. I argued that to leave would mean all those who had been killed would have died in vain. "What about those who are going to die or get fucked up? Don't you think we owe them something?" he had replied. A hand touched my ankle and I jumped.

"How you doing?" shouted a medic, over the roar of the aircraft engines and my ringing ears. "About three hours, we'll land."

I nodded my head, okay. How did he think I was doing— hooked to an I.V., not able to see? The nurse had said I would see again, but the horror of blindness consumed me. I tried not to think of never seeing another sunrise or monarch butterflies hovering over red clover fields; or hunting—ducks streaking across a gray autumn sky as I led them with my 12 gauge; or deer hunting. What about my salt-lick?

I thought back to a Sunday after church. I was ten that summer, when I dissolved salt in a few gallons of boiling water. I lugged it about a mile into the woods to a stump I'd selected. It was a white pine stump—the tree harvested by loggers near the turn of the century. The top was porous and moss-covered, spongy in the center. I poured the brine onto the face of the stump—watched it seep into the decaying heart—not letting any spill down the sides. I had fantasized about monster bucks I would shoot. Now I might never see them. Blindness terrified me and I recalled that moment of light and yearned for its embrace.

25

106th General Army Hospital, Yokohama, Japan

22 August 1968

A nurse bathed my eyes in warm solution, removing salve and sloughed tissue. Then an eye specialist examined me. The doctor—Japanese by his accent—said to me, "Can you see my light?"

"I see gray, not black, like when the bandages were on." He gently probed, creating flashes—star-like streaks that dimmed to dots and floated slowly across my dark sky, then out of sight.

"Your corneas are badly burned. I can't tell about the iris, pupils, or optic nerves."

"Will I see again?"

"Only time will tell. We'll know in a few days—there's no infection, but we'll keep them bandaged."

I listened to ward routine as the morning progressed. The stench of changing bandages gave way to a colostomy bag that worked loose. That caused someone to vomit and that smell made me sick. I jumped when a bleach mop slapped the floor between our beds.

"You're a lucky mother," the mop voice said. "They can't make you do their nigger work."

"Yeah, I'm real lucky. Want to trade? What do you mean, do their work?"

"Shit man, the minute you're sent to PT, they put you to work."

"What's PT?"

"Physical Therapy." Then he laughed as a set of wheels squeaked past. "Man, you going to the head again? You're wearing out the wheels on that I.V. rack."

"Hey," the voice in the aisle replied. "I got to pee. Then he started chanting, "I'm free, I'm free, I got the million dollar wound—left-handed I can pee."

"What else can you do left-handed?" mocked a voice farther down the ward.

My hand ached. I discovered that if I folded my pillow in half and tucked it under, elevating it, the throbbing lessened. I heard another set of wheels, heavier, rolling toward me. Then I smelled it.

"Not that shit again," said the voice in the next bed. "This is the third time this week you've fed us liver."

"Sit up," a man's voice said. "I have a lunch tray."

I sat up, slid the pillow behind me, and felt a tray set on my lap. I was apparently on my own. I ran my fingers around the edge of the tray then felt for the food. My bandaged hand was of no use and I couldn't get food to stay on the fork so I ate with my fingers. Gravy was soon dripping down my chest along with bits of crumbled liver. Screw it. I'm hungry; they'd just have to clean me up.

"That must be the secret to eating this shit—close your eyes," the voice next to me joked. "Hey, can somebody help this guy?" He called. At supper time a nurse fed me.

Slowly the ward quieted and finally I heard, "Ten minutes to lights out." My ringing ears tried to focus on approaching footsteps but they shuffled past. I lay there, hand propped on pillow.

I must have dozed. "Get down. Get down. Incoming. Incoming. What the fuck is happening?" I screamed, ripping the bandage from my eyes, lashing out with my feet and hands as I dropped to the floor and rolled under the bed.

"Settle down. Nobody's going to hurt you," said a woman's voice. "A bedpan fell."

"Where am I? Who are you?" I shouted. The deck was warm. Cradling my injured hand, I curled up, ready for another rocket.

"You're in a hospital—nobody can hurt you." A hand reached down and touched my arm. "Let me help you up. I need to get you to the station."

They rebandaged my hand. Then I was rolled back to the ward and spent the night listening for intruders. In the morning they moved me to a corner bed. I could feel the wall at my headboard and the right side of the bed—there were only two directions I had to guard. Nurses and medics spoke softly from a distance, warning me of their approach. Through the window, morning sun warmed my face, mocking me. In the afternoon I heard a lawnmower and asked to have the window opened. Beneath the bandages, I wept at the smell of the fresh-mown grass and wanted to die if I couldn't see again.

I lay awake nights terrified of what the future might hold. When I was a kid a blind piano tuner used to come to our house—the old timers said he'd been gassed in World War I. His fingers reminded me of butterflies, how they had floated over keys—adjusting wires—ear cocked. But I knew I'd rather be dead than go through life blind. Doctor's exams, dressing changes, cleaning dead tissue from wounds, eating, bathing, feeling helpless and alone, no longer in control. The sweet stench of decaying flesh, antiseptics, last night's sweat, nightmare jungle chases.

Opaque shadows emerged as my vision returned. Light

increased and images formed. I received eye drops several times a day to moisten them as I blinked away burned tissue. The I.V. tube was removed from my arm. I talked a medic into a set of crutches.

I went to find the two guys I'd been between the first day on the ward—they'd shipped home. Each day a few men were transferred out, but their beds were quickly filled. My eyes improved, and again I was reminded how fortunate I was. Booby traps were the cause of most injuries on this ward, often resulting in blown off limbs—traumatic amputations, they were called. Light hurt my eyes, so each day I spent hours in bed dozing. Nights were bad. Hysterical screams—usually from new arrivals—echoed through the ward. And I remembered my first night, under the bed. Medics and nurses moved about the darkened ward, white specters drifting in the night, calming shattered nerves with a soothing word and an injection.

A young soldier in the bed next to mine had been on the ward for several days. His unit had been operating in South Vietnam's central highlands when they were ambushed. Walking point, he took two AK-47 rifle rounds in the stomach. He had a shit bag that had a life of its own; farting, belching, rumbling.

A gurgle, like a cow's wet grass fart, made me glance over at him.

"You want to play a game of checkers?" he asked.

"Why not?" I stole a last moment of sun warming my face. I recalled the thousands of games I'd played against my brothers and sisters. "Set'em up."

He slid a cart between our beds and set the board up. "You move first."

I couldn't concentrate. After three lost games I told him my eyes ached and I lay back on my pillow as his bag gurgled.

"I hate this fucking thing," he said with a catch in his throat. "It's so gross. I know my girlfriend won't be able to listen to it. They said I'd have to wear it the rest of my life." He kicked the checker cart and sent it skidding out into the aisle. He laid back, crying quietly. What could I say?

My wounds were healing. My eyes improved each day but my ringing ears still drained. The bone infection in my leg seeped, but I could walk with crutches. Scar tissue formed around the edges of holes on my hand and arm; some stitches were removed. Each day, small bits of iron worked their way out.

Whenever I dozed, *he* appeared—some nights we just looked at each other, his dark eyes piercing, questioning—other nights he chased me. Each night, I told him I was sorry. I'd wake up panting from my run. Lying silent, listening for his approach, I'd watch the sky turn from dark to gray and doze off when the ward awakened—in my twilight mindset I was comforted, knowing he'd be stopped before he got to me.

Afternoons I visited other wards, shuffling along, searching for anybody from the boats. I found the cox'n from another Tango boat. He was lying on his stomach, his back a mass of bandages. A rocket had detonated on the mast above him, showering him with shrapnel. He was sedated, not interested in visiting.

On the ward below mine, I found Mays. He'd always been easy-going and friendly. He had about eight years in the Navy and had planned to make it a career—impossible now. He'd lost a foot. He told me that a rocket had come through an open door and detonated on his ankle. He blamed it on a kid that had recently been assigned to his boat.

"Useless little honky," he raged. "I should've thrown the little fucker overboard the first time I saw him. Little shithead didn't shut the door behind him when he went to his gun mount. I wish the little fucker had been in the forward turret."

"Why's that?" I asked.

"Because, the first rocket that hit us went into that turret and cut my forward gunner in half."

I remembered him—a heavy-set black guy; always laughing. He and Mays had been close friends. "I'm sorry. I didn't know," I told him. I recalled the Alpha boat I'd seen pushed sideways by rockets and machine gun fire. I felt somehow guilty because I was white and he seemed to be attaching blame on whites.

"Man, I could sure use some smokes," he said absently, his eyes closed. He was still on an I.V. and I wondered if they were putting morphine in it and that was why he seemed different.

The soldier who drove the army skimmer—the small fiberglass outboard shuttling troops to the medevac boat on August 18—was on the same ward. He'd been hit deep in the shoulder by a sniper round, fracturing several bones. He said that day was a screw job, shuttling wounded on the open river when everybody knew snipers were there. I was supposed to ride that army skimmer to the medevac boat but Buddha had refused to let me go—too risky he'd said.

Each night I replayed the ambush, creating different scenarios that would save us. I felt guilty about trying to kick the wounded sergeant down the hole to the well-deck, but I thought he was dying anyway, and I had to escape from him. It was Crow's fault. If he'd stayed in his gun mount and done his job, that wouldn't have happened. Then I would somehow be on the riverbank in the jungle, running. I could hear whispers from the nurse's station as shifts changed at midnight and the bag sloshing in the next bed as he turned restlessly and whimpered.

I told my checker-playing friend about Mays needing cigarettes. He loaned me three dollars and I talked a ward medic into buying a carton of Kools. After lunch I shuffled to the ward below and delivered them to Mays and was rewarded with a hint of smile and the old humor. I met the boat captain of Tango 9. A piece of shrapnel had ripped a hole in his upper arm. He was from Idaho and planned to make the Navy his career. The boat cox'n with the back injury had been on Tango 9 also; the same rocket had wounded both of them. But there was a distance between us all—like we were in a play and didn't know our lines or what we were supposed to do.

One Sunday morning I attended church service. I wanted to keep the promises I'd made while lying on Tango 11's bloody deck. I knew I could never explain that moment of peace—that glimpse of eternity—so I pulled it close, treasured it and listened to the chaplain. I recalled the memorial service for the Tango 7 crew. Memorial services I'd witnessed flashed by, for Marines at Cua Viet and the Navy and Army services on the pontoon barges alongside the *Benewah* down in the Delta. I wondered what right I had to be alive. I hobbled out of the chapel when they began serving communion.

On Monday morning, three army guys, patients on the ward, received orders to return to Vietnam.

"Motherfuckers won't be happy 'til I'm in a body bag," said a black guy. "Two 'Hearts' I got already. What the hell they got to send me back for? I only got ninety-two days left. Motherfucker."

"This is just bullshit," said another soldier. "I can't even bend my knee I got so much metal in it. What the hell good am I going to be? Cocksuckers didn't even fix my teeth— said I could get it done in Danang."

"They can kiss my fuckin ass," said the third soldier. "I'm heading out the gate tonight and not coming back. Tokyo's a big place. I can get lost." In the morning he was gone.

Rumors circulated that some of us were going back to our boats. I asked Mays what he thought.

"I got my ticket home," he said, pointing at his bandaged stump. "I'd be surprised if they sent anybody back. Rumor has it the Vietnamese Navy is taking over the boats after the first of the year. Besides, they're still training classes at Mare Island. Lots of fresh meat. I doubt if you'll go back." Mays was right. Next morning my name was on a list for return to the United States.

My last night in Japan. I felt guilty going home, seeing so many others so grievously wounded. I was healing, I could return to Tango 11. Buddha needed me—who would cox'n the boat? The jungle night chase replayed, again, as each night, filled with nightmare terror of capture, only to jerk awake as *he* stood above me. I lay in the dark and thought about the crew on August 18. Professor had proven steady. Buddha had challenged his courage when we first met, yet Professor's steady nerves had calmed me when I panicked after that third rocket had knocked us down.

The army sergeant was a true hero. He'd come up and gotten terribly hurt. But I recalled seeing him still breathing in my rack in the well-deck. I couldn't imagine he had survived. If ever somebody deserved a medal for bravery, it should be him. Dennis and Stonewall and Buddha—they'd done their jobs. I never did see Snipe or Crow after the boat was beached. I wondered why Snipe hadn't released the safety latch for the ramp—why Crow had gone below instead of staying in his gun mount.

26

Starlifter Flight

28 August 1968

We were up at 0400 hours for final doctor inspections and fresh dressings. I was anxious about leaving the security of familiar surroundings, but excited about returning home. I'd said goodbye to Mays—the kid next to me had gone home the week before. I had requested to be sent to a Seattle area hospital but my transfer orders said Great Lakes Naval Hospital, north of Chicago.

Loaded buses pulled off the army base and past a crowd of Japanese waiting beneath a sea of umbrellas. As we drove through Yokohama I remembered the man on the water-wheel pedaling water up to his paddy and recalled how Professor was always talking about the perseverance of oriental people. At the airport, we wolfed down breakfast while the stretcher cases were loaded, then we were shuttled to the airfield.

Our plane was a C-141 Starlifter—a huge cargo plane. The front third of the hold was loaded with walking wounded, packed into aft facing seats; the middle third, filled with stretcher cases stacked five high, I.V. bottles hanging. Many of these patients were critical—amputees, burned, stomach, head, and chest wounds—nightmarish wounds. Medics and nurses were in constant attendance. The idea of facing family with such traumatic injuries must have been terribly stressful.

The rear of the plane was loaded with caskets. They were palletized, banded together, and loaded with a forklift tractor. I recalled the flight from Vietnam to Japan when my eyes had been bandaged and I couldn't see the coffins. Now I sat and stared at their gray sheen.

As the plane gained altitude, I drifted back to the beginning—that rainy Monday morning at Coronado, gathered in the auditorium for orientation with a map of Vietnam projected onto the screen. We had been bent on saving the world. So gung-ho. So naïve. Now I closed my eyes and saw *him*—and farmers and fishermen, their only desire, to live in peace and raise their families. They really didn't care what government was in charge. Professor was right. They didn't want or need us.

The aircraft's hum carried me to a plateau filled with foggy apparitions. Staring out the darkened window, I imagined I was on my R&R flight to Australia. The pressurized cabin, the sounds of the aircraft, my stuffy ears added to the sense of realness. The guys I traveled with—in my dream-state—were swathed in bandages. I watched them through the darkened porthole, yet I was with them. One attempted to lift a beer can to his lips, held between bloody stumps. Another was lying in a corner, blood puddled about him— it was me. I jerked awake, elbowing the man next to me, clammy sweat draining down my face. Again, I wondered what happened to the guys on Tango 11. I hadn't seen any of them in the hospitals. I watched as two medics walked up the aisle between the rows of stretchers, checking swaying I.V. bags, shouting to the patients over the plane's turbines.

I looked past the stretchers to the shadowed coffins and recalled a conversation with Professor about a philosophy book he'd been reading.

He had talked about Just War and principles of Just Cause and Just Conduct and said how we—the United States—had perverted the concept. The whole thing was too abstract for me and I had only half listened as I'd slapped mosquitoes. It had been one of the nights during the U Minh Forest operation. He'd talked about the civilians we were killing. I had argued with him about that. We'd never fired on any. But he continued on, saying that we didn't know where all those bullets we fired ended up. And the bombs we heard in the distance on still nights—they were from B-52s, dropped from 30,000 feet. What were they hitting? I only knew that I had never hurt a civilian and was thankful for that.

I recalled what the tour boat director had said that first afternoon I met Dennis while we were crossing San Diego Harbor. "Off our starboard side secured to a mooring buoy you will see a warship similar to the USS *Maddox*, the destroyer that started the Vietnam War. It was three years ago this month that she fired on a North Vietnamese patrol boat in their territorial waters. Since then, over 15,000 Americans have been killed and over 100,000 Vietnamese civilians and soldiers have been murdered by American bombers and ground troops." That was almost a year ago. I wondered if he'd adjusted his numbers since then. I thought I'd tuned him out that day. Some people opposed the war—I considered them ignorant. As I reflected, I was surprised. Professor and the tour guide had said basically the same thing. Would the tour guide use the bodies at the back of this plane as part of his statistics?

Rain gusted in the open door as we sat on the tarmac in Anchorage, Alaska. Patients and coffins destined for the west coast were transferred to different aircraft; the rest of us continued on.

Hours passed and finally engine pitch changed as we began our descent to Scott Air Force Base in southern Illinois.

We were shuttled to a mess hall, then waited for our flight. I watched the television mounted high in a corner. The Democratic National Convention was in Chicago and the world seemed to have gone crazy. Protesters and policemen were battling in the streets. A pig had been nominated to run for president.

"What the hell is going on?" I asked one of the mess hall workers cleaning a nearby table.

"Who knows? From what I hear the protesters are getting the crap beat out of them."

"But there are thousands of them. Where did they come from?"

"They've been talking about it for two weeks—the protesters started coming to Chicago and it seems like it got out of hand. They want peace in Vietnam—sounds good to me, I don't want to go." He nudged my crutches with his foot, "Look at you. What good did it do?"

I looked at him and recalled the Vietnamese farmers and fishermen again. But in my mind I justified being there— fuck him—what did he know? Friggin scullery rat had probably never been out of Illinois.

Red Cross ladies offered us one free phone call to our families, to let them know we were home. But there wasn't a telephone at the farm in Minnesota. We boarded our last flight for the short hop to Glenview Naval Air Station (GNAS) near Chicago.

We seemed to barely reach cruising altitude before we began descent. We touched down and taxied to the hangar. Everybody was silent, no doubt lost in his little universe of memories as the aircraft rolled to a stop. Hydraulics hummed, cargo bay doors opened, and the rear ramp lowered. First off, caskets. Next, stretcher cases were transferred to ambulances and buses. Last, we walked out the rear door of the plane.

27

Greeted by
Antiwar Protesters

29 August 1968

It was a bright autumny day. Cool, clear—I was surprised not to smell burning leaves. We loaded onto gray navy buses for the ride north to the hospital. As our bus meandered across the base, I smelled fresh-mown grass along the boulevards where marigolds and pansies sparkled in the breeze. Sailors, working slowly, picked weeds from flower patches—tending lawns seemed somehow surreal. Nearing the gate, we stared at men in crisp uniforms saluting each other, shiny cars passing through—it was a world we'd forgotten. Then we were beyond the security of the base.

"Well kiss my ass. We got a welcoming committee out here," said a small man sitting near the front of the bus.

I was farther back, behind the stretchers that flanked both sides. I moved forward in the aisle. A large group of people stood on the sides of the street holding signs welcoming us home.

Eggs and tomatoes splattered the windshield. Wipers smeared a pasty reddish yellow crescent.

The bus slowed and a ripple of noise washed over us. Antiwar protesters blocked the street, in front and behind the bus. We couldn't move—we were surrounded by the mob. They screamed and waved signs. They attacked with rotten fruit, tomatoes, bricks. As they gained courage they begin hitting the bus windows with clubs, fists, and protest signs; screaming obscenities and lies.

I thought of the pack of wild dogs that had attacked a doe when I was twelve. It was early winter—I was out checking muskrat traps. First I heard the yapping, then the doe burst through a clump of willows and out onto the ice, where she stood quivering. A few seconds later, five mangy-haired dogs broke from the slough, skidded onto the ice, and surrounded the trembling deer. The protester shouts blended to an indistinguishable blur in my ringing ears.

Beyond the stretcher, beyond the garbage-splattered window, a girl's hate-filled face twisted as her mouth stretched wide screaming at us. I caught snatches. "…fucking killers …rot in hell. Fucking pig lackeys..."

She reminded me of the prostitute in Saigon—the way her face had twisted after the drunken soldier stomped it. But then I recalled the girl sitting beneath the eucalyptus tree in Golden Gate Park the weekend Professor, Dennis, and I had visited Haight Ashbury. This screaming girl beyond the bus window was so angry. The one beneath the tree had smiled at me. Had that been only nine months ago? How could people change so fast?

Bricks thudded against the bus. It edged forward when the mob tried to force the doors open. I was at a loss when I looked into the raging faces of the young people banging fists against the windows. Professor had talked about people protesting the war, but nothing about hating us. These were people my age. What had I done to them?

The confrontation was over as abruptly as it had begun. Eggs and tomatoes splayed back windows. I watched through splattered yokes as protesters shrank in the distance.

I stood beside a stretcher holding a blind soldier. "What is it?" he shouted. "Who's out there—why are they scream-ing—what's going on?"

"It was antiwar protesters. They can't get us. We're past them," I said, my hand on his shoulder.

He reached up, grabbed my hand and squeezed. "Don't let them get me." Then his voice rose in panic, "Don't let them get me. Shoot me first! Promise me, don't leave me."

I recalled the sense of helplessness the dark days my eyes were bandaged. How I'd flash back to jungle night-mares at noise threats. His words angered me. Who were these people, terrorizing a blind man; attacking injured peo-ple; betraying us? The confrontation was like a firefight, but in this nightmare we had no weapons. We'd been ambushed and wounded again. There were about twelve of us, walking wounded, on the bus and some shouted at the driver.

"Turn this fucking bus around. We want a piece of those assholes."

The driver pulled to the curb. "I'd love to, but there's a standing order—military personnel that assault antiwar pro-testers will be court-martialed. We'd be infringing on their first amendment right to free speech. Welcome home."

"Don't leave me," the blind man sobbed.

I looked down. I'd forgotten him and he was still clutch-ing my hand. I squeezed his fingers. "Don't worry, nobody's going to hurt you." A slight tremor passed through his body and he rolled his face toward the tomato-stained window, his fingers clutching mine.

Afternoon sun baked us as we traveled north on Inter-state 94. I watched the faces of people on their way home in the rush-hour traffic and I recalled Buddha's words. "Frig-gin civilians. They're a bunch of sheep, don't know any-thing better." They turned off to peaceful sounding towns like Highland Park, Deerfield, Lake Forest, Lake Bluff. Our convoy turned off the Interstate and we passed a sign—VA Medical Center. Old men in wheelchairs stared at us from behind the cyclone fence.

That night I had a dream. I was on a stretcher, my eyes bandaged. Protesters poked at me with sticks and laughed. They took turns, sneaking up beneath cover of the screamers, poked me with glowing sticks, then jump back laughing. I lashed out with my feet. A corpsman woke me up. It was a strange dream. Crow stood in the crowd, laughing at my torment. The other face, Vietnamese—*his* face, tried to shield me.

28

Great Lakes Naval Hospital

15 September 1968

I began physical therapy. My right hand was bent up, back, from tissue and skin that had been damaged. The fingers were undamaged—they had been curled around the throttle, protected by the thick brass handle when the rocket burned through. Each morning, a therapist massaged my hand and wrist, pushing slowly downward, stretching, strengthening skin and muscles, improving range of motion. My right leg was still sore from the infection, still seeping, but I spent an hour each morning stretching and walking to strengthen it. Dark specks of metal—shrapnel—continued to surface. I watched other patients struggle to rebuild their lives without limbs, sightless. One young man had no forehead yet seemed mentally alert. For the thousandth time I wondered about war's capriciousness and how Professor and I had so miraculously been spared.

At night, the screams and moans and smells from earlier wards were replaced by low moans and nightmares. In the darkness I willed thoughts to peacefulness yet, on the periphery, August eighteenth lay in wait to ambush me. Always the game ended with the rocket entering the cox'n flat at a different angle, making a direct hit on me, like the rocket that had maimed the sergeant. Then it would get fuzzy, and I'd be crawling on the riverbank. Then the dream would come—always the same—alone, chased through the jungle, thorned vines snagging tattered fatigues, slowing me down. Crashing behind me—throwing myself behind a tree as *he* loomed over me.

In the early morning hours I'd creep from my bed to the darkened dayroom and—with others— watch lighted ships inch across Lake Michigan.

An escape was the Magnavox television donated by the Disabled American Veterans. Mounted high on the wall in the dayroom, it tantalized us with a fairytale world of luxury autos, easy-to-use household goods, liquor, cigarettes—all promoted by beautiful women.

"Give me an hour with that girl—the moon would be flashing on my bare ass in the back seat," was a typical reply to the mini-skirted model promoting the Mustang convertible.

Then there was the girl standing on her head, demonstrating how simple the new and improved floor wax was to apply. "For women with more exciting things to do than scrub floors," bragged the commentator. In response, somebody would shout, "Stand on your head Honey—I'll eat you like an ice cream cone."

Liquor and cigarette commercials brought a mixed response, the way they were set in romantic and peaceful settings, especially when men were in the scenes.

"Look at that faggoty cocksucker ride off into the hills with a Marlboro hanging from his lip. Probably fucks his horse when he gets over the ridge. Bet he's never had leeches in his crotch."

"That fuckin idiot. You can tell she wants it, and all he

does is stare at the sailboats," in response to a Scotch whis-key commercial, the setting, a seaside pavilion.

Soap operas commanded silence; each show had its au-dience. Men hung on the dialogue and nuances of the day's events then rehashed them for hours afterward, musing on what might develop the next day.

News of the war had a strange, silencing effect. We watched, but nobody discussed it. Henry Kissinger was get-ting more involved in the Paris Peace Talks and I recalled what Professor had said—the war would drag on for years if he became a participant. I'd never really watched much television. On the farm, we had a small black and white but reception was terrible. During my four years in the navy I'd mostly been on ships or overseas.

I received a thick manila envelope; return address, Washington DC. Inside was a Purple Heart Medal. It was water-damaged—the gold tarnished, the white portion of the ribbon stained gray. It reminded me of the stale left-over-from-Korean War C-rations we'd been fed; one of the guys on the ward joked that the Purple Heart should have gotten a Purple Heart. I quietly tucked it away.

I began getting passes from the hospital and my two old-er brothers, who lived nearby, took turns picking me up. I spent weekends at their apartments. They were both married and each had a child, but I was an excuse to party. I wasn't old enough to drink in Illinois, so we often crossed the bor-der into Wisconsin to visit a small bar and dance joint called The Pit. It was a happy, noisy place packed with young beer drinkers. Vietnam seemed another world, yet afterwards I'd feel guilt that I was having such a grand time when so many were dead.

One evening, on the Illinois side of the border, my brother and I stopped at a greasy-spoon where they didn't card me.

We began with a pitcher of beer then ordered supper; baskets of shrimp and fries, soggy with cooking oil. We ate, drank another pitcher of beer, then went to the bathroom. With the door locked, we crawled out the window and squealed out of the parking lot in his new Mustang convertible, howling with laughter. Two blocks later we were pulled over for speeding—they didn't know about our dine-and-dash and we talked our way out of the ticket. The patrolmen were veterans. We told them we were out celebrating. I showed them my hospital wrist tag—told them I'd been wounded in Vietnam. For the rest of that autumn we joked about the locals lined up at the locked bathroom door, their legs crossed waiting to pee.

I went to see *Valley of the Dolls* one of my first evenings away from the hospital. The line at the theater—the people joking, talking about things important to them—their jobs, high gas prices, a weekend party—troubled me. Didn't they realize there was a war going on? Didn't they give a fuck? It was a different world from mine and I felt adrift. There was a comfort level back with the guys on the ward that was missing here. Inside the darkened theater I didn't trust people sitting behind me. I moved to the back row. Life was not what Magnavox portrayed.

I was staying with my brother and his wife in Woodstock, IL, one weekend. My younger brother and his friend were down from northern Minnesota visiting and we were walking around downtown. Woodstock had a quaint farm town atmosphere and the town square was a community gathering place. Afternoon sun flashed through crimson maple leaves in sharp contrast to the plush grass below them.

A large crowd was gathered in the square. As we drew near I heard amplified voices haranguing the group, vehemently denouncing the war. "Bomb schoolhouses—napalm hospitals. American troops raid villages at night, drag young girls into the jungle, rape them—kill the parents. The American CIA accuses Vietnamese of being traitors and tortures them, claiming they are Viet Cong. American helicopters shoot at farmers working in rice paddies. Stop them. Stand up. Unite. The North Vietnamese want only peace and freedom. America must get out of Vietnam," shouted the speaker.

I looked around in disbelief. Students sat on the grass in front of the podium; crowds surrounded the square, standing on the cobblestone walkways listening to the diatribe. Protest organizers sat in chairs on one side of the stage while one protester, older than the others—scrawny, long haired, with intense dark eyes—choreographed the speakers. One by one they rose, approached the microphone and began their spiel with the phrase "I'm not a scheduled speaker, however..." As each speaker retreated from the platform, the leader cheered and clapped, motioning others to join him, attempting to stir the crowd's enthusiasm. They were telling lies—distorting truths.

Our boat crew hadn't killed women and children. We didn't rape women. We hadn't destroyed Vietnamese homes or villages. I never witnessed bombing or napalming of innocents. We never shot at farmers in their paddies. Often times we didn't return fire because ricocheting rounds might injure innocent civilians. We never tortured prisoners. We turned them over to the ARVN for interrogation. Anger rising, I moved forward.

"You're a bunch of fucking liars," I screamed up at them from beyond the police cordon. In my mind, I was back on the bus—these were the same people who had assaulted me. "Let me through," I said to a policeman holding a baton between us. "Those bastards are lying. They don't know what the fuck they're talking about. I just got back from Vietnam. I want to talk."

A police sergeant came over, listened to my story, and

agreed. The protesters all claimed they weren't scheduled speakers. They felt it their moral obligation to speak up. I also should have that opportunity. The policemen escorted me to the podium. The protesters stood to block us from the stage. This was not part of their plan. The policemen pushed them back with batons. Strange how they didn't resist, I thought absently.

"Give me the microphone, asshole." I said it softly as I reached out toward the greasy-haired protester.

"You're not a scheduled speaker here," he shouted, pulling it back.

My hand shot forward, grabbed the microphone. "None of you are scheduled from what you're telling this crowd," I shouted.

He grabbed for the microphone. A policeman hit the protester's arm and pushed him into a chair with the rest of the group.

"Who of you has been to Vietnam?" I shouted into the microphone. I approached them and pointed. "Have you? You? You?" Glares answered me.

The eight protesters rose—the policemen raised batons. "Stay back—don't give us a reason," the sergeant said.

I scanned the crowd. "I have been there." And I began repeating what I'd been taught. "We're protecting the South Vietnamese from communist aggression. Viet Cong are the terrorists, killing their own people. They kill village leaders, rape and torture family members in front of parents before executing them. They extort money from farmers and fishermen to finance their terrorism. They force young men and women to serve with them under threat of killing family members."

"Baby killer. Baby killer," shouted the protesters. The police line advanced, batons raised. The protesters went silent.

"These people are cowards," I shouted, pointing. "Several weeks ago a planeload of wounded flew into Glenview Naval Air Station. We were assaulted when our buses left the base. They knew they could do it without being stopped— protected by the first amendment, freedom of speech. They so terrified a blind soldier he committed suicide that night. Hung himself in a toilet stall. This scum hasn't been to Vietnam. They're cowards hiding behind peaceful intentions. Look at them. If they believed, would they let a few policemen stop them? They're chickenshit."

"You bastard! I'm glad you were shot. Too bad they didn't aim better," shouted the chorographer. "We'll get you."

I dropped the microphone to the stage and crushed it under my heel as I turned to walk away. The crowd began milling, talking in hushed tones, and wandered off. Sun still sparkled through red-leafed maples. Next morning, my brother told me that he heard on the radio that some protesters had been caught with a trunk load of dynamite. Late afternoon I returned to the base and found orders waiting for me—a thirty day leave.

That night I lay awake replaying the confrontation. I hadn't given it any thought then, but now, after watching the Democratic National Convention fiasco on television and listening to the protesters in Woodstock, I was confused. Even my brothers were careful not to ask about the war. I wasn't the only one; men talked about it on the ward. The most common complaints were from guys returning from leave— they no longer felt comfortable—everybody had changed.

29

Convalescent Leave-
Return to the Farm

2 October 1968

As the Greyhound passed through Wisconsin dairy country I watched Holsteins going out to pasture after morning
milking. Leaves turned from reds to golds as we crossed the
St. Croix River into Minnesota. Riding north, they faded to
wind-blown browns, to naked trees like the ones artillery
had stripped at Cua Viet. We passed Lake Bemidji toward
the Greyhound station at the Markham Hotel. I wasn't wearing my uniform— that was another thing guys returning to
the hospital said. Don't wear a uniform when traveling. Assholes would insult you.

Nobody knew I was coming—no phone at the farm—so
I started hitchhiking, duffle bag in hand. It was a clear day
but I shivered, not used to the late autumn north wind. About
four miles north of town a neighbor picked me up.

"Didn't hear you were home," Tom said. "Thought you
were in the hospital."

"I got a thirty day convalescent leave—just got it yesterday. Didn't have time to send a letter." He was quiet for the
next sixteen miles.

Near the farm we passed my stepfather, Herman, bent

over, pawing through the dirt, picking potatoes at the edge of a cornfield. He didn't see us when we passed. He looked so alone out there—small and old. The kids were in school.

"I'll get out at the end of the driveway." I looked over, thanked him and climbed out. He nodded in silence. The old neighbors were men of few words. I waved as he drove away. Not much of a dust cloud on this clay-packed road, just oil fumes from worn piston rings.

I limped the quarter mile up our driveway toward the homestead. My mother, Barb, saw me about half way and came out. I hadn't heard from her since I'd been wounded. Now she ran her hands down my pant leg and sleeve as if to see if I was missing anything. Apparently one of my brothers had told her where I'd been injured.

"My dearest, darling son. I was so worried about you."

"Yeah, yeah," I said slipping away. "I'm thirsty and tired and need to sleep. I'm fine."

"You can stay in your old room. How long are you here for?"

Everything seemed the same. The loud, slamming screen door—like the ones on the hooches in Cua Viet. The flypaper ribbons hung over the table, black with the summer's catch. The withered plants, long-dead from lack of water. The old-lived-in-house-smell. The humming flickering fluorescent tubes that never got changed until they went dark. I walked through the house to the front room—the piano piled high with sheet music of Bach, Beethoven, Mozart, and Lutheran church hymnals. I looked out the picture window to Maple Lake. Past the fort Randy and I had built in a huge birch tree. Most of the little treehouse was on the ground now, a section of roof wedged in the fork near a broken limb—like a body after an artillery barrage.

I jumped when the screen door slammed and turned to see Herman standing in the kitchen looking at me. He was carrying a wire basket of potatoes in each hand. His shoulders sagged under the weight. His sweat-wilted engineer cap shaded his eyes. He set the baskets down and came toward me. Silently he put his arms around me and hugged. Tears came unbidden. He had never shown affection to anybody. He stepped back quickly, turned, and blew into his wrinkled gray handkerchief. "I gotta get these spuds to the basement," he said, and walked back to the kitchen.

Barb watched silently.

The kids came home from school—not much had changed with them. They treated me the same as ever. That night we played cards and visited like the old days. I think they were warned not to ask me about the war.

After the house went dark, I slipped out and walked to the bluff overlooking Maple Lake. Beneath the harvest moon I listened to geese wing south. Twice flocks passed between me and the moon. Frost settled and I remembered and wept and didn't understand why. I felt guilty because I was alive when so many others weren't and I recalled Professor's words, "What about those who haven't died yet?" Now many of them were dead. I drifted off—that was the first night I felt happy to greet those faceless ones in my dreams—I felt safe with them. I woke up shivering, stars fading in the east and mallards feeding on wildrice near the boggy shoreline. I crept back to the house and filled the stove. Herman heard me and got up and shuffled out into the living room in his ancient leather moccasins and droopy-bottomed long johns, putting the coffeepot on to boil.

"You were picking spuds yesterday when Tom and I drove past. I'll help you today," I told him as he sprinkled coffee into the bubbling water.

"That's good. I got nobody to ride the digger and raise it at the end of rows. I was forking'em yesterday." He stood for awhile, back to me, looking down at the pot as grounds rolled in the boiling water. "Do the mallards still feed below the hill at night?"

I nodded silently.

Slowly he turned, handed me a mug of coffee, grounds still swirling. "How long you home for?"

"Thirty days. Then I go back to Great Lakes. You planted quite a bit of corn this year—cob corn or silage?"

"Silage. It froze early. Kernels didn't dent."

"I'll help get it chopped—it'll go fast with both of us— maybe Randy can help get wood up on the weekends before I go back." He had aged. The halo of hair surrounding his pale bald skull had gone from gray to white. His shoulders drooped, as though he were still holding the potato baskets. He nodded as he shifted the handleless mug between palms. He got dressed then and went out to do the morning milking and chores before breakfast.

The week passed. We finished the potatoes then got the silage chopping machinery greased and ready to go. I fell into my old routine. For brief moments I forgot, but a whiff of kerosene, wood smoke, the slamming screen door or a thousand other things sent me back. One day my little sister showed me a pair of glasses the army had sent to the farm and I remembered them testing my eyes back in Japan before they'd healed. I looked through them and laughed. With the dark frames and thick lenses they truly were the proverbial Coke-bottle glasses. The kids had fun playing with them.

On Friday night Randy and I went to a bonfire beer party at a neighbor's house. People I'd known all my life seemed uncomfortable when I came near—edged away after a brief greeting. One guy praised me for being a Black Beret. I looked at him in silence and thought what an ass he was. He'd weaseled out of the draft by claiming to be a farmer, now he praised me. Black Berets sounded mysterious. He probably thought they must be greater than the fabled Green

Berets. Little did he know that Black Berets were PBR sailors—PBRs were small, water-jet propelled patrol boats that had caught the media's fancy—like the mystique of World War II PT boats—totally unlike the slow, heavy workhorse I was on. I didn't bother explaining the difference. I grabbed a handful of beers and sat in the shadows away from the noise. Sparks showered skyward as kids poked at the bonfire, chanting, "Come on baby light my fire." Crow liked that song and I could see him sitting on the edge of his rack in the well-deck, a can of warm whiskey in his hand, tapping his foot and humming along, mouthing a lyric now and then.

Each day I walked the woods around the farm. Randy and I used to take turns climbing young maple trees. When the climber was about fifteen feet in the air, the one on the ground chopped the tree and it was an exhilarating ride down. Now I kicked at the rotting stumps. The bloated cows' legs I'd used as teeter-totters were now scattered bones.

Herman asked me to ride into town with him. We delivered two cans of cream to Land O' Lakes Creamery, then drove around on errands; Co-op store, Red Owl, Surge Milking Machine dealer. It was the same at each stop. "This is my boy—just got back from Vietnam." He didn't see the silent nods and fixed-grin responses. He was proud.

We got out of the car at the little gas station downtown. "Put in a dollar's worth," he told Dale, the owner. We walked over to a truck with bushel baskets of apples pyramided from ground to tailgate. It was an unspoken rule—if you bought gas you got a free apple. Dale came over, Herman handed him a dollar and said, "This is my boy, he just got back from Vietnam."

I'd begged apples from Dale since I was a little kid. He looked at me, frowned, and said, "Take two." Dale had been in the Korean Conflict.

Later we went out to the John Deere dealer on the west

side of town and went in back to find a part for the silage chopper. "This is my boy, he just got back from Vietnam," he said to the mechanic.

The mechanic had been a Marine Raider during WWII and lost a hand during the assault on Tarawa, so the story went. As little kids, we had peeked in the open overhead door at him in awe—the story was that a Jap hacked it off with a sword, but one-handed the mechanic had clubbed him down. Now he looked at me, nodded, and said, "Howdy." Then he turned back to his work.

At home the kids found it humorous that I jumped at unexpected noises. I learned to sit facing the door so they couldn't surprise me with the slamming screen door. One evening after supper Randy came around the table behind me—I caught a hint of burned cordite then a string of cracks like an AK-47 exploded under my chair. I hit the deck. Herman jumped, too. "Take those damn firecrackers outside." He'd served in the army during WWII. The kids thought the whole thing hilarious.

We harvested corn that week. I drove the Allis Chalmers tractor, pulling a wagon alongside the chopper while Herman drove the Farmall pulling the harvester that diced the corn stalks. Each day after a late lunch he took a nap—he seemed to tire easily. On the weekends Randy helped cut firewood.

Many nights I crept out of the house and sat above the lake. The first flakes of winter brushed my cheeks and I recalled a strange thought I'd had during the memorial service for the Tango 7 crew. How that past winter they'd flown west, died and come home before the frost was out of the ground. This would be their first full season beneath the soil. Why them and not me? We were supposed to lead the column that morning.

I wandered north one sleeting afternoon, beyond the

barn, over a fence, into the woods—stopped to check the twine box on an abandoned oats binder—yes, the wrens had used it again this past season. My feet carried me back, beyond the thickets of the sumac maze we'd played in, down through a gully carved by glaciers, up the far side where I shuffled through dank leaves until I found the Hills Brothers coffee can. I sat against a birch tree and sobbed the racking cries of the little boy whose puppy had been murdered; for everybody—the pilot in the Gulf of Tonkin, the crew of Tango 7, the Marines at Cua Viet, the army troops in the Delta, the sailors, the Viet Cong soldier, the little dog. I wept as I stared at the rusted can I'd used as a headstone that morning so many years ago when I buried Shep.

Early one morning near the end of my thirty-day leave, Herman got up while I was filling the stove. He put coffee water on to boil then kneeled at the bottom step of the stairs, opened a hinged step, and pulled out a .50 caliber ammo box he stored his treasures in. The box held medals, paperwork, pictures—a lifetime accumulation of memories. He removed an antique silver cigar cutter attached to a hand-made silver chain.

"When I returned from the war, my father gave me this and the homestead—now I want you to have it." He held it out and lowered it gently into my open palm, chain links flashing beneath the flickering fluorescent, then turned back to the stove and filled our coffee mugs.

My last day at home, clouds scudded overhead, spitting snowflakes that sparkled in the sun. Deer season opened that weekend and I decided to try for one. I loaded the 30-30 Winchester and walked back to Horseshoe Lake—to the deer lick I'd drifted back to under anesthesia after I'd been wounded. I spotted the two white pines. Entering the tree line, I paused every few steps to listen and look.

Deer had completely destroyed the lick. There was a

leaf-covered hole two feet deep with arms reaching out like giant tentacles. They'd devoured the root system, digging twelve feet out from the base of where the stump once stood, seeking traces of salt that had leeched down over the years.

I crept along the lakeshore through thickets of new aspen shoots, past gnawed barkless gray stumps with lichen clinging to the north side, past an overgrown beaver run—the beavers had moved on because they'd depleted their food supply. On a high point of land poking out into the lake—like the small salient Tango 7 had angled out from in the river—I crouched, peeked over a blow-down, and spotted a flock of canvasbacks bobbing in the middle. Beyond them, on the far side of the lake, wind created long ocean-like swells in reed canary grass. Near the shore below me, water-lily leaves danced on slow rolling waves as they battled new-forming ice while chickadees flitted from leaf to leaf. Nestled out of the wind, bathed in early winter sun, I dozed off with the Winchester between my knees, barrel resting against my shoulder.

I jerked awake, sweat-drenched and shivering, with a hollow feeling—an ache for the tranquility of that numinous glow. Through the haze of the remembered dream I saw Buddha squatting in the soft light. He frowned, rattling a pair of dice in his hand, chanting, "Seven come eleven, seven come eleven." A one-legged Vietnamese man crouched in the sand next to him, eating a can of C-rations and grinning, nodding encouragement. Professor, Dennis, Stonewall, and I stood in a dusty village square visiting with a group of peasants. Everybody laughed. Smiled. Their faces radiant. Snipe and Nancy sat in the dusty red clay laughing at a little girl as she played with my puppy, Shep. A wrinkled mamason squatted at a cooking fire ladling bowls of fish soup her Viet Cong soldier son passed to me with a smile and a bow. Our boat drifted in the river. Crow hung from the top of the ramp, feet twitching above dark water. Mamasan's son held out a bowl of *nuoc mam*-scented rice to me with a smile as she nodded for me to accept it—I felt at peace as she welcomed me home.

Remembering, gazing into early winter radiance flashing off wind-swept water, I flicked salty droplets from my lip with the smooth cool muzzle of the Winchester.

Epilogue

As the years passed, I thought of my fellow crewmen often. In 1991, when I discovered Buddha's telephone number through a Mobile Riverine Force Association (MRFA) reunion bulletin, I decided to contact him. I hoped to finally lay to rest my yearning to know what had happened to my old crewmates.

During the time we served together, the rest of the guys and I had thought of Buddha as a tyrannical alcoholic who made unreasonable demands upon us. We would gather on the boat's stern as he snored in his bunk in the well-deck, and complain about his dictatorial ways, shaking our heads. My hand trembled as I dialed Buddha's number. When I finally said his name into the phone, I wasn't prepared for his reaction.

"Hello?" A gravelly voice answered.

"Buddha?"

"This is Ed Thomas," he answered. Silence for a moment. Then he said softly, "Some people called me Buddha long ago."

"Buddha. This is Afe. From Tango 11."

"Afe?" he said very quietly. "Afe?" he said again, this time his voice gruff, the same as I remembered. "I've been looking for you for twenty-four years." The phone went silent. I thought I had lost the connection. Then he coughed and continued. "They told me your medevac chopper got shot up but nobody knew what happened to you." Another pause. I heard Buddha's sharp intake of breath. "When we got back to the *Benewah* two days after the ambush, nobody knew what had happened to you."

He pulled his breath in again and let it out in a sob. "I tried to find you. You were gone."

I was shocked by his emotion. This was not the same person I had known on the boat. After he regained his composure, after we had caught up on our lives, he told me it was the anniversary of Tango 7—the day she had hit the mine. "It should have been us," he whispered.

Buddha lived ten hours from me, in the Upper Peninsula. That autumn, as I drove north on Forest Highway 13 through afternoon drizzle, my mind drifted back to Vietnam. Saturated maple branches hung low in the overhead canopy like nipa palms on jungled riverbanks. Ferns and tag alders provided perfect camouflage for ambushers along the shoulders. I caught myself watching for trails in wet grass, unnatural branch configurations, braced for that first rocket. I stopped behind a jackknifed logging truck. Exhaust permeated the haze, and again I tasted our boat's diesel fumes as we idled on fog-shrouded rivers.

Buddha's cabin was rough, unpainted chipboard inside and out. A hand pump supplied water to the sink which drained onto the sand just beyond the wall. No hot water. An outhouse. We spoke long into the night, Buddha drinking Johnny Walker, ice, and Coke, while I nursed a warm beer. He told me what he knew of the men, the rumors he had heard over the years.

Buddha said he heard a rumor that Crow had committed suicide after he got out of the Navy and the black sergeant had recovered from his wounds—receiving the Silver Star. He didn't say anything about Snipe, just shook his head when I asked a second time. Buddha said he saw Stonewall in Norfolk about a year after they returned from Vietnam. They had a few drinks, agreed to get together, but Buddha never saw him again. He had no idea what happened to Dennis or Professor.

Buddha seemed to go for days without eating. On the woodstove that heated the cabin, there was an open pot of bean soup simmering. I ate some the first day and found it laced with dog hair. Three days later, after the soup had gone cold at night when the stove burned out and warmed again in the morning when rekindled, the soup had fermented. Buddha swore it was okay.

During one of my visits, Buddha and I attended the MRFA reunion in Chattanooga and renewed acquaintance with crewmen from other boats. I listened as a radioman who was on a boat behind us related how he remembered August 18th.

Steve told the story to a group of guys, each holding a can of Budweiser, perched on chairs in a circle around him. Steve had watched our boat, in the heart of the kill zone, receive countless rounds of enemy machine gun fire and seven rocket hits. His arms exploded into the air with each description of another rocket blast, his beer foaming over the top and down his knuckles. He slurped the bubbling head, licked the foam from his drooping mustache and described the wildly careening boat. His voice lowered, his tone changing as he described the radio commands, the three times other boats were ordered along side, believing us dead.

That weekend, among the old crewmen, we were young again, back on the river. Laughing at good memories, going silent when bad times reared their head. Buddha seemed nervous—tremors in his hands at times. And I recalled those mornings in the well-deck of our boat when his hands shook as he poured sugar into his C-ration coffee. On our drive back to Michigan at the end of the reunion, Buddha talked animatedly about the addition he planned for his cabin. He seemed to have a new spark after visiting old friends. But it didn't last.

I'd get over to the U.P. at least once a year, hoping for a meaningful visit. Each time I turned onto Old Plank Road near Wetmore, I knew I was entering a quagmire. Visits blurred together, always the same. Buddha would drift back to our arrival in the Mekong Delta at the height of the Tet Offensive in early February 1968, our time up north on Task Force Clearwater, keeping the Cua Viet River open. And always he would amplify memories of countless combat operations and patrols, slurring sentences, trailing into silence. About 4:00 a.m., he'd drop his tobacco wad on the counter, shuffle off to bed, and begin snoring. He would sleep until late in the morning, stretching and coughing as he crawled from beneath the single wool blanket. He'd pack yesterday's chew under his lip, walk Izzie and Yooper—two chocolate Labradors—then return to the cabin and mix a drink.

It was disconcerting how our roles had reversed. As boat captain he had attempted to micro-manage every facet of our lives. Now, from his isolated cabin in the U.P., he was seeking reassurance, a validation for our time in Vietnam. During one visit I suggested he make an appointment at a VA hospital and talk to somebody about his Vietnam memories. I mentioned an article I had read, about a new diagnosis for vets experiencing flashbacks—post traumatic stress disorder (PTSD). "Only pussies go crying to a shrink," had been his response. I didn't bring it up again.

Over the years, between my visits to the U.P., he'd call

me in the early morning hours, incoherent, lost in the past. A past so distorted I no longer recognized it. A past he drank himself into, alone. He wanted closure. He needed to see the old boat crew. He gave me a list—their full names and service numbers. Asked me to help find them. In his midnight ramblings he became obsessed with our time in Vietnam. Early winter 1999 I received a package. A large, hand-painted plaque with the Mobile Riverine Force symbol, my name, and T-112-11, our boat number. On the back, it said, *To Afe— A River Rat. A Long Awaited Thanks. Edward W. Thomas.*

During our last visit, Buddha was tormented by the smells of Vietnam. "Do you remember that stink?" he said. "Christ. I'll never forget it." He looked down at his whiskey, his eyes wide and staring. "Sometimes I wake up at night and smell it—the smoke, the charred flesh, the rotting vegetation. Then he started to laugh as if he were telling a good joke. "Do you remember that old papason who tried to sell us dope from his sampan? I think he shit himself when I pulled my .38 and yelled *didi mau.* Fuck he stunk of *nuoc mam.* Crow was pissed. He wanted to sell the pot in Dong Tam," Buddha said, his eyes almost closed, his drink sloshing over the glass as he tried to steady himself against the chipboard wall. "But I fixed that chickenshit bastard good after we got back from the August 18th ambush. Stuck the .38 barrel in his mouth and made him clean the well-deck, cox'n flat, and the 50 cal where that sergeant got splattered. Made him scrub out every speck of blood and meat." He laughed again, as if the image of Crow scrubbing blood off the deck was funny. Then he dropped into his chair. Just when I thought he might have fallen asleep, he lifted his head again, squinting, slurring his words. "Blow-flies, fat blue bastards—had to get rid of them."

When I left the next day, Buddha walked me to my truck. He reached through the pickup window to shake my hand, hanging on a little too long. "Thanks for coming, Afe. I mean it."

A few months later I opened the summer edition of *River Currents*, our MRFA newsletter. There, staring at me was a picture of Boat Captain "Buddha" Edward Thomas III clutching the M60 machine gun I had retrieved from a helicopter knocked down during a North Vietnamese artillery bombardment on Cua Viet Naval Base in March 1968. The caption below the picture read, "The association mourns the loss of one of its founding members." Buddha had died alone in his cabin, a victim of diabetes and a brain aneurysm.

Once again, I felt like that twenty-year-old cox'n. Cut off. Not privy to details, my world limited to the view through one inch slits in the armor surrounding the cox'n flat, asking questions without answers. Why, since the dawn of civilization, are leaders so eager to send young men and women off to war? Why were some veterans able to shake the trauma off and go on with their lives? Why had Buddha wasted his last years on whiskey and memories?

I came to realize how much I cared about Buddha. He changed from that tyrannical boat captain he had once been. He was a touchstone to my past—our past. I felt guilt. If I had made an effort—found some of the old crew—maybe Buddha might have taken a different tack. Perhaps he would have chosen a better life. Perhaps he would have moved beyond the memories of Vietnam.

The seasons pass. Each time I see my children and grandchildren, guilt rises, like bile in the throat. Guilt that I'm alive, have lived a full life when so many others didn't have a chance. Spring, my grandchildren and I search for purple May flowers and pink trilliums. Summer, the little girls have cow-calling contests and we're quickly surrounded by the herd. Autumn, we feed the ponies acorns and cob corn and carve jack-o-lanterns. Winter we make snow angels, let the pony pull us on sled rides, and come in to steaming mugs of hot chocolate.

Over the years, in my mind, I speak to those silent ones, those ghosts, always asking why I have been allowed this time. Why I am here to hold my wife and grandchildren close, to cherish each day.

Acknowledgments

This memory journey began with a series of essays I wrote while attending writing classes taught by Dr. Mark Christensen at Bemidji State University (BSU). His suggestions and prompts were instrumental in illuminating those nocturnal conversations I had with "Buddha" Ed Thomas. Mark's encouragement allowed me to explore depths I had shied away from. Feedback from fellow students provided valuable insights.

James Bishop, a fellow Vietnam veteran who is like a brother to me, has been a constant pillar of encouragement.

Susan Carol Hauser, retired chair of the department of English at BSU, is a source of wisdom and advice.

Dan O'Brien taught a writer's workshop I attended—he invited me to his ranch in South Dakota. One evening, during a conversation over shots of Crown Royal, as I defended our adventure in Vietnam, he said in astonishment, "You can't possibly believe it was a Just War." His stark statement forced me to explore a possibility I had shied away from.

Steve Almond, in another writer's workshop—his comments were the genesis of my quest to discover and finally lay to rest an incident that had troubled me for years.

Michael A. Harris, a former crewman aboard ATC 152-1 and owner of Legacies of Honor (see last page) provided excellent technical advice when he read my manuscript.

Angela F. Foster, Pine City, MN is the editor every writer hopes to find. She tightened my prose, and pointed out layers and insights I had overlooked.

Patti, my wife, has endured decades of silence about my time in Vietnam—it takes a special lady to carry that burden. Perhaps now we can lay it to rest.

To order *Muddy Jungle Rivers*, go to
www.hawthornpetalpress.com

Or write
Hawthorn Petal Press
PO Box 652
Bemidji, MN 56619-0652

Also available at on-line bookstores.

About
The Author

In January 1968 Wendell Affield went to Vietnam as the cox'n of Armor Troop Carrier 112-11 with the Mobile Riverine Force. Part of his tour of duty was in the Mekong Delta with the Army 9th Infantry Division and, for four months, with the 3rd Marine Division on the Cua Viet River just south of the DMZ as a member of Task Force Clearwater.

At seventeen, he enlisted in the navy. He was half way through his first tour in Vietnam aboard the destroyer, USS *Rogers* DD 876, in 1966, when his class graduated from high school. Affield, the third of nine children, grew up on a small farm in northern Minnesota. After leaving the navy in 1969, he found work as a meatcutter apprentice in the Chicago area and, a few years later, became a manager, a position he held for almost thirty years. In 1980 he and his family returned to northern Minnesota. After retiring in 2001 Affield enrolled in Bemidji State University, where, over the years, his Vietnam essays evolved into *Muddy Jungle Rivers*.

He and his wife, Patti, live on a farm in northern Minnesota. They have three children and several grandchildren. Affield is a freelance writer and is working on a collection of poetry and memoirs of his childhood. He is a member of the National Writers Union.

LEGACIES *of* HONOR

Michael Harris served with Mobile Riverine Force—
Vietnam - Task Force 117 on Armor Troop Carrier 152-1,
with River Assault Squadron 15/River Assault Division 152.
Today, Michael is an accredited Veteran Service Officer
with Vietnam Veterans of America. Michael has assisted
many Vietnam veterans in acquiring their authorized but
undocumented military awards and decorations. One day he
and his wife, Connie, decided they could take the mission
a step further by starting a small business to sell military
medals, ribbons, attachments and compose Shadow Box
display cases. "Legacies of Honor" became a reality in 2006.

http://www.legaciesofhonor.org

Also visit Michael's award-winning **http://www.riverinesailor.com**

*After visiting Legacies of Honor, after over forty years, I had Michael and
Connie gather my information and build a Shadow Box. It is a touchstone
to my past—a past my wife and children are fascinated by. I commend
Michael and Connie for this keepsake they have created for my family.*

Wendell Affield